Opening the Parables

Opening the Parables

M. D. Hayden

WIPF & STOCK · Eugene, Oregon

OPENING THE PARABLES

Copyright © 2024 M. D. Hayden. All rights reserved. Except for brief quotations in critical publications or reviews, no part of this book may be reproduced in any manner without prior written permission from the publisher. Write: Permissions, Wipf and Stock Publishers, 199 W. 8th Ave., Suite 3, Eugene, OR 97401.

Wipf & Stock
An Imprint of Wipf and Stock Publishers
199 W. 8th Ave., Suite 3
Eugene, OR 97401

www.wipfandstock.com

PAPERBACK ISBN: 979-8-3852-0030-6
HARDCOVER ISBN: 979-8-3852-0031-3
EBOOK ISBN: 979-8-3852-0032-0

VERSION NUMBER 07/05/24

Biblical citations throughout (unless otherwise noted) are from the *New Revised Standard Version Updated Edition* (NRSVUE). Copyright © 2021 National Council of Churches of Christ in the United States of America. Used by permission. All rights reserved worldwide.

Extracts from *Through the Valley of the Kwai* by Ernest Gordon used by permission of Wipf and Stock Publishers, www.wipfandstock.com.

Pine Creek Meeting story used by permission of the Meeting and individuals involved.

To the Southern Baptists of my childhood who gave me a firm, though flawed, foundation.

To the Early Friends whose writings confirmed my belief in the Inner Teacher/Spirit of Truth.

To the Pen Man who helped me write this book.

At another time I saw the great love of God, and I was filled with admiration at the infinitude of it; I saw what was cast out from God, and what entered into God's kingdom; and how by Jesus, the opener of the door, with his heavenly key, the entrance was given . . .

—George Fox, *Journal of George Fox*, 1647

God hath communicated and given unto every [one] a measure of the light of his own Son, a measure of grace, or a measure of the Spirit, which the Scripture expresses by several names, as sometimes of the "seed of the kingdom," "the Light that makes all things manifest," "a talent," "a little leaven" . . .

—Robert Barclay, *Apology*, Proposition VI

Contents

Preface | ix
Acknowledgments | xii
Introduction | xiii
Abbreviations | xvi

BOOK I: THE SEARCH FOR CONSISTENCY
Chapter 1: Influences on this Book | 3
Chapter 2: The God of the Good News | 14
Chapter 3: Why Parables? | 23
Chapter 4: Ears to Hear | 32
Chapter 5: Traditional Interpretation vs. Quaker Application | 39

BOOK II: THE PARABLES IN REAL LIFE
Chapter 6: The Kingdom Within | 53
Chapter 7: The Good Samaritan | 60
Chapter 8: Lost and Found | 71
Chapter 9: The Pharisee and the Tax Collector | 85
Chapter 10: The Vineyard Workers | 90
Chapter 11: Who's Welcome in the Kingdom? | 97
Chapter 12: How the Kingdom Grows | 108
Chapter 13: The Parable of the Talents | 115
Chapter 14: The Unmerciful Servant | 128
Chapter 15: The Dishonest Manager | 134

BOOK III: THE CHURCH, THE QUAKERS, AND THE PARABLES

Chapter 16: George Fox and Experiential Christianity | 143

Chapter 17: Jesus Un-Churched | 149

Chapter 18: Opening Parables: Discussion, Advices & Queries | 156

Appendix: Traditional Interpretations vs. Quaker Applications | 167

Bibliography | 207

Subject Index | 215

Scripture Index | 223

Preface

When I was five, I went to church and heard about Jesus for the first time. Grandma took me to the Prince Street Baptist Church in Clovis, New Mexico. We went downstairs where she left me in the Sunday School classroom with a nice teacher who gave me crayons and a little picture to color. A few more children my age gathered and then it was time to start. The teacher read stories from a picture book about this wonderful, kind, and loving man named Jesus who only helped people. It made me feel good to hear those stories.

Just as she finished and it was time to leave Sunday School and go upstairs to church, one of the kids said, "And then they crucified him."

"What does crucified mean?" I asked.

Another kid volunteered cheerfully, "It means they killed him by driving nails into his hands and feet and hanging him up on a cross."

What??! Why would anyone kill such a good person? I wouldn't believe it. A couple of kids followed me down the hall, insisting it was true. *Why did they tell about it with such apparent glee?* I was angry and outraged.

This was the beginning of my doubts about the Church.

I kept going to church with Grandma though. She died when I was nine, and I changed to another Baptist church where my parents dropped me off each Sunday morning. When I was eleven, my non-churchgoing mother gave me a little zippered Bible so I could participate in Bible drills at Sunday School, but I don't remember reading it. Around that time, I became more and more aware of hypocrisy in the church. Some of the adults I knew from Sunday mornings, who warned us kids against smoking, drinking, dancing, movies, etc., my Aunt Connie knew from Friday and Saturday nights at the bootleg joint where she tended bar. When the church fired its beloved minister because he and his wife were getting a divorce, I felt sorry for their daughter whom I knew slightly from school. She looked so sad all the time. And then the church decided to take away the car they had given the minister because they loved him so much. In a small, strange way, it was Jesus all over again. Once again I was outraged. I stopped going to the Baptist church. That fall, I switched to the liberal church in town, Trinity Methodist, in part because some of my friends were Methodists.

The summer I was thirteen, between the Baptists and the Methodists, I decided to read the Bible on my own. Much of it just confused me, but the cynicism of Ecclesiastes spoke to my early teen self (I memorized passages like "For in much wisdom is much grief: and he that increaseth knowledge increaseth sorrow"). Skimming through the pages, I finally became curious about the red letters. Why were some sections of the New Testament printed in red? I discovered they were supposed to be the words Jesus spoke! I searched the red-letter passages and read them carefully. Some parts in red letters seemed to be clear instructions for how to live. Some parts in red rankled; they contradicted other parts that seemed more like I imagined Jesus to be.

A year later, I told a minister at a youth retreat that I could not be a Christian because I could not do what Jesus said I should do. I could not give up everything to follow Jesus. I wanted to have fun, go to college, and travel the world. I was pretty sure I could not love my enemies. I was too selfish to be a Christian. The minister smiled broadly and said, "Oh, don't worry about that. Jesus didn't really expect *us* to do those things. *He* could because he was the son of God. But it's beyond human beings to do things like love our enemies."

If the minister's intent was to win me over to Christ, his words had the opposite effect. I was more certain than ever I could not join the Church. My sense was that if God sent a beloved child to earth with a singular message of love, compassion, mercy, and forgiveness, can he have known what humanity would do with that message? I still have that question: did God know that we would modify Jesus' message to justify wars and hatred, advocate for judgment and punishment, and establish hierarchies in "heaven" and earth? I have always struggled to reconcile the Christ the Church promotes with Jesus the teacher whose words, when we find them, are so simple and so powerful.

When I was nineteen, I left the Church for good, but not God, and not the teachings of Jesus. For decades I avoided Christianity, but I could not dismiss all the words in red letters. Some of them were simply too good and too true.

More than forty years later—in one of the Divine's fine ironies—I was led to attend a Quaker seminary. Inspired in large part by the early Quaker understanding of scripture and Jesus' message, I am today a follower of the *way of Jesus*. The essence of Jesus' way remains in scraps of his authentic parables, proverbs, and aphorisms, fragments preserved by the gospel writers. It remains in stories passed on by early Christians and included in the gospels about the way his life "preached" what he taught: his compassionate treatment of people regardless of their social status, his insistence on love as the highest value, his challenges to authorities (religious and political), his willingness to die rather than to kill or provoke violence. It remains in individual spiritual experiences and direct encounters with the Divine by any name: the Light, the Holy, the Spirit, God . . . Such is the way of Jesus, from whose spoken teachings over two thousand years ago came a paradigm shift we humans still struggle to absorb.

Opening the Parables is a work of considered opinion about what Jesus taught in his parables. I make no pretense of being a biblical scholar, theologian, or historian. My qualifications for writing this book are (1) I am an educated, experienced, and curious reader; (2) I have always mistrusted interpretations made by religious authorities with a theological agenda; and (3) I am convinced Jesus' parables contain a key to his intentional and consistent message.

I encourage you, the reader, to question my conclusions and explore for yourself the thousands (probably millions) of interpretations of Jesus' parables. I hope this book will lead you to look more closely at what Jesus said (as far as we can know) and to question what the Church has said he said.

—MDH, 2024

Acknowledgments

MY DEEP GRATITUDE TO those who shepherded me through the writing of this book. Thank you to my daughter and grandsons for their patience and loving support. To my Quaker seminary friend and pool-player extraordinaire, Debbie Faith Stanley, who provided invaluable feedback, great conversations, and sorely-needed encouragement. To my Scottish Zoom friend, Valerie Dearnley, (who lives in the Light and reads from the heart) who inspired me to make insightful changes and additions. To my brilliant Buddhist historian friend, Tom Davis, who apparently found nothing to disagree with in what he read, an encouragement in itself. Finally, thank you to Shelley Newby, who introduced me to the Pen Man; to Eric Muhr of Barclay Press who encouraged me to contact Wipf & Stock Publishers, and to Wipf & Stock editor Matthew Winer, who patiently answered my many questions.

Introduction

"The Kingdom of God is like . . ." Jesus taught his Kingdom of God lesson consistently and repeatedly, inductively, deductively, in as many ways possible, to address all learning styles. His lessons focused on his students, on ways to behave, here and now, in a way beneficial to humanity and pleasing to God. Many of his first students seemed to grasp the concept and applied it to their lives.

As time passed, however, other teachers took over Jesus' lesson plan, often without fully understanding his lesson or intention. Beginning with the gospel writers, these later teachers changed the focus of the lesson from the students to Jesus himself, and from the Kingdom of God to Jesus as Christ/Son of God. Eventually they added material about Church doctrine and practices based on worshipping Jesus, modifying his original lesson for their different intentions. Perhaps by the grace of God, the essence of Jesus' original lesson remains—buried, hidden, and obscured—but still there in the New Testament text.

In seminary, almost everything I read about Jesus and his teachings, even scholarly works by agnostics, was filtered through what the Church said about him. When I read *The Five Gospels: What Did Jesus Really Say? (The Search for the Authentic Words of Jesus)*, it became my New Testament. The work is based on the research and findings from over a decade of work by more than two hundred biblical scholars from various denominations. Using specific objective criteria to identify words Jesus probably said (or very close to something he said), the scholars were able to separate what Jesus said from what the Church said he said. Roughly 80 percent of the New Testament contains words by others ascribed to

Jesus. The words *most* likely to be authentic to Jesus are found in his unique aphorisms and puzzling parables.

In my own journey with the parables, from the red letters I found as a teenager to *The Five Gospels* I found in seminary, I am convinced that Jesus meant what he said about love and the Kingdom of God, a concept at once so simple but so difficult we still don't fully grasp it.

Concentrating only on what Jesus said in the parables, without the accoutrements of traditional Christian interpretation, what do his parables teach us? Surely someone has done this. In searching, however, I found no interpretation that focused *only what Jesus focused on* in his authentic teachings, i.e., compassionate love and the God of the Kingdom (which is Love itself). Scholarly works spend a lot of time analyzing the historical background of the parables as used by early Christians; on language issues in translation; on the structure of and figurative language in the parables. Theological works focus on the parable's meaning in Christianity (which did not exist when Jesus told the parable); spiritual writings too use language and images from the Christian tradition to talk about Jesus' parables.

Every interpretation I found looked at the parables, one way or another, through the filter of Christian tradition and doctrine. Of course, I could not possibly read all the millions of interpretations of Jesus' parables, but if an interpretation using only the authentic words of Jesus (as far as we can know) does exist, it seems to be not readily available. *Opening the Parables* is my attempt at such an interpretation. Others may exist; others may do it better; but for those who have not yet found the parables interpreted using the unadulterated words of Jesus, this is a beginning. Since many, if not most, of his remaining authentic teachings begin with "The Kingdom of God is like . . . " we will take him at his word, i.e., that he wants to teach us to understand a divine dimension or realm unlike our normal reality but intertwined with it, the part that compassionate love plays there, and how we can become conscious citizens in that realm.

The power of the parables, of course, is that they work in different ways for different people; the Holy speaks to us in whatever language we can hear. Many who love the traditional Christian religion, who are deeply moved by its rituals and liturgies, who are lifted by its symbols of glory and majesty, who resonate with its central figure, Christ the sacrifice, may prefer the allegorical interpretations of traditional Christianity. This book may not be for them. But for those put off by what Christianity has become, my hope is that this book will open discussion of the original source of that faith, the way of Jesus.

Opening the Parables is really three books, so I divided it that way. Book I: "The Search for Consistency" is written from my intellect and education. Book II: "The Parables in Real Life" is written from my heart and personal experience. Book III: "The Church, the Quakers, and the Parables" is written from the spiritual understanding and affirmation I found in the writings of Early Friends. The Appendix, "Traditional Interpretations vs. Quaker Applications," is for those interested in the Early Friends' approach to using scripture.

Throughout the book I capitalize the word "Church" to signify the institution of Christianity (Catholic and Protestant) as it developed over the centuries, becoming more and more distracted from the teachings of Jesus about love in the Kingdom of God, which he said is *here, now, among us*—not there, then, with the elect.

Abbreviations

NRSVUE   New Revised Standard Version Updated Edition
YLT   Young's Literal Translation
QBI   Quaker Bible Index

BOOK I   **THE SEARCH FOR CONSISTENCY**

1

Influences on This Book

> [I would] that all women [could] read the Gospels and Paul's epistles, and that they be translated into the common language so that they be read and known not only by the Scots and Irish, but also by the Turks and Saracens. . . . I would that the plowman sing a text of the Scripture at his plow, that the weaver at his loom use it to drive away the tediousness of time, or that the traveler make the time pass and rid his journey of weariness . . . [1]
>
> —DESIDERIUS ERASMUS, 1529

The Bible, George Fox, and Early Friends

FOR CENTURIES, THE NEW Testament existed only in various Latin translations used by the Church and inaccessible for anyone who did not read or understand Latin, which was most people. Handwritten translations of the Bible into English existed as early as the 1300s, and the 1560 Geneva Bible translation into English (based on Erasmus' earlier translation into Greek and updated Latin) was the "Bible of choice" for educated English-speaking Christians for a hundred years or more. (Shakespeare, for instance, quoted from the Geneva Bible.) But the translation commissioned by King James I of England and published in 1611 (i.e., the "King

---

1. Erasmus, *Exhortation*.

James Version") was the first Bible printed in a form small enough for an individual to own and read it.

Widespread availability of individual Bibles in English allowed even common people to read the text for themselves, among them, George Fox, son of a weaver in the English Midlands. Fox was a religious seeker in Puritan England and is acknowledged as founder of the Religious Society of Friends (also known as Quakers). For centuries, those like George Fox and early Friends who sought and found consistency in the teachings of Jesus, also found themselves at odds with Christian doctrine and the institutional Church.

Fox knew the Bible so well, tradition says, that if it were lost he could have written it down from memory. Having studied it deeply, Fox became suspicious of religious "authorities" who knew church doctrine but struggled to explain Jesus' teachings. Disappointed, and in a period of intense seeking, he heard a voice tell him there was one who could "speak to his condition" (address his concerns), and that was Jesus Christ himself.

Fox went to scripture with new eyes to see what Jesus said, alert for a consistent Truth rising out of the words. Fox wrote in his journal that he esteemed "the Holy Scriptures" highly: "they were very precious to me, for I was in that spirit by which they were given forth, and what the Lord opened in me I afterwards found was agreeable to them."[2]

"What the Lord opened" in him led Fox to emphasize that scripture is understandable only if read in the same spirit in which it was written, i.e., a Spirit of Truth ("the Spirit of Christ," "the Light of Christ Jesus"). Fox and early Friends called spiritual insights gleaned from this Spirit of Truth "openings," beckoning entrance to a higher understanding. One such "opening" held that Truth, unlike humanity, is consistent, unchangeable, and does not contradict itself. As Fox wrote in his journal:

> But while people's minds run in the earthly, after the creatures and changeable things, changeable ways and religions, and changeable, uncertain teachers, their minds are in bondage; they are brittle and changeable, tossed up and down with windy doctrines and thoughts and notions.... the Light of Jesus Christ ... would keep them to the unchangeable.[3]

---

2. Fox, *Journal*, 34.
3. Fox, *Journal*, 13.

The group of early Friends, including Fox, who wrote a letter to King Charles II in 1660 to assure him they were not involved in a plot against him, did so by declaring their abhorrence of all violence, saying:

> That Spirit of Christ by which we are guided, is not changeable, so as once to command us from a thing as evil, & again to move unto it;[4] And we do certainly know, and so testify to the world; that the spirit of Christ which leads us into all Truth, will never move us to fight and war against any man with outward Weapons neither for the Kingdom of Christ, nor for the kingdoms of this world.[5]

Early Friend William Penn described Fox as having "an extraordinary gift in opening the Scriptures. He would go to the marrow of things and show the mind, harmony and fulfilling of them with much plainness and to great comfort and edification." When Penn says that Fox's approach to scripture led to "harmony," "much plainness,"[6] "great comfort and edification," this suggests Fox could interpret in simple language the often disquieting or baffling inconsistencies in biblical text.

Those who followed him called themselves "Followers of the Way," "Publishers of Truth," and eventually "The Religious Society of Friends." George Fox "opened the scriptures" in a way that led them to read the Bible for the teaching of Jesus and to question interpretations imposed by church doctrine. In essence, if it wasn't specifically in the Bible, or if it contradicted what Jesus said about the Kingdom of God, it was debatable.

To early Friends, baptism, communion, etc. were sacred, inward, spiritual events—sacramental because they came from inward conviction, not simply because it was on the church calendar. John the Baptist had differentiated between the water baptism he performed and the spiritual baptism Jesus brought,[7] and Friends understood baptism to be an inward experience of the Holy Spirit that could happen any time, especially when a person was still and attentive. Communion, too, was understood as an inward encounter with the divine, a direct spiritual experience more

---

4. "So as once to command us from a thing as evil, and again to move unto it"— that is, tell us not to do something because it is wrong, and then urge us to do it. This is an argument against the concept of "holy war."

5. Fox, et al., "Harmless and Innocent People."

6. "Plainness in dress and address" was a Quaker expression that meant wearing simple unadorned clothing and using clear simple language.

7. "I have baptized you with water, but he will baptize you with the Holy Spirit" (Mark 1:8; Matt 3:11).

powerful than any ritual imposed by the Church. When Jesus told his followers, "Remember me when you eat and drink," that meant remembering Jesus (alive and teaching) and his message several times every day. Shattered by Jesus' crucifixion, early Christians made the communion meal a reminder of his death. But to Fox and early Friends, "communion" was a spiritual encounter with the living Inner Teacher/the Inner Christ, who, Fox said, "has come to teach his people himself."[8]

Ultimately, the first Friends rejected much of what the Church taught, which was mostly about itself, its doctrines, rituals, sacraments and even terminology. The word "church," for instance, a translation of the Greek word, *ekklēsia*, is used in the New Testament to mean a "gathering of those summoned" but "never refers to a building."[9] Purists that they were, Fox and early Friends did not refer to places they gathered as "churches," but simply as "meeting houses." They reserved "church" for the people called together by God/the Holy Spirit/the Light—something holy, and wholly beyond humans.

Early Friends allowed space for the Inner Teacher/Inner Christ/God to work in individuals rather than through church structure, doctrine, and authority. In the two quotations below, William Penn expresses the Quaker understanding of faith and worship:

> God visits and appears to people in ways that are appropriate to their spiritual states and conditions and in ways in which they are prepared to receive him. For some it has been outward and sensibly; for others inward and spiritually."[10]

and:

> The humble, meek, merciful, just, pious, and devout souls everywhere are of one religion and when death has taken off the mask, they will know one another, though the diverse liveries [different costumes] they wore here make them strangers."[11]

Understanding scripture required reading it at the same spiritual level as its source, and teaching people why and how to do this was part of Fox's gift for "opening scripture." As he wrote in his journal:

---

8. Fox, *Journal*, 8, 48, 78, 80, 90, 98, 104, 107, 112, 143, 149 and more.
9. Mounce, "*Ekklēsia*": "In the NT a church is never a building or meeting place."
10. Penn, *Twenty-First Century Penn*, 303.
11. Penn, *Fruits of Solitude*, Vol. I, Part 3: Religion.

> I turned the people to the Spirit of God, which led the holy men of old to give forth the Scriptures and showed them that they must also come to receive and be led by the same Spirit if ever they came to know God, and Christ, and the Scriptures aright.[12]

By 1678, this was an established and fundamental belief of early Friends, as Robert Barclay explains in his *Apology*: "This is the great work of the Scriptures, and their service to us, that we may witness them fulfilled in us, and so discern the stamp of God's spirit and ways upon them, by the inward acquaintance we have with the same Spirit and work in our hearts. . . . it is only the spiritual man that can make a right use of them."[13]

The ways Fox opened scripture led his followers and other seekers to find consistency in what Jesus taught that resulted in "testimonies" like these:

- In the eyes of Jesus' God, everyone, regardless of status, race, or gender, is equally loved and valued. This divine Love extends to all creation.
- Jesus' emphasis on truth leads to integrity in dealing with each other.
- Jesus taught that shedding "the burdens of abundance" enables us to enter more easily the Kingdom of God. No one should profit from the hardship of others.
- Early Friends embraced simplicity in all its aspects: language, behavior, clothing, possessions. Simplicity was central to Quaker worship. Friends eliminated anything outward that could interfere with direct inward communion with the Divine: "no altar, no liturgy, no pulpit, no sermon, no organ, no choir, no sacrament, and no person in authority."[14] The Holy Spirit was in charge, and Friends worshiped by listening for its divine guidance.
- Jesus' emphasis on love of God, love of neighbor, love even of enemies, makes war and violence indefensible in the Kingdom of God, and is thus foundational to the Quaker peace testimony.

Fortunately, a wonderful resource exists which shows how early Quakers understood and used the Bible in speaking and writing: *The Quaker Bible Index: A key to biblical allusions in early Quaker writings and early Quaker*

---

12. Fox, *Journal*.
13. Barclay, *Apology*, "Third Proposition."
14. Brinton, *Friends for 350 Years*, 77.

uses of biblical phrases, by book, chapter, and verse: a work in progress begun by Esther Greenleaf Mürer.[15] This title and description are taken from the introduction written in 2005 at which time Mürer said she had thirty-five thousand such allusions and counting. The Quaker Bible Index (QBI) is the primary source used in this book for early Quaker references to material from the parables of Jesus.

The Jefferson Bible, Red Letters, The Complete Sayings of Jesus

Aside from Jesus' own voice, the oral tradition of the earliest days, both before and after his death, was the most authentic version of his teachings. People sharing Jesus' words orally could be held accountable by others who had heard him speak in person, but with the passage of time, fewer and fewer people remained who had heard Jesus' voice. With the transition to written accounts, new kinds of errors became possible: misspellings, omitted words, and even intentional editorial changes. More and more words surrounded the words of Jesus; more and more his words were modified or rearranged or buried in context to fit the needs or assert the agenda of certain religious groups. Even while his teaching continued to spread through the oral tradition, there must have been those who wished they had heard him in person, those who longed to know his words unfiltered through other voices.

Centuries later, Thomas Jefferson was one who sought to uncover the authentic words of Jesus. Though Jefferson was not a theologian, he had studied the New Testament text in Greek, Latin, English and French, all languages he knew, and he was convinced there was more to the gospels than met the eye. Having isolated as much as possible what Jesus said and did from what was said about him, Jefferson created a singularly consistent version of the gospels. In a letter to John Adams, Jefferson described what he discovered in "the very words only of Jesus" as "the most sublime and benevolent code of morals which has ever been offered to man." Jefferson continued:

> I have performed this operation for my own use, by cutting verse by verse out of the printed book, and arranging, the matter [i.e., material; words and actions] which is evidently his, and which is as easily distinguishable as diamonds in a dunghill. The result

---

15. Mürer. QBI, Introduction.

is an 8vo[16] of 46 pages of pure and unsophisticated doctrines, such as were professed & acted on by the unlettered apostles, the Apostolic fathers, and the Christians of the first century.[17]

Jefferson concludes that separating the words and teachings of Jesus as much as possible from surrounding interpretative text leads to a gospel far superior to the gospel promoted for centuries by Christian tradition and dogma, cluttered as it is with inconsistencies and contradictions. Jefferson's "cut-and-paste" version of the New Testament, which he titled *The Life and Morals of Jesus of Nazareth Extracted Textually from the Gospels in Greek, Latin, French & English*, though shared with his friends, was not published in his lifetime. First published in 1904 by the United States Congress, Jefferson's book, now known as *The Jefferson Bible*, remains in print and continues to speak to seekers today.

A longing to lift Jesus' teachings out of the gospel writers' context is found as early as the fourteenth century in a document which may be the first "red-letter edition" of the New Testament. That document, known as "Codex 16," is an ancient manuscript of the four gospels in Greek and Latin, in which "the words of Jesus, the genealogy of Jesus, and the words of angels are written in crimson."[18]

At the turn of the nineteenth century, the idea for a "red-letter edition" of the New Testament was the brainchild of Louis Klopsch, an editor of the *Christian Herald*, who was inspired by the words in Luke 22:20: "This cup is the new testament in my blood, which is shed for you." That sentence, which "provided the name for the second major division of the Bible—the New Testament—also offered Klopsch the idea for printing the words of Jesus in the color of his blood."[19] In 1899, Klopsch published his first edition of a red-letter New Testament; this was followed in 1901 by a red-letter edition of the entire Bible. In an Explanatory Note, Klopsch wrote:

> Modern Christianity is striving zealously to draw nearer to the great Founder of the Faith. Setting aside mere human doctrines and theories regarding Him, it presses close to the Divine Presence, to gather from His own lips the definition of His mission to the world and His own revelation of the Father . . . . The Red

16. "8vo," abbreviation for "octavo," printer's term referring to a book about 8 inches x 5 inches.
17. Letter, Jefferson to Adams, 1813.
18. Funk, et al., *Parables of Jesus*, vii.
19. "Origins Red-Letter Bible."

Letter Bible has been prepared and issued in the full conviction that it will meet the needs of the student, the worker, and the searchers after truth everywhere.[20]

Today, most Bible publishers include a red-letter edition among their offerings, but the criteria for what to include in the red letters is an editorial decision, so selections vary depending on the editor and publisher. Red-letter selections may include all text "universally accepted as the utterances of our Lord and Savior," as the first red-letter edition did, which includes words attributed to Jesus by others, even "in people's dreams or visions and after he was resurrected,"[21] or—as the Jesus Seminar red-letter edition does—may restrict selections to words that scholars have determined to be something Jesus probably said or close to it.

Around the same time as publication of the first red-letter bibles, Arthur Hinds,[22] an early twentieth-century American businessman (another non-theologian, like Thomas Jefferson) sought consistency in the "bare sayings" of Jesus. The lengthy title of Hinds' 1927 book—also like Jefferson's, still in print—makes clear his intent: *The Complete Sayings of Jesus: The King James Version of Christ's Own Words Without Interpolations and Divested of the Context, Excepting the Brief Portions of the Gospel Narratives Retained to Establish the Place, Time, or Occasion, or a Question the Reply to Which is the Master's Own Answer*. In "The Compiler's Purpose," Hinds writes:

> The shelves of the libraries and of the bookstores bend beneath the tomes of the sayings, the bare sayings, of all the other great men; but one will not find in library or bookstore, in any published book, the complete sayings of Jesus, the bare sayings in simple sequence, Christ's own words, separate.
>
> . . .
>
> Many a reader, arrived at FINIS in the New Testament itself, has but a hazy picture of Christ on his daily walks as a circuit preacher everywhere within walking distance; has but a sketchy outline of the times and occasions—so many biographers!—Matthew, Mark, Luke, John, Paul—each essaying not a biography as such,

---

20. Klopsch, "Explanatory Note," xvi.
21. "Origins Red-Letter Bible."
22. Hinds was, at one time, owner of the bookstore in New York that eventually became Barnes & Noble. In 1917, Clifford Barnes bought out Hinds' ownership of the store and partnered with William Noble.

not the record of the Teacher's sayings as such, but intent upon launching each his own conception of Christ's mission.[23]

Theologians who study God and biblical scholars who study the Bible most often do so through the lens of Christian tradition and church doctrine. Perhaps non-experts like Jefferson and Hinds have less difficulty in separating Jesus' words from the teachings of the church than do religious experts. Sometimes what we are sure we know gets in the way of what we can see or discover. The fact that both Jefferson's and Hinds' books are still in print (as well as many newer books that focus on lifting Jesus' words from surrounding text), indicates the longing still exists to hear Jesus' singular and authentic voice free from the clutter of centuries of confusion and Church doctrine.

The Jesus Seminar, *The Parables of Jesus, Red Letter Edition*

In 1985, New Testament scholar Robert W. Funk retired from his position as a distinguished professor of religious studies and founded the Westar Institute, an independent, non-profit research organization, not "*affiliated with any religious institution or denomination*" and not advocating "*a particular theological point of view.*"[24] Its first project was formation of The Jesus Seminar whose mission was, as Funk put it, "to inquire simply, rigorously after the voice of Jesus, after what he really said."[25] The Jesus Seminar research project began in 1985 and continued in three phases to 1998, with the cooperation and collaboration of more than two hundred biblical scholars representing diverse Western religious traditions.

Three years after it began, the Jesus Seminar published *The Parables of Jesus, Red Letter Edition*, its initial report on the "search for the authentic words of Jesus." In this edition, scholars began with C.H. Dodd's definition of a parable as "a metaphor or simile drawn from nature or common life, arresting the hearer by its vividness or strangeness, and leaving the mind in sufficient doubt about its precise application to tease it into active thought,"[26] and added the following characteristics as "marks of the genuine parables" typical of Jesus' voice:

---

23. Hinds, "Compiler's Purpose," 192.
24. Westar Institute, "About Us."
25. Westar Institute, "Bob Funk."
26. Quoted in Funk, et al., *Parables of Jesus*, 16.

- [The listener/reader] "must always look for the surprising twist in the story, the unusual figure, the paradoxical pattern."
- "The parable has no conclusion. . . . Jesus himself never explicitly tells us how he meant them to be understood."[27]
- "The genuine parables of Jesus are narratives. . . . A common plot involves the reversal of roles."
- "Genuine parables of Jesus will exhibit the marks of oral composition," i.e., "a tight, lean, compressed style. No more words than necessary"; "uncomplicated plots and the use of pairs and sets of three"; "concrete, vivid images."
- "If the parable itself is at odds with the context in which the evangelist places the parable, we have weak evidence that the parable predates the work of the evangelist."[28]

Five years later in 1993, the final "report" on this project from the Jesus Seminar (*The Five Gospels* published by Polebridge Press) included these additional characteristics of Jesus' parables:

- "Jesus' sayings and parables cut against the social and religious grain. [They] surprise and shock: they characteristically call for a reversal of roles or frustrate ordinary, everyday expectations."
- "Jesus' sayings and parables are often characterized by exaggeration, humor, and paradox."
- "Jesus does not as a rule initiate dialogue or debate, nor does he offer to cure people."
- "Jesus rarely makes pronouncements or speaks about himself in the first person."
- "Jesus makes no claim to be the Anointed, the Messiah."[29]

---

27. Because the explanation of the parable of the sower given in Matt 13:18–23, Mark 4:13-20, and Luke 8:11-15 goes against this quality in other parables of Jesus, and earlier versions of the parable do not have it, scholars determined it to be the work of the gospel writer.

28. Funk, et al., *Parables of Jesus*, 16–17.

29. Funk and Hoover, *Five Gospels*, 31–32.

Consistency in the Parables

How can we know what Jesus really said? We can't, of course. But his parables—simple stories that have puzzled, intrigued, and confused hearers/readers for centuries—seem to offer the best possibility for hearing Jesus' authentic voice. The parables consistently make "a comparison between God's kingdom, actions, or expectations" and "things in this world."[30] If we cut away centuries of interpretative text to find words as close as possible to what Jesus said, we find one key that opens the meaning in all his parables and other teachings.

Over a hundred years ago, German parables scholar, Adolf Julicher (1857–1938), broke with the tradition of "allegorical interpretation of the parables, which had been dominant for all previous centuries of the Christian era."[31] Instead of parsing the parables for allegorical symbols about Christianity, Julicher said, "[the hearer/reader] must draw from the parable only one thought." Rather than a complicated allegory, the Jesus parable "is there only to illuminate . . . one point, a rule, an idea, an experience that is valid on the spiritual as on the secular level."[32] A point, rule, or idea accessible to the common people who listened to Jesus speak when he walked the Galilean countryside over two thousand years ago.

Opening the Parables is based on the premise that Jesus taught a singular spiritual truth which appears consistently in all his teachings, especially in his parables. In the best-possible way, Jesus was a one-subject teacher (one subject, using various teaching techniques, both deductive and inductive), a one-sermon preacher (one message, told in various ways). Everything he taught or preached was about love in the infinite, here-and-now Kingdom of God.

All his parables, proverbs, aphorisms, and direct statements teach one lesson: in the highest realm we can imagine, compassionate love is all that matters.

---

30. Hultgren, *Parables of Jesus*, 3.
31. Hultgren, *Parables of Jesus*, 13.
32. Quoted in Hultgren, *Parables of Jesus*, 13.

2

The God of the Good News

> Jesus came to Galilee proclaiming the good news of God and saying, "The time is fulfilled, and the kingdom of God has come near; repent and believe in the good news."
>
> —Mark 1:14–15

For centuries, Jesus' parables have been—and still are—extensively interpreted by religious experts who impose Christian dogma and tradition on a parable told decades before Christianity *per se* even existed. There was no Christian tradition when Jesus was teaching his followers, and he was teaching regular people, not theologians. No wonder then that after two millennia, Jesus' parables, coated with an overlay of Christian dogma, still puzzle readers of the New Testament.

Although the Hebrew tradition foundational to the New Testament posits a single, all-powerful God responsible for creation and involved in the affairs of human beings, that God reflects many characteristics of powerful humans: anger, jealousy, vanity,[1] judgment, punishment, and revenge. Scattered through Hebrew scripture are hints that this God had another side, but before Jesus came along we have no record, at least in Western thought, of anyone teaching common people about an all-loving divinity intimately concerned with all creation, all people, and all individual lives.[2]

---

1. For example, requiring worship, offerings, and sacrifice of the purest animals.
2. Perhaps the *bodhisattvas* of Buddhist thought came close; a bodhisattva was an enlightened being, but not a god or deity, who reincarnated on earth "to work for the

"Not Your Father's God"

In the Hebrew scriptures[3] that Jesus would have studied as a boy, references to God loving his people, the Israelites, are intertwined with vivid descriptions of ways he punishes their enemies, or worse, his own people who displease him. For Jesus' first followers (who were also Jewish), the one God of Israel was a god of one people, his chosen people, their ancestors, the Israelites. (An intimation that this God cares about peoples other than his own, however, appears in the story of Jonah. God commands Jonah to warn the Ninevites to change their immoral behavior or risk destruction. Nineveh was the capital city of Assyria, a long-time enemy of Israel, and Jonah despises the Ninevites. He tries to avoid God's command because he knows God will forgive the Ninevites if they repent. Sure enough, they do, and God does.)

Based on the idea that what would please a human ruler will please God, scripture in the books of Genesis, Exodus, Leviticus, Numbers, and Deuteronomy are filled with references to offerings, sacrifices, and instructions for what, when, where, and how to make an offering or sacrifice pleasing to God.

Some of the most powerful language in scripture, however, deals with God's rejection of offerings and sacrifice.[4] For instance, consider these verses from the prophet Micah which begins with a "mortal's" questions about how to please God: Will burnt offerings of expensive livestock or precious oil be enough? What if I sacrifice my firstborn child? Would that be enough for God?

> "With what shall I come before the Lord and bow myself before God on high? Shall I come before him with burnt offerings, with calves a year old? Will the Lord be pleased with thousands of rams, with ten thousand of rivers of oil? Shall I give my firstborn for my transgression, the fruit of my body for the sin of my soul?"

---

benefit of all sentient beings," according to Chögyam Trungpa Rinpoche.

3. The *Tanakh* (The Hebrew Bible) includes the Torah and nineteen other books of the Bible referred to in Christianity as the "Old Testament."

4. For examples, see Ps 40:6; Ps 50:7–14; Isa 1:11–17; Isa 56:1–8; Isa 66:1–4; Jer 6:19–21; Jer 7:21–22.

> He has told you, O mortal, what is good, and what does the Lord require of you but to do justice and to love kindness, and to walk humbly with your God?
>
> —Mic 6:6–8

God responds with remarkable simplicity and clarity through the prophet Micah, "He has told you, O mortal" what he requires from you: justice, kindness, humility. This message occurs in Jesus' teaching throughout the New Testament. (How ironic that Christianity developed into a religion based on the idea of a god who required the sacrifice of his own son.)

Jesus refers to Hebrew scripture that focuses on God's love and forgiveness, alluding to passages about what God requires of us, i.e., not offerings and sacrifice, but to love God with all our hearts, minds, souls, and strengths; to love our neighbors as ourselves;[5] to care for the "widows and orphans and foreigners" among us. Jesus goes a step further, adding that we are to love *all* others, enemies as well as neighbors.

How Many Commandments?

For centuries, the Ten Commandments in Exodus and Deuteronomy have been considered (by Jews and later by Christians) a comprehensive guide to pleasing God. But Jesus doesn't really talk about the Ten Commandments. In fact, one of the most surprising things he says to his first-century Jewish listeners is his answer to the question, "What is the first commandment?" when a group of Jewish religious authorities (priests, scribes, Pharisees, etc.) question him to see if he knows what he is talking about. "One of the scribes came near and heard them [i.e., religious experts] disputing with one another, and seeing that [Jesus] answered them well, he asked him, 'Which commandment is the first of all?'" (Mark 12:28).

In the Hebrew scriptures Jesus and his first followers would have been familiar with, there are six-hundred-thirteen commandments, including the first ten which established the Torah, the foundation of Jewish religious and civil laws.[6] In the order the commandments are given

---

5. "You shall not take vengeance or bear a grudge against any of your people, but you shall love your neighbor as yourself: I am the Lord" (Lev 19:18).

6. Those listening to Jesus speak would have known the story of the ten commandments, told twice in Exodus and twice in Deuteronomy. The commandments are first given directly to the Israelites at Mt. Horeb/Mt. Sinai through fire, darkness, and the disembodied voice of God, with Moses as mediator. God carves the commandments

in Exod 20:2–3 and Deut 5:6–7, the first commandment on the list is (1) "You shall have no other gods before me." The commandments then follow in this order: (2) Do not make or worship idols. (3) Do not misuse the name of God. (4) Observe the Sabbath. (5) Honor your father and mother. (6) Do not murder. (7) Do not commit adultery. (8) Do not steal. (9) Do not "bear false witness against your neighbor," i.e., lie about someone. (10) Do not covet anything your neighbor owns, not his wife, house, field, slave, ox, donkey, or anything else.

In answer to the scribe's question, "Which commandment is the first of all?" Jesus makes no mention of these ten commandments. Instead, he quotes Moses in Deut 6:4–5, admonishing the Israelites: "Hear, O Israel: the Lord our God, the Lord is one. You shall love the Lord your God with all your heart and with all your soul and with all your might."[7] All three canonical gospels report Jesus repeating Moses' summarizing admonition as the first, and therefore, the primary, or greatest commandment (see Mark 12:30, Matt 22:37, and Luke 10:27).

Prōtos, the Greek word translated as "first," can also mean "foremost" or "chief," which makes Jesus' answer both pithy and surprising to those who first heard it. When the scribe affirms that this is indeed the first or foremost commandment, he acknowledges Jesus' cleverness, but also his wisdom and insight.

A list of rarely-if-ever-quoted other commandments appears a few chapters later in Deut 10:4. When Moses brings the second set of tablets to the Israelites, he tells them that God "wrote on the tablets the same words as before, the ten commandments that the Lord had spoken to you." And then he says: "So now, O Israel, what does the Lord your God require of you? Only to fear the Lord your God, to walk in all his ways, to love him, to serve the Lord your God with all your heart and with all your soul" (Deut 10:12). He follows this with six more "commandments"!

> and to keep the commandments of the Lord and his decrees that I am commanding you today, for your own well-being. Although heaven and the heaven of heavens belong to the Lord your God, the earth with all that is in it, yet the Lord set

---

into stone tablets which Moses brings to the people. The story is long and involves golden calves being worshipped while Moses is still up on the mountain and results in his smashing the first set of tablets. Eventually the Israelites convince Moses to ask God to give them another chance, but they are afraid of hearing anything directly from God, so they ask Moses to "translate" the tablets for them. The second time, before Moses repeats the list of commandments, he prefaces it with the admonition in Deut 6:4–5.

7. Mark's version adds "mind."

> his heart in love on your ancestors alone and chose you, their descendants after them, out of all the peoples, as it is today. Circumcise, then, the foreskin of your heart,[8] and do not be stubborn any longer. For the Lord your God is God of gods and Lord of lords, the great God, mighty and awesome, who is not partial and takes no bribe, who executes justice for the orphan and the widow, and who loves the strangers, providing them food and clothing. You shall also love the stranger, for you were strangers in the land of Egypt. You shall fear the Lord your God; him you shall serve; to him you shall hold fast; and by his name you shall swear (Deut 10:13–20).

Notice the quality of these commandments: The mighty and awesome God loves and has chosen you, so (1) be stubborn no longer, but believe the God who loves you is not partial, cannot be bribed (by offerings and sacrifices), accomplishes justice for the oppressed, loves and provides for strangers (those who are not your people). (2) Love the stranger as God does. (3) Respect and revere your God. (4) Serve your God. (5) Hold fast to your God. (6) Bind yourself with his name.

These are the commandments reflected in all of Jesus' authentic teachings, but often unknown, omitted, or ignored in traditional Christian interpretations.

Gospel = Good News?

To his focus on a God of love and forgiveness, Jesus adds the startling "good news" that the place ruled by God is accessible to each of us.

The gospel writers refer to his teachings in general as "the good news of the kingdom," using the New Testament Greek word *euangelion*,[9] which means "good tidings." From Greek, the word made its way into Latin as *bona adnuntiatio* ("good announcement") and then into Old English as "*godspel*" meaning "good message," or "glad tidings," and thence to the English word "gospel."

Jesus begins almost every parable or proverb with "the Kingdom of God is like . . . " In fact, this near and accessible "kingdom" "is just about

---

8. "Circumcise then, the foreskin of your heart" is a metaphor based on the practice of cutting away a thickened layer of skin which is possibly unnecessary and potentially unclean. In Hebrew tradition, the heart was the seat of the will and the intellect. This metaphor suggests that it too may be covered by a layer of unnecessary "protection," such as mistaken beliefs that make it more difficult to understand the truth about God.

9. From which we derive the word "evangelize," i.e., "spread the good news."

all he talks about."[10] He talks about it so much, it seems like he thinks that *it* is the good news he is bringing to people.

By the time Paul was writing his letters to early Christian churches in the 50s CE, and well before Matthew, Mark and Luke wrote their "Gospels According to" a few decades later, the understanding of Jesus' "good news" had changed. Instead of Jesus' message that God's kingdom "has come near," and indeed, is within each of us right now, a shift occurred; the kingdom of God became "near" in time, a future event that hasn't happened yet but will soon.

One can imagine that after his crucifixion, his followers—baffled and grieving—came to terms with his cruel death by deciding that *it* was the "good news" and the *really* good news was that he rose from the dead and ascended to live with God in the Kingdom (which now they understood was in heaven, not here on earth). It almost makes sense: while Jesus was with them, so was the Kingdom of God. When Jesus left, God and his kingdom left also. Determined that his death have meaning, early Christians decided that the God they knew from Hebrew scripture had demanded (and provided) a sacrifice because humans were so vile. The good news (now) was that we had been saved from the wrath of God through Jesus' death and resurrection. In the decades after his death, Christian tradition began forming around the assumption that in all his teachings Jesus referred to his own upcoming death and rebirth as "good news," a sacrifice to redeem sinful humanity.

God's Kingdom of Love

While he was alive, Jesus talked consistently about God, God's Kingdom, and love, always relating them to "good news." He did not talk about death, but life. He did not tell his followers they had to die to enter the Kingdom of God, not even figuratively (Paul did that.) Instead, Jesus taught them how to live, here and now, among humans and in the Kingdom of God. All they had to do was to give up arrogance, violence, anger, and greed; to focus instead on humility, kindness, and compassion; to be satisfied with (and make sure others had) enough food, shelter, and material goods. A simple message at odds with human nature, human culture, and human religion; a message so challenging, we still can't fully grasp it. (We can, apparently, grasp a powerful king

---

10. Rohr, "Mystical Holism."

God who requires the blood sacrifice of his most beloved child and will let us into his kingdom if we just acknowledge that.)

Jesus' earliest followers understood the whims of power, and their understanding of deity reflected what they saw in themselves and other humans, particularly those who ruled them. Like us, they had difficulty with the concept of Jesus' consistently all-loving God who ruled the counter-intuitive kingdom described in "the good news."

Jesus brought his good news in simple direct language to ordinary people, not religious authorities nor the educated elite. He avoided intellectual/theological exposition. Rather than explaining or defining God's love, he taught inductively, using parables that blurred the lines between God's realm and the earthly realm. He showed love in action with images from ordinary life but extraordinary reality.

He brought this good news to the common people, not the wealthy or powerful. In fact, Jesus' God of the Good News was a threat to those with power because it posited a power higher than theirs that was not necessarily on their side. (As it played out, those with power were also a threat to his message once they were able to control it and change it.)

Jesus framed the concept of a loving God in the shared experience of having a ruler and living in his kingdom, but the kingdom he describes does not operate the way human kingdoms do—time, quantity and size have no meaning in this kingdom where the last shall be first. In fact, many of Jesus' teachings make no sense or seem patently wrong in the world as we know it; people still struggle to understand what he meant. Nowhere does Jesus say specifically "God is Love,"[11] yet his teachings make perfect sense if we grasp that the highest value in God's kingdom is compassionate love. And, because this is a deity we are talking about that love includes the following attributes: it is abundant, universal, unconditional, merciful, compassionate, infinite, and eternal.

Ironically, traditional Christianity has never been comfortable with Jesus' message about the unconditionally loving God of the Good News and his Kingdom, perhaps because it diminishes the Church's power and control over people. The earliest written accounts of his teachings (Paul's letters, the gospels, etc.) already include modifications that qualify or limit the Love of God. Worse, for two millennia, Christian transcribers or editors have "rectified" Jesus' puzzling teachings about the Kingdom of God to fit more closely what we humans know of kingdoms and rulers.

---

11. This phrase occurs in the New Testament only in the Gospel of John, written a hundred years or so after Jesus' death.

Through the centuries, however, individuals have intuitively or experientially grasped the nature of God and God's Kingdom as Jesus taught it, i.e., as boundless love for all creation. Mystics inside or outside the Church are often a good source for insights into Jesus' God of the Good News. George Fox is one of them. Below is an "opening" or "revelation" he describes in his journal:

> Though I read the Scriptures that spoke of Christ and of God, yet I knew Him not but by revelation, as he who hath the key did open, and as the Father of life drew me to his Son by his spirit. And then the Lord did gently lead me along, and did let me see his love, which was endless and eternal, and surpasseth the knowledge that men have in the natural state or can get by history of books....[12]

Julian of Norwich (1342–c.1416) is another, who even from within the embrace of the Church, beautifully expressed her experience of the Creator God who loves every lily in the field, every falling sparrow, and every human being.

> I saw that [God] is to us everything which is good and comforting for our help. He is our clothing who wraps and enfolds us for love, embraces us and shelters us, surrounds us for his love which is so tender that he may never desert us. And so in this sight I saw that he is everything which is good, as I understand.
>
> And in this he showed me something small, no bigger than a hazelnut, lying in the palm of my hand, as it seemed to me, and it was as round as a ball. I looked at it with the eye of my understanding and thought: What can this be? I was amazed that it could last, for I thought that because of its littleness, it would suddenly have fallen into nothing. And I was answered in my understanding: It lasts and always will, because God loves it; and thus everything has being through the love of God.
>
> In this little thing I saw three properties. The first is that God made it, the second is that God loves it, the third is that God preserves it.[13]

Such "openings" and "revelations" still happen,[14] though our contemporary materialistic and physicalist culture, including Christianity, tends

---

12. Fox, *Journal*, 11–12.
13. Julian of Norwich, "Highest Form of Prayer."
14. For example, see "Awakening" in Chapter 6.

to dismiss them. Understandably, those who have these experiences are reluctant to speak of them. The fact that "openings" and "revelations" keep breaking through in individuals (everywhere on the planet), however, may be an explanation for why human beings still believe in something higher than themselves.

3

Why Parables?

> When he was alone, those who were around him along with the twelve asked him about the parables (Mark 4:10).
>
> Then the disciples came and asked him, "Why do you speak to them in parables?" (Matt 13:10).
>
> Then his disciples asked him what this parable meant (Luke 8:9).

EVEN JESUS' DISCIPLES WERE mystified by his parables.

Jesus' response in all three synoptic gospels is to describe parables using a trope from Hebrew scripture about seeing but not perceiving and hearing but not understanding:

> "they may indeed look but not perceive, and may indeed hear but not understand . . ." (Mark 4:12).
>
> "To you it has been given to know the secrets of the kingdom of heaven, but to them it has not been given. . . . The reason I speak to them in parables is that 'seeing they do not perceive, and hearing they do not listen, nor do they understand'" (Matt 13:10, 13).
>
> He said, "To you it has been given to know the secrets of the kingdom of God, but to others I speak in parables, so that 'looking they may not perceive and hearing they may not understand'" (Luke 8:10).

Not only did Jesus use riddle-like parables, but he did not write anything down. His teachings about the God of the Good News and the Kingdom of God/Heaven were passed along via the oral tradition until, decades after his death, other people began writing them down, sometimes in Aramaic, sometimes in Greek, and then Latin. Three hundred years later, of the written versions of Jesus' teachings in existence at the time, three narrative accounts of his life and teachings—Mark, Matthew, and Luke (the "Synoptic Gospels")—became part of the New Testament canon, along with a fourth version, "The Gospel According to John" which is less biographical and more poetic.

In the more than two thousand years since Jesus last told a parable in person, millions of words have been written interpreting his sayings and parables which have puzzled and intrigued hearers/readers from the beginning. In his excellent book, *The Parables of Jesus: A Commentary*, biblical scholar, theologian, and seminary professor Arland J. Hultgren cautions us against approaching a parable as an "actual event." For instance, he says that interpreters of the Parable of the Vineyard Workers (Matt 20:1–16) may:

> raise the question why the landowner has to go out more than once to hire workers. Why did he not hire a sufficient number when he went out early in the morning? Scholars have speculated as to the reason. One proposal is that the work was particularly urgent; it had to be done prior to the onset of the rainy season. A second proposal is that it was late August or early September; the grapes must be picked; it is probably a Friday; and the work has to be finished by sundown, the onset of the Sabbath. But neither of these proposals is sound. For one thing, they turn the parable into an account of an actual event.

Hultgren concludes:

> The only sufficient reply to the question of why the landowner hired workers at different times is that it makes a grand story consisting of a crescendo of events that leads up to the end that has been planned all along. . . The story has been composed with its end in view. It has not been composed as the narration of events in real life, starting from the beginning and ending in due course.[1]

---

1. Hultgren, *Parables of Jesus*, 37.

To understand Jesus' parables, it helps to remember that they are fictional stories—characters and situations set in the everyday life of human beings—that Jesus uses *to make a point* about love and/or the Kingdom of God which is more important than whether all the details make logical sense. Zooming in on factual details allows us to miss (or ignore) the (sometimes uncomfortable) higher truth in Jesus' parables.[2]

Secrets, Mysteries and Parables

Occasionally Jesus gave us a parable, such as the one below, that is so direct it is difficult to miss the meaning (though practicing what it preaches is still difficult for human beings to do).

> Someone in the crowd said to him, "Teacher, tell my brother to divide the family inheritance with me." But he said to him, "Friend, who set me to be a judge or arbitrator over you?" And he said to them, "Take care! Be on your guard against all kinds of greed, for one's life does not consist in the abundance of possessions." Then he told them a parable: "The land of a rich man produced abundantly. And he thought to himself, 'What should I do, for I have no place to store my crops?' Then he said, 'I will do this: I will pull down my barns and build larger ones, and there I will store all my grain and my goods. And I will say to my soul, Soul, you have ample goods laid up for many years; relax, eat, drink, be merry.' But God said to him, 'You fool! This very night your life is being demanded of you. And the things you have prepared, whose will they be?' So it is with those who store up treasures for themselves but are not rich toward God" (Luke 12:13–21).

The parable itself occurs only in verses 16–20. Traditional interpretations of the parable, however, may include references to material added by the gospel writer before the parable (verses 13–15, the odd dialogue about dividing a family inheritance and Jesus' admonition to beware of all forms of greed) and after the parable (verse 21). From what we know of Jesus' habitual practice of telling parables without explaining them, it is more likely that the writer of Luke or another source added the pointed summary statement.

---

2. "Facts" are lodged in the earthly, material world; they can be proven to be true or false. Truth exists in a higher plane that speaks to the spirit or soul; for instance, Shakespeare's play *King Lear* about an old man and his children contains universal truths about human relationships, even if the events didn't happen in the "real" world.

In the non-canonical Gospel of Thomas the parable is stripped to its essence and probably closer to the way Jesus told it, i.e., without details like building bigger barns or eating, drinking and being merry, and without explanation.

> Jesus said, "There was a rich man who had much money. He said, 'I shall put my money to use so that I may sow, reap, plant, and fill my storehouse with produce, with the result that I shall lack nothing.' Such were his intentions, but that same night he died. Let him who has ears hear"[3] (Thomas 63).

Here we find Jesus' consistent message that earthly wealth, possessions, and status matter only in the physical realm and serve us only while we are alive. The security of having wealth does not last beyond the body itself. Implied but not stated in the parable is that something else may last beyond that. If we've heard other lessons from Jesus, we know to consider it might be the love in the Kingdom of God.

The gospels were written in first-century Greek, but some biblical scholars think Jesus' use of the parable form reflects its use in Hebrew scripture. The English word "parable" translates the Greek word *parabolē*, which means essentially what the word means in English, as well as the Hebrew word *mâshâl*. According to *Strong's Definitions*, though, translated as "parable" or "proverb," *mâshâl* has other connotations as well; it is "apparently from [a word meaning 'dominion or rule over'] in some original sense of superiority in mental action; properly, a pithy maxim, usually of metaphorical nature; hence, a simile (as an adage, poem, discourse) . . . ."[4] The phrase "superiority in mental action" suggests something like *koans* in Zen Buddhism, i.e., paradoxical statements or questions "inaccessible to rational understanding," but which "may be accessible to intuition" and thus lead to spiritual enlightenment.[5]

When people reach enlightenment, have powerful spiritual awakenings, or perceive higher truths, it is often difficult for them to describe what happened. Such experiences are ineffable, i.e., beyond words. Perhaps one reason Jesus used parables the way he did was to push his followers past logical reasoning and provoke them into an intuitive grasp of higher truths. Placing his stories in the "Kingdom of God" with its

---

3. *Gospel of Thomas*, 63.
4. "H4912—*māšāl* - Strong's Hebrew Lexicon (kjv)." Blue Letter Bible.
5. "*Koan*," Buddhism Guide.com.

different reality provides us a key to access spiritual realms not perceived through ordinary literal language.

Many who saw Jesus and heard him speak may have responded to his charismatic teaching without understanding what he was really saying, hearing his parables as simple stories that didn't make much sense but were compelling nonetheless. (A practice still true today.) Even the disciples had to be given a key to the parables, and even with that key, they sometimes did not understand. And even when Jesus was quite direct, he said things people found difficult to grasp. For instance, in the following proverbs Jesus speaks very directly about how to live in the Kingdom of God:

> Love your enemies (Matt 5:44).
>
> If anyone strikes you on the cheek, offer the other also (Luke 6:29).
>
> From anyone who takes away your coat do not withhold even your shirt (Luke 6:29).
>
> Give to everyone who asks of you (Luke 6:30).
>
> Forgive and you'll be forgiven (Luke 6:37).
>
> Let the dead bury their own dead, but as for you, go and proclaim the kingdom of God (Luke 9:60).
>
> Ask, and it will be given to you; search, and you will find; knock, and the door will be opened for you. For everyone who asks receives, and everyone who searches finds, and for everyone who knocks, the door will be opened (Matt 7:7–8).

Passages in which Jesus speaks directly like this are called "the hard sayings" because what he says seems beyond reason, beyond what is humanly possible. The gospel writers and later editors often added explanatory or elaborative text around the hard sayings to "soften" them.

In his lifetime, Jesus' direct teachings and puzzling parables might be dismissed as nonsense by some, but to authority figures listening on the literal level, what he said about the Kingdom of God was zealous and dangerous: it challenged the authority of both Roman and Jewish power structures.

The core of his message referred to a dominion *greater* than Rome. To suggest that such a place existed was bad enough, but Jesus went further: he advised people to obey the ruler of that dominion! This clearly was to oppose Rome and the Emperor, and any opposition was considered treason, a serious crime in the Empire. Only three types of criminals were executed by the painful, prolonged, and shameful death of crucifixion: pirates, rebellious slaves, and traitors. Jesus was not a pirate and did not lead a slave rebellion. His crucifixion meant that Rome, at least, considered him a traitor and punished him accordingly.

The synoptic gospels include an account which may attempt to explain why he was executed in this manner: it is the scene in which Pilate tries to get Jesus to say he is "King of the Jews," which Jesus adroitly avoids admitting by saying essentially: "Your words, not mine." Given his fate, however, Jesus must have refused to deny the existence of the divine ruler and realm that he described in all his teachings and in every parable: a dominion greater than Rome's empire, ruled by a benevolent "king" not terribly interested in human-made rules, including religious ones.[6]

Jesus' teachings also threatened Jewish religious authority, the Sanhedrin, a council which combined religious, political, and educational functions in the Jewish community and included both Sadducees and Pharisees. The Sadducees were priests, elite religious leaders with high social status, education, and authority. Scribes could be Sadducees or Pharisees; they were often teachers with some theological training, valued because they could not only read but write.

Jesus frequently warned his disciples against the "righteousness" of the Pharisees and the "chief priests and scribes," referring to them as hypocrites. They seemed to be everywhere Jesus was, watching and listening, waiting for him to make a mistake, challenging him every time he "broke a law" (commandment of the Torah). Jesus responded to the Pharisees' accusations directly, saying that their understanding was limited and did not reflect knowledge of a higher law. For instance, when they scold him for doing "unlawful" things on the Sabbath, like healing people or allowing his disciples to "pluck heads of grain to eat," Jesus replies: "The Sabbath was made for humankind and not humankind for the Sabbath, so the Son of Man is lord even of the Sabbath" (Mark 2:27–28). Essentially, he says, humans made the Torah with its rule about the sabbath. But humans were created by God before the Torah, so even children[7] have authority over its rules about the sabbath.

---

6. For example, see Mark 2:27, "And Jesus said to them, 'The Sabbath was made for [hu]mans, not [hu]mans for the Sabbath.'" Such challenges upset Jewish religious authorities and seem to have led them to cooperate with the Romans in getting rid of him.

7. The phrase "Son of Man" is loaded with meaning in the Christian tradition

Another thing about Jesus that must have been maddening for the priests, scribes, and Pharisees, who considered themselves experts on Hebrew scripture, was his ability to quote it to make his own points. For instance, Jesus stresses in a new way the near presence of God, an idea that appears in Deut 30:11–14 when Moses says to the Israelites:

> "Surely, this commandment that I am commanding you today is not too hard for you, nor is it too far away. It is not in heaven, that you should say, 'Who will go up to heaven for us and get it for us so that we may hear it and observe it?' Neither is it beyond the sea, that you should say, 'Who will cross to the other side of the sea for us and get it for us so that we may hear it and observe it?' No, the word is very near to you; it is in your mouth and in your heart for you to observe."

Jesus alludes to this passage when he tells his followers:

> ". . . The coming of the kingdom of God is not something that can be observed, nor will people say, 'Here it is,' or 'There it is,' because the kingdom of God is [within] you." (Luke 17:20–21).

His emphasis on this idea was worrisome to religious authorities because, if the Kingdom of God is within us, we have no need of temples and intermediaries like priests or scribes; if the Kingdom of God is within *everyone*, no one has a corner on true righteousness. This was the most radical "good news" Jesus taught, i.e., this kingdom and the loving God who rules it are eternal, but also here, now, and most disturbing of all, *accessible to everyone*. As Jeremias phrases it, Jesus' "proclamation of a God who was at the present moment offering a share in salvation to the despised, the oppressed, and the despairing, ran counter to all the religiosity of his time . . ."[8] Such a concept is still too radical for human beings to accept, particularly those with power who have the most to lose. How can power structures possibly control people who believe this? Obviously Roman and Jewish authorities in Jesus' time had to get rid of the peasant teacher spreading such ideas.

Another reason Jesus taught obliquely may have to do with human nature and our desire to pin down meaning and thus, control it. In the form of parables, Jesus' teaching is counter-intuitive and resists logic or linear thinking. Its continued power may rest in its very elusiveness and

---

which interprets it as Jesus referring to himself as the Messiah. But the phrase in Aramaic and Hebrew can simply mean the child/children of a human being.

8. Jeremias, *Jesus and the Message of the New Testament*, loc. 231.

ambiguity: "What we can fully understand, what we can make ourselves, we don't have to have any reverence for, we can replicate it."[9] For more than two millennia, traditional Christianity has "controlled" Jesus' message by imposing on it Christian dogma and doctrine. Despite all the Church has done through the centuries to interpret, fix, and thus control Jesus' words, those who "have ears to hear" still suspect that Jesus' good news is radically different from the Church's good news.

Characteristics of Jesus' Parables

The classic definition of a "Jesus parable" comes from Welsh theologian, C. H. Dodd, in his 1936 work, *The Parables of the Kingdom*:

> At its simplest the parable is a metaphor or simile [i.e., comparison] drawn from nature or common life, arresting the hearer by its vividness or strangeness, and leaving the mind in sufficient doubt about its precise application to tease it into active thought.[10]

Biblical scholars of the Jesus Seminar identified specific and consistent qualities in an authentic Jesus parable—"authentic" in the sense that Jesus probably really said this, or something very close to it. An authentic Jesus parable contains all the following:

a. a narrative or story

b. metaphor/simile

c. simple language

d. concrete words, as few as possible

e. a surprising ending with no explanation of its meaning

f. inner consistency—elements in the parable do not contradict each other[11]

---

9. Attributed to E. F. Schumacher (1911–77), author of *Small Is Beautiful: A Study of Economics As If People Mattered* (1973) and *A Guide for the Perplexed*. I copied this quotation for myself years ago but did not indicate its source. I have been unable to find it in either of the above books or online.

10. Dodd, *Parables of the Kingdom*, 5.

11. Funk, et al., *Parables of Jesus*, 16–17. "If the parable is at odds with the context in which the evangelist places the parable, we have weak evidence that the parable predates the work of the evangelist. . . . When in doubt, scholars put the parable under review to the final test of a reading: can one read or interpret this parable in a way that

Reading Jesus' parables for an "inner consistency" requires that we question any element that violates his consistent message about the Kingdom of God and the importance of Love, especially if an introduction, ending, or explanation includes elements antithetical to love, such as judgment, punishment, violence, rejection, cruelty, etc. In the early days of Christianity, when different factions were trying to evangelize and convert new followers, such additions by the gospel writer or later editors may have been added to soothe potential converts frustrated by stories they didn't understand.

---

coheres with other authentic (or inauthentic) parables in the tradition?"

4

Ears to Hear

> And he said, "If you have ears to hear, then hear!" (Mark 4:9)
>
> Do you have eyes and fail to see? Do you have ears and fail to hear? (Mark 8:18)
>
> The reason I speak to them in parables is that 'seeing they do not perceive, and hearing they do not listen, nor do they understand.' (Matt 13:13)

ALL THREE OF THE synoptic gospels describe the crucifixion, so their accounts must have been written after Jesus' death. Biblical scholars disagree on the dates these gospels were written,[1] but generally agree that the writers were probably not among those who heard Jesus speak in person. The writer of Luke's gospel says as much at beginning of his account:

> Since many have undertaken to *compile a narrative* about the events that have been fulfilled among us, *just as they were handed on to us by those who from the beginning were eyewitnesses and servants of the word*, I, too, decided, as one having a grasp of everything from the start, *to write a well-ordered account* for you, most excellent Theophilus, so that you may have a firm grasp of the words in which you have been instructed (Luke 1:1–4). (Italics added for emphasis.)

---

1. Estimates range from circa 69 CE (Mark) to circa 85 CE (Matthew) to circa 95 CE (Luke).

Notice the phrases in italics above that indicate conscious manipulation of material "handed on to us" from eyewitnesses. "Compiling a narrative" is not just writing down a known sequence of events; "compiling" requires ordering and structuring of information so it results in "a well-ordered account." Though the three synoptic gospels follow the same general biographical narrative, each gospel writer includes details intended to give newcomers "a firm grasp" of Jesus' teachings.

All three writers worked from material preserved in the oral tradition—teachings, sayings, parables, and stories—Jesus' words memorized, collected, and passed on. In some cases, all three include similar material, such as using the same phrase to identify what Jesus did as "preaching the good news of the kingdom." In his version, Luke adds as context, Jesus in the synagogue at the beginning of his ministry, unrolling a scroll and reading aloud a passage from the prophet Isaiah (61:1–2a) which begins:

> The spirit of the Lord God is upon me because the LORD has anointed me; he has sent me to bring good news to the oppressed, to bind up the brokenhearted, to proclaim liberty to the captives and release to the prisoners, to proclaim the year of the LORD's favor.

Jesus then declares "Today this scripture has come true in your hearing."[2] Neither Mark nor Matthew recounts this incident.

New Testament scholars believe we find the most authentic remnants of Jesus' words in his sometimes puzzling, often counterintuitive parables, all of which "revolve around one central theme: the kingdom of God."[3] Jesus explains to his disciples that he uses parables so that only those "with ears to hear and eyes to see" will understand what he is saying.

Hearing/Seeing Vs. Understanding/Perceiving

The idea that eyes and ears alone do not assure understanding was common in Hebrew tradition, and the words for "hear" and "see" had more than one meaning, as they do in English today. For instance, in Ezek 12:2 ("Mortal, you are living in the midst of a rebellious house who have eyes

---

2. Isaiah 61:1–2a. It is telling that Jesus (or Luke) chose to end the quotation from Isaiah with the line: "to proclaim the year of the Lord's favor." The next phrase of the lengthy sentence continues "and the day of vengeance of our God, to comfort all who mourn . . ."

3. Blomberg, *Interpreting the Parables*, 291.

to see but do not see, who have ears to hear but do not hear"), the Hebrew word *ra'ah* used for "to see" can also be translated as "to perceive"; *shama'*, the word translated as "hear," can also be translated as "to understand, perceive the sense of what is said." Similarly, in the Greek of the New Testament, the word *blepō* can mean seeing with the eye and/or discerning, perceiving, or understanding something, as in "I see . . .". The word *akouō* can mean "to hear" and/or "to perceive the sense of what is said" as in "I hear you" indicating we understand what a person means.

"The reason I speak to them in parables is that 'seeing they do not perceive, and hearing they do not listen, nor do they understand'" (Matt 13:13).[4] The Greek word, *syniēmi,* translated as "understand" means "to set or join together in the mind," as in "to put it all together." Jesus implies that he speaks on more than one level so only the most perceptive listeners will understand *all* he says. On the material level of seeing, Jesus tells simple stories about things people see happen in ordinary life—seeds being planted, sheep cared for, travelers attacked by bandits, rich people having banquets, and so on. But these simple stories with unexpected outcomes operate on another level: Jesus sets them as comparisons to the Kingdom of God. To this day, hearers and readers of his parables are inclined to approach the parables from a more-or-less literal stance, taking situations at face-value, and floundering in the process.

The gospel writers were among those who floundered. To address confusion among early Christians, they included explanations and interpretations such as that exemplified in the Parable of The Sower. Below is Mark's rendering of the parable divided into sections: (1) the original part "authentic to Jesus"; and (2) verses added as explanation, attributed to Mark or another early Christian. Scholars of the Jesus Seminar "were virtually unanimous" that the "hardening theory" and the "allegorical interpretations of the parable" are the "formulations of Mark or the Christian community before him. They do not represent Jesus."[5] (These "formulations" also appear in the Gospels of Matthew and Luke which probably used Mark's version as a source.)

---

4. See Matt 13:13–15. The writer of Matthew has Jesus quote more from Isaiah 6:9–10 with its harsh intention to prevent healing for those who don't comprehend.
And he said, "Go and say to this people: 'Keep listening, but do not comprehend; keep looking, but do not understand.' Make the mind of this people dull, and stop their ears, and shut their eyes, so that they may not look with their eyes and listen with their ears and comprehend with their minds and turn and be healed."

5. Funk and Hoover, *Five Gospels*, 55.

Mark 4:3–9: "authentic to Jesus" (per the Jesus Seminar).

"Listen! A sower went out to sow. And as he sowed, some seed fell on a path, and the birds came and ate it up. Other seed fell on rocky ground, where it did not have much soil, and it sprang up quickly, since it had no depth of soil. And when the sun rose, it was scorched, and since it had no root it withered away. Other seed fell among thorns, and the thorns grew up and choked it, and it yielded no grain. Other seed fell into good soil and brought forth grain, growing up and increasing and yielding thirty and sixty and a hundredfold." And he said, "If you have ears to hear, then hear!"

Mark 4:11–12: "The hardening theory."

And he said to them, "To you has been given the secret of the kingdom of God, but for those outside everything comes in parables, in order that 'they may indeed look but not perceive and may indeed hear but not understand; so that they may not turn again and be forgiven.'"

Mark 4:13–20: "allegorical interpretation."[6]

And he said to them, "Do you not understand this parable? Then how will you understand all the parables? The sower sows the word. These are the ones on the path where the word is sown: when they hear, Satan immediately comes and takes away the word that is sown in them. And these are the ones sown on rocky ground: when they hear the word, they immediately receive it with joy. But they have no root and endure only for a while; then, when trouble or persecution arises on account of the word, immediately they fall away. And others are those sown among the thorns: these are the ones who hear the word, but the cares of the age and the lure of wealth and the desire for other things come in and choke the word, and it yields nothing. And these are the ones sown on the good soil: they hear the word and accept it and bear fruit, thirty and sixty and a hundredfold."

In other parables about seeds, Jesus begins by saying straight out: "The kingdom of God is *as if* someone would scatter seed on the ground" (Mark 4:26) and "With what can we compare the kingdom of God . . . It is *like* a mustard seed . . ." (Mark 4:30–31a; Matt 13:31; Luke 13:18–19). In Mark's

---

6. Mark equates the seed with the words of Jesus; in Greek, "*logos*," can be translated as "word," "speech," "talk," "discourse," "teachings," etc.

version of this parable, Jesus begins by saying it is about what happens to "the *secret* of the Kingdom of God" when it spreads. Mark does not have Jesus clarify what that secret *is* but merely refers to it as "the word." Some later Christians have found comfort in the simplicity of this interpretation, satisfied that "word" represents Jesus' teachings, whatever he said. Others, influenced by the Gospel of John ("in the beginning was the Word"), interpret "word" to mean Jesus himself as the Christ.[7]

Jesus' repetition of the word "love" provides a key to the "secret" of the Kingdom of God.

Jesus speaks of the necessity for humans to love God; doing so with all one's heart, soul, and strength, he says, is "the first and greatest commandment," i.e., what God requires of us is our love. He adds love of neighbor as second to it, saying, "All the Law and the Prophets hang on these two commandments." In other words, everything in the Hebrew tradition—laws, rules, prophecies—is subject to or depends on two commandments to *love*. Then, according to the writers of Matthew and Luke, he adds something outrageous and incomprehensible: "Love your enemies and pray for those who persecute you/do good to those who hate you" (see Matt 5:44 and Luke 6:27, 35).

Using Love as Key to Interpretation

Remember that Jesus' authentic teachings are *all* about love in the Kingdom of God. Introductory or concluding verses added by the gospel writer or later editors may include references lifting Jesus up as Savior of humanity, but these were written in hindsight. In what remains of his authentic teachings, Jesus focuses on his listeners, *not himself*. His goal is to help them understand what it means to live in the Kingdom of God, where love and compassion are abundant, eternal, infinite, and unconditional. This is always his lesson plan; it underlies everything he says, and so we should always start there.

Leaving out added interpretations and staying as close as possible to words authentic to Jesus, we find that all the images, all the situations, all the emotions and reactions in the parable connect to the Kingdom of God, which Jesus tells us, is on earth, within us, here and now. He begins parables by setting up the comparison: "The Kingdom of God is

---

7. Per the scholars of The Jesus Seminar, in his authentic teachings, Jesus does not refer to himself as the Messiah/Christ.

like . . .'." When the parables' unexpected outcome occurs—unusual in our material, earthly reality—we are to perceive that it is *not* unusual in the Kingdom-of-God reality, where love is the only influence.

Listen to the Parable of the Sower as though it happens in the Kingdom of God on earth, within and among humans.

Listen! = Hear and pay attention.

A sower went out to sow. = Let's say someone goes out to plant seeds of what they hope to reap. In the Kingdom of God, the only crop of value is Love/Compassion.

And as he sowed, some seed fell on a path, and the birds came and ate it up. = Seeds of Love may fall along the way and be destroyed by creaturely instinct or ignorance.

Other seed fell on rocky ground, where it did not have much soil, and it sprang up quickly, since it had no depth of soil. = Seeds of Love may appear to take root in people who embrace the idea with enthusiasm, who follow new fads quickly, but whose commitment is shallow and short-lived.

And when the sun rose, it was scorched, and since it had no root it withered away. = Seeds of Love may fall among people who are impatient, who lose interest and go on to something else before it can take root in them.

Other seeds fell among thorns, and the thorns grew up and choked it, and it yielded no grain. = Other Seeds of Love may fall among harsh, angry people whose hearts cannot accept love nor give it.

Other seed fell into good soil and brought forth grain, growing up and increasing and yielding thirty and sixty and a hundredfold." = Other Seeds of Love may fall and take root in people whose hearts are open, and the harvest of Love increases exponentially.

Perhaps the parable understood this way is too simple to be considered worthy advice from the Kingdom of God. Beginning with the gospel writers, the early Church seemed to have no patience for the complexity of Jesus' simplicity. On the contrary, the more complicated the interpretation, the better.

In the authentic parables, Jesus presents the Kingdom of God as co-existing with the human realm. Though our bodies live in the material realm of human reality, our soul/spirit/self can live, even now, in

God's realm. We have bodily eyes and ears, yes, but we also have spiritual eyes and ears. In the parables, the realms may overlap in the actions of the characters, e.g., the vineyard owner exhibits qualities found in the Kingdom of God while the laborers exhibit qualities found in human kingdoms (20:1–15); the Samaritan exhibits Kingdom-of-God qualities while the priest and Levite exhibit human-kingdom qualities (Luke 10:30–35). When we see compassionate love happening in a parable, we are seeing the Kingdom of God happening.

To fully understand the parables, we must hear/see them with our spiritual senses. As the early Friends phrased it, we must hear or read them in the same spirit as that in which Jesus told them.

Love God and Love Each Other

A *manifestation* of the Kingdom of God (with its emphasis on Love) in humans on the earthly realm (with its emphasis on power, wealth, possessions, and status) gives an authentic Jesus parable its unexpected twist and surprising ending.

If we use Love as a key to the hidden meaning in Jesus' parables, which contain "good news" about God's kingdom *within us*, we unlock the same message every time; every authentic parable tells the same Truth:

> In the Kingdom of God, Love rules.
>
> In the Kingdom of God, Love is the only power.
>
> In the Kingdom of God, all are equal in Love.
>
> In the Kingdom of God, all are equally Loved.
>
> Love is the only currency and only measure of value.
>
> Love is unconditional, infinite, abundant, universal, and eternal.

5

Traditional Interpretation vs. Quaker Application

> [George Fox] stood up in the face of the Christian Church, and said to it, "No, thou shalt not do this! Thou shalt not conform thyself to the world; thou shalt not go into an unholy alliance with the State; there shall still be in the midst of thee a spiritual people who shall bear their protest that Christ's kingdom is not of this world, and that religion standeth not in forms and ceremonies, but is a matter connected with the inner man, and is the work of God's Spirit in the heart."[1]
>
> —Charles Haddon Spurgeon, 1866

AMONG THE VERY FIRST *interpreters* of Jesus' teachings were the writers of the gospels of Mark, Matthew, Luke, and the non-canonical gospel of Thomas. Most traditional Christian interpretations are based on those first interpretations, and thus often on the end-times theology of early Christianity.

> When the Son of Man comes in his glory and all the angels with him, then he will sit on the throne of his glory. All the nations will be gathered before him, and he will separate people one from another as a shepherd separates the sheep from the goats, and he will put the sheep at his right hand and the goats

---

1. Spurgeon, "George Fox: An Address."

> at the left. Then the king will say to those at his right hand, "Come, you who are blessed by my Father, inherit the kingdom prepared for you from the foundation of the world . . . "Then he will say to those at his left hand, "You who are accursed, depart from me into the eternal fire prepared for the devil and his angels . . ." (Matt 25:31–34, 41).

This passage, which appears only in Matthew's gospel, was written during the formation of the early Church, perhaps to frighten people, convincing them to become Christians and thus avoid being cast aside by God. Biblical scholars recognize the "last Judgment" as an aspect of "Matthew's theological scheme, which became popular in the post-Easter community."[2] In Matthew's gospel, Jesus is a divinity who will come from his throne "in glory" to judge humanity at some future time. The simile, "as a shepherd separates the sheep from the goats" refers to Jesus separating those who are "blessed" from those who are "accursed," Those who have shown mercy will "inherit the kingdom," and those who have not shown mercy will be cast into "eternal fire." Apart from mercy, these concepts—thrones, glory, angels, "accursed," "eternal fire" and devils—are completely foreign to the Jesus who taught about the Kingdom of God, within us, here and now, where all are loved, and the sun shines on the righteous and the unrighteous alike.

Traditional Christian Interpretation

Matthew's "Last Judgment" scenario, which focuses on division, separation, judgment, and punishment, is foundational to traditional Christianity. It appears to greater or lesser degrees in all three synoptic gospels. For instance, note the focus on judgment and punishment in the following passage from Mark, versions of which also appear in Matthew and Luke (who probably used Mark as a common source).

First, the basic aphorism believed by scholars to be an authentic teaching of Jesus:

"Children, how hard it is to enter the kingdom of God! It is easier for a camel to go through the eye of a needle than for someone who is rich to enter the kingdom of God" (Mark 10:24b–25). Given that Jesus spoke always about love and the Kingdom of God, this metaphor seems to mean that those loaded down with wealth/possessions have difficulty

---

2. Funk and Hoover, *Five Gospels*, 258.

letting them go; concern for material things distracts from concern about others, a necessary quality of compassionate love, the gateway to the Kingdom of God.

To this authentic teaching, each synoptic gospel writer adds the reaction of the disciples (which is perhaps the reaction of his early Christian community): "They were greatly astounded and said to one another, 'Then who can be saved?'" (Mark 10:26). The implication is that if even rich people can't "be saved," who can be saved? (i.e., enter the Kingdom.) Mark continues: "Jesus said, 'Truly I tell you, there is no one who has left house or brothers or sisters or mother or father or children or fields for my sake and for the sake of the good news who will not receive a hundredfold now in this age—houses, brothers and sisters, mothers and children, and fields, with persecutions—and in the age to come eternal life'" (Mark 10:29-30; see also Luke 18:29-30). The interpreter and author of Matthew's gospel further adds: "Jesus told them, 'I swear to you, you who have followed me, when the son of Adam is seated on his throne of glory in the renewal of creation, you will be seated on twelve thrones and sit in Judgment on the twelve tribes of Israel" (Matt 19:28).

How far this last statement is from Jesus' teaching about love in the Kingdom of God, which is here, now, among us.

Interpretation like this has continued through two thousand years of Christianity. Good examples abound; one is a classic Christian devotional titled *Meditations for every day in the year: collected from different spiritual writers,* published in 1639 in Latin, the language of the Church, and still in print. Because it has been valued and consulted for centuries and is still used by Catholic and Protestant Christians alike, samples from *Meditations* will, for our purposes, represent traditional Christian interpretation of Jesus' teachings. As an example, the following is a "meditation" on (and interpretation of) the camel-and-eye-of-the-needle passage that appears in each of the synoptic gospels.

> I. Consider the observation which Christ made after the young man's departure: " How hardly shall they that have riches enter into the kingdom of God! For it is easier for a camel to pass through the eye of a needle than for a rich man to enter the kingdom of God." (Luke xviii. 24.) If, therefore, you wish to enter heaven with ease, divest yourself of all superfluities, and of every inordinate inclination for riches and the conveniences which they procure; for "they who would become rich," writes St. Paul, "fall into temptation and the snare of the devil." (i Tim. vi. 9).

> II. Consider the expression of St. Peter on this occasion: " Behold, we have left all things and followed Thee." Hence the holy Fathers infer that the Apostles had made a vow of poverty, and left everything, not only what they had, but what they might have, and even the desire of having. Ponder the greatness of the reward which Christ promises to all those who make these sacrifices for His sake: "They shall receive a hundred times as much now in this time, and in the world to come life everlasting." (Mark x. 30.) O incomparable purchase! Prefer eternal life to every earthly possession.

Note the assumption, both in the gospel writers' interpretations and in *Meditations*, that the Kingdom of God is in heaven, "the world to come life everlasting," i.e., eternity at some future time, and that the reward for sacrificing worldly goods for Christ's sake will be more goods in this life (shades of the Book of Job) plus eternal life in "the world to come." Most traditional Christian interpretation of Jesus' teachings include assumptions like this, which are the teachings of the Church about Jesus.

Early Quaker Application

Though they made frequent reference to passages from scripture, Fox and other early Friends did not explicate them as the Church and its preachers did. In reading the parables, for instance, Friends listened for what was consistent with the teachings of Jesus and what rang true in their hearts, trusting that the true meaning of the parable would become apparent to those open to receiving it. Their comments on the parables or other scripture rarely interpret a passage, assign meaning outside the text, or mention anything taught by the Church. They stay close to the text and apply its message to situations in real life, as they learned to do under the influence of George Fox.

Fox approached the Bible with great reverence and distrusted interpretations from ministers and clergy of the Church that contradicted the truths he found in scripture or experienced in spiritual encounters with the Inner Teacher/Inner Christ/God. In the example below, Fox talks about swearing oaths on the Bible, which was, then as now, customarily required for all sorts of legal and civil situations. In the seventeenth century, however, people took it more seriously, believing they could go to hell for lying, even by mistake, if they had sworn on the Bible. Fox

TRADITIONAL INTERPRETATION VS. QUAKER APPLICATION

pointed out to his followers that such oath-taking was against the teaching of Jesus who said, "Swear not at all."[3]

> The World saith, "Kiss the Book"; The Book saith, "Kiss the Son, lest he be angry": And the Son saith, "Swear not at all, but keep to yea and nay in all your communications; for whatsoever is more than this, comes of evil."

> The World saith, "Lay your hand on the Book"; the Book saith, "Handle the Word"; and the Word saith, "Handle not the traditions, inventions, nor the rudiments of the World"; and,

> "This is my beloved Son, hear ye him," saith God, "who is the Life, and the Truth, and the Light, and the Way to God, who saith, "Swear not at all."[4]

Notice that the World (i.e., the Church) and the Book (the "letter of the law") are contradicted by the Son (Jesus), the Word (the "spirit of the law"), and God, a succinct summary of Fox's objection to the Church.

Reading the early Friends' writing today is challenging, in part because they spoke and wrote in Elizabethan English, the same language Shakespeare used. (William Shakespeare died in April 1616, only eight years before George Fox was born in July 1624.) Words in modern English that we think we know often had different meanings in Elizabethan English. For instance, in seventeenth-century England, the word "professor" referred to someone who claimed to be an expert in some subject, and it included our modern understanding of "one who teaches a branch of knowledge." A note on the entry for "professor" from the *Online Etymology Dictionary*, however, gives us insight into the word as early Friends used it: "One professing religion. This canting[5] use of the word comes down from the Elizabethan period." Apparently English Puritans and other dissenters began using it in the 1500s in a "canting" way to mock Church authorities. Try saying "professor" in a whining, falsely pious tone of voice, and you'll hear it the way George Fox and early Friends said it.

---

3. Seventeenth-century Friends refused to take oaths and were frequently imprisoned for not doing so. Friends still have a testimony against swearing oaths, though they can *affirm* something is true. Nowadays, most instances that require oaths, even in secular venues, offer an option of using "affirm" instead of "swear."

4. Fox, "Gospel Truth demonstrated," *Works of George Fox.*

5. "Canting" means "hypocritically pious"; "the act of speaking in a whining tone; an apparently insincere use of religious or pious phraseology." *The Century Dictionary*, s.v. "canting."

Another reason the writings of early Friends' challenge us is that few of them were great wordsmiths like Shakespeare. Many, like George Fox, were not highly educated. (Brilliance and genius exist, however, in people without university degrees.) When Fox spoke or wrote, his purpose was teaching, preaching and prophecy, and his method reflected his conviction that truth spilled through him directly from the Inner Teacher and should not be edited.[6]

Like prophets of old, Fox was highly critical of the status quo, particularly the power and influence of the Church. He had experienced revealed Truth from a divine voice that told him to go to the source for answers to his spiritual questions, the source being Jesus Christ himself. What he found there, in "the very words only of Jesus,"[7] was so convincing and so obvious to him that Fox was compelled to speak out and tell others about it.

"Opening the scriptures" was the focus of much of his preaching, especially in the early days of his ministry. In 1652, for instance, at Firbank Fell more than a thousand people gathered to hear him speak from atop a large rock still known as Fox's Pulpit. For "about three hours" he spoke on the differences between what the Church said and what Jesus said. As he wrote in his journal, "I opened the parables and sayings of Christ, and things that had been long hidden; showing the intent and scope of the apostles' writings, and that their epistles were written to the elect."[8] By "the elect," Fox referred to those fortunate enough to hear Jesus speak in person, or to those throughout time who have had "ears to hear" and discern his true teachings.

As a youth, he had studied the Bible and sought out priests and preachers to ask them probing questions about scripture, but he received unsatisfactory, sometimes ridiculous advice (such as the minister who "prescribed" tobacco and singing psalms for his spiritual angst). "There were two thirsts in me," Fox wrote in his journal, "the one after the creatures [i.e., humans], to get help and strength there, and the other after the Lord, the Creator, and his Son Jesus Christ."[9] Eventually Fox began

---

6. This method continues today in Quaker worship where vocal ministry spoken extemporaneously out of the silence is valued more highly than a prepared message.

7. In his 1813 letter to John Adams, Thomas Jefferson described what he discovered in "the very words only of Jesus" as "the most sublime and benevolent code of morals which has ever been offered to man."

8. Fox, *Journal*, 155.

9. Fox, *Journal*, 84.

avoiding "professors," because he sensed "they did not possess what they professed."[10] He wandered the countryside alone, meditating, praying, gaining deep spiritual insights, having visions, and experiencing epiphanies, which he referred to as "openings."

Among those openings were realizations like these: (1) God was not to be found in churches or temples, but in people's hearts, and (2) spiritual wisdom and ministry was not obtained by attending Oxford or Cambridge for a degree in divinity. Instead, Fox wrote, there was "an anointing within man to teach him," which made it possible for the Lord to "teach His people Himself." Fox repeated this idea often in his journal, and "Christ has come to teach his people himself" became a refrain among early Friends. When Fox began his public ministry based on these and other epiphanies, he met great resistance and suffered much abuse, but nothing stopped him.

The active presence of God within each of us, a concept taught by Jesus and embraced by George Fox, is remarkably difficult for people to accept. From the beginning, what became Christianity could not grasp it and so ignored it, or reinterpreted it, often completely changing what Jesus said. Fox, who understood scripture at a spiritual level, was a fiery evangelist for the faith he learned from the Inner Christ/Inner Teacher/God Within, and a convincing critic of the Church and those who claimed to be Christian, but who did not "possess what they professed." Full of conviction that the Church had long ago fallen away from the truth and become corrupt, Fox was able to communicate the difficult concept of the Inner Christ/Inner Teacher/God Within clearly enough that thousands of people followed his teachings and became Quakers.[11]

Below is an example of his style, in 1654, rather shockingly accusing the Church of creating the scriptures in its own image.

> Now all you Priests and People that talk of these things without[12] you, from the Letter, this is a Parable to you, and you read the outside in the Letter: and from that you Imagine, and so set up a Form, or Likeness, or Image of these things; and here you Worship, and for this you contend, and would compel all to Worship your Image you have set up, and you go about to persecute and destroy all that will not bow to it with you: But it is but the Form

---

10. Fox, *Journal*, 69.

11. In 1660, the population of Great Britain was about 5.27 million. Estimates of the Quaker population range from thirty-five to fifty thousand.

12. "Without you," i.e., external reality, outside yourself, as opposed to "within you."

you have, and not the Substance; And you put the Dead Letter for the Living Word, and your own meanings of it, arising from the brain, and first Wisdom, and natural Learning . . .[13]

Paraphrased into modern English:

> Now all you Priests and People who talk of things outside you, external reality, this is what you think a parable is when you read the Scriptures: you read in the words there what you know of things outside yourselves, the external, the material world. And from that reality you create models or images, and this is what you worship. These models you created are what you argue for. And what you compel all to worship: your own image that you have created. And you persecute and destroy all that will not bow to it with you. But what you have is only something that looks like the scriptures, and not the real meaning or higher truth in them. Using your own meanings that come from your brain, your instinct, and what you've learned about the world, you substitute earthly reality for spiritual truth . . .

In seventeenth-century Quaker writings, we find numerous allusions to the parables, but few interpretations as such. Early Friends practiced what might be termed "applied" theology rather than "theoretical" theology.[14] Instances of this can be found in the online Quaker Bible Index which identifies countless references to parables used in the writings of early Quakers, such as this one about the Pearl from Isaac Penington in 1670:

> Sit down and count the cost of plowing up thy field, of searching after the hidden treasure of pure and true wisdom, and consider seriously, whether thou canst sell all for it, both inward and outward riches; that if thou do set thy hand to the plow, thou mayest not look back after anything else within or without, but mayest be content and satisfied with the pearl of true wisdom and life alone.[15]

---

13. Fox, *Word From the Lord*.

14. By the twentieth century there were Quaker exegetes, of course, such as New Testament scholar and Harvard professor, Henry J. Cadbury, known for, among many other things, his book, *The Making of Luke–Acts*, and his convincing argument that Luke was not a physician although he is identified as such in the gospel. Robert Funk writes in his book *Honest to Jesus* (p. 178): "It is said of Henry J. Cadbury, a renowned New Testament scholar and Quaker, that he gained his doctor's degree by depriving Luke of his."

15. Penington, QBI.

Penington speaks simply about the cost of changing your life after finding the "pure and true wisdom" in what Jesus taught. If you accept it, your life will change and there's no going back. Consider carefully, Penington advises, how your life will change if you accept that truth. For early Quakers, it meant joining a radical and persecuted group; it meant giving up fancy clothes, fancy words, and social status; it meant defying church and state authorities; it likely meant spending time in prison. The advice above from Penington is an example of Quaker applied theology, i.e., the application of Jesus' teachings to one's life. (For more comparisons of traditional Christian interpretation of the parables with early Quaker application, see Appendix.)

Seeking to be guided by the Source itself—God/the Inner Teacher/the Inner Christ—the first Friends went to the text of the New Testament to find what Jesus said. There they recognized Love in all its manifestations—compassion, inclusion, forgiveness, equality, integrity, universality, unity, harmony, peace—as the essence of Jesus' teachings. They rejected teachings or behavior motivated by or resulting in anything else, which meant they rejected much of what constituted the Church. For early Friends, long before John Woolman wrote it in 1761, "Love was the first motion."

"The Pearle Found in England"

In 1658, Fox wrote an eight-page epistle[16] addressed to "FRIENDS" in which he "opens" the Parable of the Pearl found in Matt 13:44–46:

> The kingdom of heaven is like treasure hidden in a field, which a man found and reburied; then in his joy he goes and sells all that he has and buys that field. Again, the kingdom of heaven is like a merchant in search of fine pearls; on finding one pearl of great value, he went and sold all that he had and bought it.

Bear in mind that Fox knew the truth of this parable from personal experience. He had risked all, given all, for the pearl of Truth he discovered in the teachings of the "Christ who," he said, "has come to teach his people himself."

In the style of the time, the title of the Fox's epistle is lengthy and includes several allusions to scripture in addition to the pearl parable.

---

16. Fox, *Pearle Found in England.*

> The Pearl Found in England.
>
> This is for the poor, distressed, scattered ones in foreign nations.
>
> From the royal seed of God, and heirs of salvation called Quakers,
>
> who are the Church of the living God, built up together of living stones in England.
>
> A visitation and uniting to the pearl of God which is hidden in all the world that everyone may turn into himself, and there feel it, and find it.[17]

Paraphrase and Comments

The following is a phrase-by-phrase paraphrase of this title into contemporary language. (The reader is encouraged to listen with seventeenth-century ears and discard twenty-first-century baggage around words like "redemption," "salvation," "Emmanuel," "hope of glory," etc.).

> "*The Pearl*" is an allusion to the parable that almost everyone at the time would have understood. To claim it "found in England" was a daring assertion.
>
> "*Royal seed of God*" = Jesus' teachings planted in each of us. "Seed" was among various words Quakers used to refer to "that of God" in everyone.
>
> "*Heirs of salvation.*" The phrase sounds innocuous to us but must have set some teeth on edge when Puritans heard or read Fox's epistle. It challenged the prevailing Puritan (Calvinist) belief in predestination, i.e., that salvation (going to heaven rather than hell) was only for "the Elect," those already chosen by God. No one knew for sure who was Elect and who was not, but if you were not predestined for heaven, there was nothing you could do to be saved from hell. For Fox to claim an "inheritance" of salvation was extremely provocative.

Saying that Quakers are "*the Church of the living God, built up together of living stones in England*" is another provocative statement. If Quakers are the Church of the living God built with living stones, does this suggest the possibility of a Church built with dead stones? And for

---

17. Spelling and punctuation have been modified for clarity.

Quakers, is this a sidelong glance at the "living Christ" who has come to teach his people himself? Fox alludes to a verse in 1 Pet 2:5: "Ye also, as lively stones, are built up a spiritual house, an holy priesthood, to offer up spiritual sacrifices, acceptable to God by Jesus Christ." Fox suggests that the spiritual practices of Quakers please God because they reflect the spiritual truths taught by Jesus.

"*A visitation and uniting to the pearl of God which is hidden in all the world that everyone may turn into himself, and there feel it, and find it.*" These final lines of the title seem, for twenty-first-century Quaker readers, rather tame. But in this statement, Fox undermines the very foundation of the Church and all governments aligned with it. Essentially, Fox repeats the astonishing teaching of Jesus that the Kingdom of God/God/Love is within each of us and accessible to all of us. We need only search within to find this priceless pearl. This statement was as troubling to religious and political authorities when Fox preached it in the seventeenth century as it was when Jesus taught it in the first century.

BOOK II **THE PARABLES IN REAL LIFE**

6

The Kingdom Within

Mind the Light in you which shows you evil, which checks you, when you speak an evil word, and tells you you should not be proud, nor wanton, nor fashion your-selves like the world, for the world's fashion passes away.

Mind the Light. It will keep your mind humble, heart lowly, and turn the mind within to wait upon the Lord, to be guided by Him.

Mind the Light. It will bring you to lay aside all evil, to wait on Christ for teaching till an entrance be made to your hearts and refreshment come from His presence there.

Mind the Light and it will not allow you to conform to the world's evil customs . . .

Mind the Lord's love for you and mind the Light above all things.

—George Fox, Epistle 17[1]

---

1. Fox, "Epistle 17."

Hidden Treasure and Pearls

THE BREVITY OF THE two parables that follow may deceive us into passing over them quickly. But within them is a vital key to understanding Jesus' message about the Kingdom of God (in Matthew's gospel, "Kingdom of Heaven").

> The kingdom of heaven is like treasure hidden in a field, which a man found and reburied; then in his joy he goes and sells all that he has and buys that field.
>
> Again, the kingdom of heaven is like a merchant in search of fine pearls; on finding one pearl of great value, he went and sold all that he had and bought it (Matt 13:44–46).

Imagine the difference if these parables just said, "the kingdom of heaven is like a treasure" or "like a pearl of great value." The words "hidden" and "in search of" highlight that something of great value is *hidden*; it must be *searched for and found*. Traditional Christian interpretation sees the treasure/pearl as representing Christ and salvation. But when Jesus was alive and teaching these parables, that notion hadn't yet been conceived. Instead, he emphasized the realm ruled by a God of Love which exists *within* each of us regardless of our external circumstances.

So how do we search for or find this hidden treasure within us? Spiritual teachers and religious practices may offer paths toward the treasure, but ultimately, it is discovered in unique and individual epiphanies. The most powerful experiences that open us to "that of God within"—and without—often occur when we are out in nature, perhaps more so than when we are in church.

Hidden Treasure and Pearls in Real Life

Individual spiritual encounters help us—to paraphrase George Fox—become aware of what is eternal, of what gathers our hearts together up to the Lord and lets us see that we are "written in one another's hearts."[2]

In my own experience, one such "pearl of awareness" occurred as I walked down a city sidewalk in Colorado Springs, Colorado, about twenty years ago. Coming toward me were three young black men. The one in the center caught my attention—something in the way he moved—a

---

2. Fox, "Epistle 24."

loose, casual, confident, jaunty athleticism. Deep in the throes of middle-age myself, I wondered, "What would it be like to be that young man, to move with such grace, to be so sure of my body?"

Suddenly, in a way I cannot explain, I *was* the young man. I was inside his head, looking out through his eyes, seeing the white-haired woman walking toward me. But I was more conscious of the two men on either side of me. For a brief-but-timeless-moment inside that young man's body, I experienced anxiety, uncertainty, the need to keep my guard up. And then suddenly, I was me again, passing the young men on the sidewalk.

The pearl revealed to me in this encounter was this: I knew without doubt that there was no separation between me and the young man, no true separation between me and anyone or anything else in creation. It is me[3] in that car wreck; me born in a Brazilian favela or Mumbai slum; me blown to bits in Gaza; me addicted to drugs and lying homeless on a sidewalk; me dying of hunger in an African village. It is me, too, in a luxurious mansion; me insisting that the Bible is the inerrant word of God, that Jesus died for our sins, that war is necessary, and that we need more guns. We are all one in the Kingdom of God, surrounded by endless grace we have done nothing to deserve and held by the boundless Love that permeates creation.

God's Pearls

For the last fifty years of their lives, my parents lived in a house on a rounded ridge of the High Plains in New Mexico, two miles from pavement and fourteen miles from the nearest town. The horizon stretched miles in every direction, the sky like a blue bowl turned upside down above us. Looking north from their house, we could see the Sangre de Cristo Mountains a hundred miles away near Santa Fe; south we could see flat-topped mesas thirty or so miles away. To the west were pinon-covered foothills and the blue Manzano Mountains. To the east, treeless yellow plains stretched over two hundred miles all the way into Texas.

With nothing to stop it, the wind on the High Plains blows constantly—sand in the summer and snow in the winter. Whistling around the house, rattling windows, banging gates, flapping tarps—wind is the

---

3. As a former English teacher, I know it should be "It is I," but in this case that sounds awkward and pretentious to me.

background soundtrack of the plains. On those rare days when the wind didn't blow, it was very quiet.

One spring when my teenaged daughter and I were visiting, there was such a day. The morning was unusually still, a little chilly, but no wind. We all took our coffee out to sit on the front porch in the early sunlight.

After a while of quiet conversation, we became aware of a sound in the distance. A rhythmical humming that we thought at first might be heavy equipment over on the highway. As the sound grew louder, it was more like a thrumming and whooshing—thrum whoosh . . . *Thrum Whoosh* . . . THRUM WHOOSH . . . Whatever it was, it was coming closer. None of us had ever heard such a sound. Unnerved, watching toward the direction of the sound, we listened and waited. Then, in the northeast, against the high blue sky, we made out a wedge of geese flying toward us. Hundreds, thousands of wild geese approached and flew directly over us, heading west toward the Bosque del Apache Wildlife Refuge near Socorro. In a wedge formation that stretched for miles across the sky, the geese kept coming, and coming, passing over us. . . . *w*hoosh thrum . . . *Whoosh thrum* . . . WHOOSH THRUM . . . the rhythmic flapping *in unison* of thousands of pairs of wings—a sound like the pumping of some great heart.

None of us were churchgoers or particularly religious, but we were all awed and silenced, something in each of us awakened to something holy in creation, something worthy of reverence in these wild geese, messengers of grace and power.

The Double Rainbow Guy

In January 2010, Paul Vasquez was at his house on the edge of Yosemite National Park just as a double rainbow appeared, arcing across the valley below. He began filming the emergence of the rainbow, recording his comments as it took perfect form before him. On the video, we see the rainbow and we hear his voice: "It's a double rainbow all the way. Whoa, that's so intense. Whoa. Oh, my God. Oh, my God. Oh, my God. . . . A double rainbow, man, a double rainbow! Wow! . . . Oh Wow. Oh God. Oh Wow. Oh Wow. What does it mean? Oh God . . . " And then we hear him weeping as he continues filming the rainbow, still saying "Oh wow . . ." He posted the three-and-a-half-minute video on the internet where it became one of the first "viral videos."

To some, the video was funny. Someone sent it to late-night television host, Jimmy Kimmel, who posted it on Twitter with the comment, "My friend Todd has declared this 'funniest video in the world'—he might very well be right," followed by a link to the video. Eventually, Kimmel had Vasquez as a guest on his show.

To those who have had similar responses to the beauty of nature, however, it is clear the man was having a religious experience. The nakedness of that experience is almost too much to watch. In an interview later, Vasquez explained the context; he had been seeing rainbows so often that earlier that morning, he sent an email to a friend saying he felt like Noah. "When I sent that email," he said, "my house filled with colors, and that's when the double rainbow started . . . I recognized I was in the presence of God." As for what came out of his mouth, he said, "That wasn't me; something was flowing through me; God was speaking through and to me." Not eloquent, not smooth, but deeply felt. And for those who can hear it, the immediate experience of the divine comes through his voice in its intensity and gratitude.

When Vasquez died in 2020, media coverage was international; tributes and obituaries for him appeared in sources like *The Washington Post*, *The Los Angeles Times*, *The Chicago Tribune*, *USA Today*, *The Baltimore Sun*, etc., as well as newspapers in the UK, Australia, and elsewhere, and in local papers across the country. Tributes and obituaries appeared in magazines like *The New Yorker*, *Variety*, *Rolling Stone*, *People*, and *Billboard*; on Facebook, Twitter, and dozens of online sites; and in news stories on all the major networks, including CNN, CBS, ABC, NBC, and Fox. When he died, his video had been viewed more than forty-five million times. As of this writing, the video has almost fifty-one million views and counting.

Though he became something of a folk hero and celebrity, Vasquez never permitted his video to be used for advertising. Today when you watch it, no YouTube ads pop up. He considered the Double Rainbow video his "gift to humanity," explaining that "the video is me understanding I'm in the presence of God. So it's like the first video of God someone put on the internet. You can't put an ad on God."[4]

Amen.

---

4. Quoted by Feliks Garcia, "6 Years Later."

The Ugly Pearl

The Pearl of Truth is not always pleasant or lovely; sometimes it is harsh and ugly; but truth is always necessary for change and growth. Below is an entry from the *Journal of John Woolman* describing a powerful and tragic truth about slavery that came to him in a dream. The impact of the truth in his dream still affects those who read his account of it.

> In a time of sickness with the pleurisy, a little upward of two years and a half ago, I was brought so near the gates of death that I forgot my name. Being then desirous to know who I was, I saw a mass of matter of a dull, gloomy color, between the south and the east; and was informed that this mass was human beings in as great misery as they could be and live; and that I was mixed in with them, and that henceforth I might not consider myself as a distinct or separate being. In this state I remained several hours. I then heard a soft, melodious voice, more pure and harmonious than any I had heard with my ears before; I believed it was the voice of an angel, who spake to the other angels. The words were: "John Woolman is dead." I soon remembered that I once was John Woolman, and being assured that I was alive in the body, I greatly wondered what that heavenly voice could mean.
>
> I believed beyond doubting, that it was the voice of an holy angel; but, as yet, it was a mystery to me.
>
> I was then carried in spirit to the mines, where poor oppressed people were digging rich treasures for those called Christians; and heard them blaspheme the name Christ, at which I was grieved; for his name, to me, was precious.
>
> Then I was informed, that these heathen were told, that those who oppressed them were the followers of Christ; and they said, amongst themselves, if Christ directed them to use us in this sort, then Christ is a cruel tyrant.[5]
>
> —*Journal of John Woolman*

"Awakening"

Federico Faggin[6] is an Italian physicist known for his work in Silicon Valley. Among other things, he developed the world's first microprocessors

---

5. John Woolman, *Journal*, 164–65.
6. Pronounced "Fah-jeen."

and served as CEO for several high-tech startup companies. A recipient of many international awards (including the 2009 National Medal of Technology and Innovation presented by President Obama), Faggin is currently president of a foundation dedicated to the study of consciousness. Below he describes something that happened in 1990 while he was on holiday with his family:

> I woke up around midnight to drink a glass of water. When I went back to bed, while waiting in silence to fall asleep again, I felt a powerful rush of energy-love emerge from my chest, the like of which I had never had before and couldn't even imagine was possible. This feeling was clearly love, but a love so intense and so incredibly fulfilling that it surpassed any possible idea I had about what love is. Even more unbelievable was the fact that I was the source of this love. I perceived it as a broad beam of shimmering white light, alive and beatific, gushing from my heart with incredible strength.
>
> Then suddenly that light exploded and filled the room and then expanded to embrace the entire universe with the same white brilliance. I knew then, without a shadow of a doubt, that this was the "substance" of which all that exists is made. This was what created the universe out of itself. Then, with immense surprise, I knew that I was that light! The entire experience lasted perhaps less than one minute, and it changed me forever.[7]

Faggin discovered the hidden treasure, the pearl of great price: the Kingdom of God that Jesus taught us about, the one that is here, now, within us, though most of the time we are not conscious of it. Our physical bodies cannot stay there all the time, but having once experienced it, our hearts and minds are forever changed. This is the realm Jesus talked about, a dimension of complete unity with God and all creation and love beyond imagining.

---

7. Faggin, "Awakening," 79.

7

The Good Samaritan

> A certain man was going down from Jerusalem to Jericho, and fell among robbers, and having stripped him and inflicted blows, they went away, leaving [him] half dead. And by a coincidence a certain priest was going down in that way, and having seen him, he passed over on the opposite side; and in like manner also, a Levite, having been about the place, having come and seen, passed over on the opposite side. But a certain Samaritan, journeying, came along him, and having seen him, he was moved with compassion, and having come near, he bound up his wounds, pouring on oil and wine, and having lifted him up on his own beast, he brought him to an inn, and was careful of him; and on the morrow, going forth, taking out two *denarii*, he gave to the innkeeper, and said to him, Be careful of him, and whatever thou mayest spend more, I, in my coming again, will give back to thee" (Luke 10:30–35, YLT).

THIS WELL-LOVED PARABLE OCCURS only in the Gospel of Luke, which was written decades after Jesus' death (estimates range from 60–130 CE). Though no other or earlier versions exist, most biblical scholars consider the parable to be authentic to Jesus. The version above of Luke 10:30–35 from Young's Literal translation (Greek to English) may be as close as we can get in this case to authentic words of Jesus.

Verses before and after the parable were added by Luke, who set the story in the context of an "expert in the law," i.e., the Torah, asking Jesus how he can inherit eternal life. Jesus asks him what the law [Torah] says, and the man replies with the commandment to "love the Lord your God with all your heart and with all your soul and with all your strength and with all your mind and your neighbor as yourself." Jesus agrees that is the way to eternal life, but the man pushes for more: "Who is my neighbor?" In other words, who am I supposed to love as myself?

At this point, Luke inserts Jesus' parable of the good Samaritan.

His Jewish listeners would have certain expectations as Jesus began telling the parable. First, priests and Levites were religious authority figures who could be counted on to know the laws about helping others in the Torah. The many references to hypocrites in the New Testament, however, make it clear that these early religious leaders were only human and no better than religious leaders of any other time, so Jesus' listeners wouldn't have been too surprised that neither the priest nor the Levite responded to a wounded stranger in the ditch.

The Samaritan, however, would have been a shock to Jesus' audience. Samaritans didn't have a good name among Jews, and vice versa. The two groups had, in the distant past, been "fellow Israelites," until historic events divided them. By the time Jesus was teaching in Galilee, the Jews and Samaritans co-existed with disdain and bitterness.

Jesus made the most admirable character in his parable the hated "other" of his listeners, which fits with his tendency to turn expectations upside-down. But there is an unasked/unanswered question in the Good Samaritan parable. Is the man in the ditch a Jew? If so, is it obvious from his appearance? The parable says he has been stripped by those who robbed him and left him beaten and bloody in the ditch, so his clothes would not identify him. Do the priest and Levite knowingly pass by a fellow Jew and does the Samaritan knowingly help an "enemy"? Or could the man in the ditch be a Samaritan? We who read the story, like Jesus' Jewish listeners, assume the man in the ditch is Jewish, probably because of the way the parable is taught. But a person who is naked, injured, and vulnerable could be anyone.

In the Torah "loving your neighbor" refers only to those in one's own tribe or group; it says nothing about loving your enemy.[1] This startling idea was original to Jesus.

---

1. Only one verse in the Torah comes close to the idea of helping an enemy, and it has nothing to do with mercy: "When you encounter your enemy's ox or ass wandering, you must take it back to him. When you see the ass of your enemy lying under its burden and would refrain from raising it, you must nevertheless raise it with him" (Exod 23:4–5).

Luke inserts the parable into a dialogue between an "expert in the law" and Jesus about the greatest commandment as the way to "inherit eternal life." Focusing on the phrase "love your neighbor as yourself," the Torah expert asks for a "definition" of "neighbor," and Jesus responds with a parable about a good Samaritan. When Jesus finishes telling the parable, he asks the Torah expert which of the three who passed on the road—the priest, the Levite, or the Samaritan—is the neighbor of the man in the ditch. The expert responds, "The one who showed him mercy."

Jesus may have told the parable in a different context, however, such as when he was teaching this lesson: "love your enemies, do good, and lend, expecting nothing in return. Your reward will be great, and you will be children of the Most High, for he himself is kind to the ungrateful and the wicked. Be merciful, just as your Father is merciful" (Luke 6:35–36). Show mercy as God shows mercy. As the Samaritan shows mercy.

Love as Key to The Good Samaritan

Two-thousand-plus years ago, Jesus spoke to ordinary people who did not think of him as a Savior, but as a teacher bringing them what he called "good news."

The most radical thing Jesus taught is that all of us live in both a physical, material world and a spiritual world, and that the simplest of us have access to, and a place in, the highest realms of divinity; in simpler terms, we can live in "the Kingdom of God," where Love is the ruler, and the only value is abundant love; infinite love; universal love.

Each parable (and most of what Jesus said) teaches us what "the Kingdom of God is like." To know this, you don't have to wait until you die (that concept hadn't even occurred to anyone when Jesus was alive and teaching his followers). You can live in the Kingdom of God here and now because, as he said, it is all around you and within you, co-existing with the material realm, the human kingdom.

In Jesus' parables, characters who live in the spiritual realm of God interact with characters who live in the material realm of humans. The robbers who beat up the man and leave him in the ditch to die, and those who claim religious status like the priest, or legal authority like the Levite, all operate in the human kingdom of power, greed, cruelty, indifference, prejudice, and arrogance.

Jesus' listeners also (now as well as then) often respond, at least initially, from the human kingdom. So those hearing Jesus tell this parable would not expect help from a Samaritan, and, if the tables were turned, most of them would be disinclined to help a Samaritan.

In Jesus' parable, however, co-existing with these representatives of the human kingdom, is the Samaritan who acts from the Kingdom of God and whose actions represent the God of the Good News. The Samaritan stops immediately when he sees someone who needs help and responds with mercy and compassion. He doesn't ask who the man is, what tribe he belongs to, what faith he follows, what political party he belongs to, who he sleeps with, or any other question about his nation, tribe, or faith.

When he has rescued the man from the cruelty and indifference of the material world, the Samaritan enlists the help of the innkeeper to continue the care of the man, paying him well to do so. He generously and without hesitation spends his own resources to help the man. As a representative of God's Kingdom in the story, the Samaritan "pays" with the currency of God's realm, i.e., compassionate love. The Samaritan's actions represent the inclusiveness of the Kingdom of God, something Jesus mentions in other teachings about enemies and neighbors. In the Sermon on the Plain (Luke)/Sermon on the Mount (Matthew), for instance, he says:

> "You have heard that it was said, 'You shall love your neighbor and hate your enemy.' But I say to you: Love your enemies and pray for those who persecute you, so that you may be children of your Father in heaven, for he makes his sun rise on the evil and on the good and sends rain on the righteous and on the unrighteous.... Be perfect, therefore, as your heavenly Father is perfect (Matt 5:43–45, 48).

When Jesus says, "Be perfect as your heavenly Father is perfect," he does not refer to being sinless and without flaw. Jesus is talking about love and how the God of the Good News loves. Look at what "be perfect" refers to, which is: "love your enemies and pray for those who persecute you" so you may be children of God, i.e., like God. The word translated from Greek as "perfect" means being complete, whole, finished, comprehensive, all-inclusive. Following as it does the comments about loving enemies and the sun and rain falling equally on the righteous and unrighteous, Jesus' lesson, very clearly is: "Be as complete and inclusive *in the way you love* as God is in the way God loves."

The Good Samaritan parable directly relates to this teaching. The Samaritan makes no distinction between "neighbor" and "enemy," acting as God does, or as those who live in the Kingdom of God do, with comprehensive love and mercy for the injured man. He spends generously the currency of God's kingdom—love and compassion—on someone who might consider him an enemy. And this, according to Jesus, is how things are in the Kingdom of the God of Good News, whose abundant and merciful Love falls on everyone without judgment or exclusion, as completely unbiased as the rain and the sun's light.

The Good Samaritan in Real Life

In the parable, Jesus teaches us how things work in the dimension he calls the Kingdom of God, the dimension of goodness, compassion, and kindness—even to enemies—which even now exists smack-dab in the middle of "real life." This Kingdom of God/Good Samaritan behavior occurs in the most extreme human circumstances such as war, and it happens in our ordinary and daily lives more often than we think.

We are quick to identify with someone like us who performs a Good Samaritan deed, but we rarely if ever recognize it when someone we consider an enemy or opponent does so.

The Pashtun Villagers

War provides many dramatic examples of Good Samaritan behavior, acts of loving compassion, astonishing because they are so unexpected. The following quotation from the blurb on the back of the book, *Lone Survivor*, by U.S. Navy SEAL Marcus Luttrell, sets the scene for one such example:

> On a clear night in late June 2005, four U.S. Navy SEALs left their base in northern Afghanistan for the mountainous Pakistani border....
>
> This is the story of team leader Marcus Luttrell, the sole survivor of Operation Redwing, and the desperate battle in the mountains that led ultimately to the largest loss of life in Navy SEAL history. But it is also, more than anything the story of his

teammates, who fought ferociously beside him until he was the last one left—blasted unconscious by a rocket grenade, blown over a cliff, but still armed and still breathing. Over the next four days, badly injured and presumed dead, Luttrell fought off six al Qaeda assassins who were sent to finish him, then crawled for seven miles through the mountains before he was taken in by a Pashtun tribe, who risked everything to protect him from the encircling Taliban killers.[2]

While acknowledging the heroism, determination, courage, and stamina of Luttrell and others who trained and served with him, I was most moved by what happened when the young man found himself stripped (his clothing literally blown off him), wounded, and alone among his enemies in the high mountains of Afghanistan.

After four days of evading the Taliban, Luttrell passed out briefly and awoke to find himself surrounded by a group of armed Afghanis. He roused up enough to shoot at them, but something, he said—something—stopped him. The men kept their distance, calling and motioning to him until he finally understood they would not hurt him. When he calmed down and lowered his rifle, they helped him up and took him back to their village. For weeks, they tended the wounds of this American soldier whose army continued to drop bombs near their village. And when local Taliban leaders returned again and again to the village demanding him, the villagers refused to give him up. Finally, Gulab, one of the village elders, walked miles over steep mountain ranges to the nearest U.S. military base to let them know the young American soldier was in their village.

Marcus Luttrell was flown home, given the best medical care, and awarded medals for bravery. Gulab, the "enemy" who helped him, however, could not leave the American military base. He might never be able to return to his village, he might never see his wife and six children again—even if he got back to the village, they might be killed by the Taliban or blown up in an American bombing raid.

Luttrell describes his childhood as patriotic, but "non-religious," so perhaps he doesn't know the Good Samaritan parable nor recognize himself as the man in the ditch.

---

2. Luttrell and Robinson, *Lone Survivor*. This quotation comes from the blurb on the book's first edition cover. Later editions omit mention of the Pashtun villagers and focus only on the heroism of Luttrell and his teammates.

The Jews who first heard Jesus tell this parable were surprised and not entirely pleased to hear their enemy, a Samaritan, as the "hero" of the story. Likewise, contemporary American Christians may prefer to gloss over the actions of the Pashtun villagers who were Muslims. These non-Christians, however, who risked their lives to show mercy and compassion for an enemy soldier most clearly demonstrate, in real life, what Jesus wanted us to learn from the parable of the Good Samaritan.

Good Samaritans in Bovina, Texas

In 2006, CrossWalk America happened: six self-identified "progressive Christians" were inspired to walk as Jesus did, spreading his good news about love. They walked from Arizona to Washington, DC, to call attention to the fact that those who most loudly proclaim themselves to be "Christian" do not speak for everyone. The source of their inspiration, the work of clergy and laypeople in Phoenix, Arizona, was a set of belief statements known as the Phoenix Affirmations, which asserted the "other" voice of Christianity—the voice in the authentic teachings of Jesus—the one being drowned out by conservative and Evangelical voices of traditional Christianity. Walking twenty-five hundred miles across the country generated news coverage of their purpose, and when the walkers arrived in Washington, DC, they were part of a rally to "nail the affirmations to the doorway of America."[3]

The introduction to the Phoenix Affirmations includes this summarizing statement: "As people who are joyfully and unapologetically Christian, we pledge ourselves completely to the way of Love. We work to express our love, as Jesus teaches us, in three ways: by loving God, neighbor, and self."[4] Organized around those three "ways of Love," the affirmations include the ideas like the ones paraphrased below.

a. fully embracing the path of Jesus, while acknowledging other paths to God;

b. celebrating "the God whose Spirit" pervades and is reflected in all creation;

c. expressing love of God in worship;

d. remaining humble while seeking the best in others;

3. Garner, "Progressive Christians Spread Message in Clovis."
4. "Phoenix Affirmations Summary."

e. resisting the "commingling" of religion and government;

f. basing our lives on the belief that all people are loved eternally and beyond imagining;

g. seeking truth through heart and mind, faith and science;

h. standing with the oppressed, seeking justice and peace.

The language throughout the Phoenix Affirmations may be somewhat challenging for conservative and Evangelical Christians, but one affirmation raises high the red flags and hackles:

> Engaging people authentically, as Jesus did, treating all as creations made in God's very image, regardless of race, gender, sexual orientation, age, physical or mental ability, nationality, or economic class.[5]

The phrase "regardless of sexual orientation" is a deal-breaker for Christians who believe homosexuality is a sin, and who interpret any suggestion that Jesus would accept such people to mean that God would also, and thus would not condemn them to hell.

In August, when the CrossWalk America folks walked along I-70 north of Richmond, Indiana, where I lived, I joined them for a while. I learned that in May they had stayed a few nights in my hometown of Clovis, New Mexico, a bastion of conservatism and Evangelical Christianity. Having grown up in Clovis, I was not surprised to learn they had been denied hospitality by all the churches in Clovis. Except one. (For more on this story, see Chapter 13.)

The day the CrossWalkers left Clovis, they walked about twenty miles northeast to spend the night at "a small, predominantly Hispanic Catholic church in Bovina, Texas,"[6] where they met a very different reception.

In organizing their journey, the CrossWalk team called or sent letters and emails to pastors of churches along their route, identifying themselves as progressive Christians, explaining that they were walking as Jesus had walked to bring a message of love, and requesting hospitality for a night or two. It would take them a full day to walk from Clovis to Bovina, where they had contacted the Catholic priest who responded with a wholehearted welcome. He offered to house the walkers in a motel

---

5. "Phoenix Affirmations Summary."
6. Elnes, *Asphalt Jesus*, 65.

at the church's expense, invited them to join his church at Mass that evening, to be followed by a meal with the congregation. When asked if he would like more information about CrossWalk and the Phoenix Affirmations, Father Chavez responded without hesitation, "You're walking for Jesus. That's all I need to know."

In the parable, the Samaritan—a "foreigner," someone from a group looked down on by Jesus' listeners—showed compassionate generosity to a stranger in need. This was in striking contrast to the behavior of the Pharisee and Levite, religious leaders who showed unwillingness to help the man in the ditch. Likewise, the generosity of the small, predominantly Hispanic, Catholic congregation in Bovina stands in marked contrast to the closed doors of larger, predominantly Anglo, Evangelical congregations in Clovis.

The Viet Nam Vet and Me

What follows is a less dramatic example of the Good Samaritan lesson Jesus taught, but a story of how any of us may find ourselves, without intending to, being kind to "our enemy."

One morning about ten years ago, I went to Sam's Club to buy a bunk bed mattress for my oldest grandson. The mattress wasn't heavy, though a bit floppy and unwieldy. I loaded it standing on its edge on a long flat cart, wheeled it through the checkout stand, paid for it, and was pulling the cart across the parking lot, holding on to the mattress with one hand to keep it upright. But the far end of it started flopping and soon it slipped off the cart. A man who had just gotten out of his car stopped to help.

As he hefted it back on the cart, I said, "It's not heavy—I just need to get it upright again . . ."

"I'll help you load it in your car," he said and took the cart handle from me. "Where are you parked?"

"Over there," I waved toward my car an aisle over, and he was already on his way.

Oh no, I thought. He was wearing a "Vietnam Veteran" baseball cap, and he was headed for the back of my car where I had two bumper stickers: "War is Not the Answer" and "Peace Be with You." I had friends from high school who had served in Vietnam, though I came to oppose the war. Knowing how fiercely defensive my friends still were about serving in the military, I didn't want to upset this man, or start an argument in the middle of the Sam's Club parking lot.

I called after him, "I don't want you to be offended by my bumper stickers." Feeling awkward, I adding lamely by way of explanation, "I'm a minister . . . "

He was already standing at the rear of my car and might not even have noticed the bumper stickers if I hadn't called his attention to them. He was silent for a minute. Then, as I clicked my key to unlock the car, he said, "So you're a preacher, huh?" He grinned at me as we lifted the mattress into my hatchback and wrestled with it. Then he said, "Guess I know who you're going to vote for!" (This was 2012, when Obama was running for re-election against Mitt Romney.)

Glancing at his Vietnam Veteran cap, I said, "I guess I know who you're going to vote for, too."

He looked puzzled for a minute, then said, "Oh, no, I'm going to vote for him, too. That other'un hasn't done nothing."

"Oh . . . no . . . " I said, realizing we had both assumed the other would vote for Romney. "I, uh, I'm a *Quaker* minister." As though that would explain everything. I couldn't think of what else to say. I really didn't want to talk politics with this man.

We struggled in silence for a few minutes with the mattress that was too long to fit in my car. Finally, he said, "Well, I didn't want to go to Viet Nam."

"I know." I said. "I know. I remember what it was like. If I'd been a young man in that place and that time, I'm sure I'd have gone, too." And that's true; given who I was in 1965, if I'd been male, I would have enlisted even if I didn't want to.

He seemed to be trying to make sense of what was happening; he was talking to a preacher, but one who opposed war—clearly he expected criticism. I just wanted to get the mattress packed and end this uncomfortable conversation.

In a minute he said, "I didn't go to church for a long time, but now I go to the Southern Baptist church."

"I started out with the Southern Baptists," I said (which was true) bending the mattress down in the front seat so he could push it from the back to slide all the way in my car. Trying to think of a way to be more honest, I added, "And went on from there . . ."

"I'll go to any church as long as they teach moral values," he said heartily as I went around to the back of the car to help him push and squeeze the mattress. Finally, it was in the car far enough that I could slam down the hatchback door.

"Thank you for your help," I said with sincere warmth as I reached for his hand. "Thank you very much. May God be with you."

"And you," he said, holding my hand in both of his and shaking it. "May God richly bless you."

Would he have refused to help me if he'd known I was a liberal and a "peacenik"? If I'd needed help, would I have asked him to help me, having noted his baseball cap? I like to think so, but perhaps I would have looked for someone else to approach. As it was, we were—each of us—caught in a real-life "Kingdom of God" moment, being kind rather than being right. A "Good Samaritan" moment of seeing not an enemy but a neighbor.

8

Lost and Found

> God is not too hard to believe in. God is too good to believe in, we being such strangers to such goodness.
>
> —William Sloan Coffin

Coins, Sheep, and Sons

Parable of the Lost Coin:

"Or what woman having ten silver coins, if she loses one of them, does not light a lamp, sweep the house, and search carefully until she finds it? And when she has found it, she calls together her friends and neighbors, saying, 'Rejoice with me, for I have found the coin that I had lost' (Luke 15:8–9).

Parable of the Lost Sheep:

What do you think? If a shepherd has a hundred sheep and one of them has gone astray, does he not leave the ninety-nine on the mountains and go in search of the one that went astray? And if he finds it, truly I tell you, he rejoices over it more than over the ninety-nine that never went astray (Matt 18:12–13).

The Parable of the Prodigal Son:

Then Jesus said, "There was a man who had two sons. The younger of them said to his father, 'Father, give me the share of the wealth that will belong to me.' So he divided his assets between them. A few days later the younger son gathered all he had and traveled to a distant region, and there he squandered his wealth in dissolute living. When he had spent everything, a severe famine took place throughout that region, and he began to be in need. So he went and hired himself out to one of the citizens of that region, who sent him to his fields to feed the pigs. He would gladly have filled his stomach with the pods that the pigs were eating, and no one gave him anything. But when he came to his senses he said, 'How many of my father's hired hands have bread enough and to spare, but here I am dying of hunger! I will get up and go to my father, and I will say to him, "Father, I have sinned against heaven and before you; I am no longer worthy to be called your son; treat me like one of your hired hands."' So he set off and went to his father. But while he was still far off, his father saw him and was filled with compassion; he ran and put his arms around him and kissed him. Then the son said to him, 'Father, I have sinned against heaven and before you; I am no longer worthy to be called your son.' But the father said to his slaves, 'Quickly, bring out a robe—the best one—and put it on him; put a ring on his finger and sandals on his feet. And get the fatted calf and kill it, and let us eat and celebrate, for this son of mine was dead and is alive again; he was lost and is found!' And they began to celebrate (Luke 15:11-24).

"Now his elder son was in the field, and as he came and approached the house, he heard music and dancing. He called one of the slaves and asked what was going on. He replied, 'Your brother has come, and your father has killed the fatted calf because he has got him back safe and sound.' Then he became angry and refused to go in. His father came out and began to plead with him. But he answered his father, 'Listen! For all these years I have been working like a slave for you, and I have never disobeyed your command, yet you have never given me even a young goat so that I might celebrate with my friends. But when this son of yours came back, who has devoured your assets with prostitutes, you killed the fatted calf for him!' Then the father said to him, 'Son, you are always with me, and all that is mine is yours. But we had to celebrate and rejoice, because this brother of yours was dead and has come to life; he was lost and has been found'" (Luke 15:25-32).

The lost coin and lost sheep parables, which appear only in Luke and Matthew, teach essentially the same lesson: someone dedicated to finding something precious that has been lost rejoices when it is found. In the Gospel of Luke, the lost coin and sheep are clustered in Chapter 15 along with the Parable of the Prodigal Son, indicating the writer connected the parables through the idea of being lost and found. Traditional interpretation sees the woman looking for a missing coin and the shepherd searching for a lost sheep as metaphors for God searching for lost sinners and rejoicing when they are returned.

In the Gospel of Matthew, however, the lost sheep parable appears in the context of Jesus teaching about protecting children. In that time and place, children of the poor were virtually without status and were especially vulnerable to abuse of all kinds. In Matthew's version of the lost sheep parable, Jesus begins by declaring the value of all children in the Kingdom of God, and then he warns his listeners to avoid sin at all costs. He specifically warns against causing a child to "sin." One verse in this section of Matthew also occurs almost word-for-word in Mark 9:42 and Luke 17:2 "If any of you cause one of these little ones who believe in me to sin, it would be better for you if a great millstone were fastened around your neck, and you were drowned in the depth of the sea" (Matt 18:6). Traditional Christianity has managed to claim that "these little ones" means "all of us who believe in Jesus," and "shame on anyone who puts a stumbling block in our way." Of course, when Jesus said this, "believing in him" did not yet have the connotation it does after twenty-one centuries of Christianity. Rarely are there sentences from Jesus that are so emphatic as this one. Maybe he means something else.

Throughout the verses of Matt 18:6–14, as well as in Mark and Luke, the word translated as "sin" is the Greek word, *skandalizō,* clearly related to the English words, "scandal," "scandalize," "scandalous," and defined in *Strong's Greek Definitions* as "to entrap . . . or entice to sin, apostasy or displeasure."[1] Is it possible that Jesus was warning his listeners against child abuse, including sexual abuse, in no-uncertain terms?

In Matt 18:10–12, we find the lost sheep parable: "Take care that you do not despise [i.e., think little or nothing of] one of these little ones, for I tell you, in heaven their angels continually see the face of my Father in heaven. What do you think? If a shepherd has a hundred sheep and one of them has gone astray, does he not leave the ninety-nine on the mountains and go in search of the one that went astray?" Occurring as it does in relation to being careful of children, this parable is more powerful and more poignant than when it follows the lost coin parable.

The Parable of the Prodigal Son is one of the best-known and best-loved parables of Jesus, probably because we commonly interpret it at

---

1. "G4624 - *skandalizō* - Strong's Greek Lexicon (kjv)," Blue Letter Bible.

face-value, applying it to our relationship with God in terms of family relationships. Asked who the main character is, we would probably say the younger son because in New Testament translations, the parable is most often titled "The Prodigal Son." But the parable has also been referred to as "The Parable of the Two Brothers," "The Lost Son," "The Loving Father," "The Lovesick Father," and "The Forgiving Father." Consider how each title emphasizes a different aspect of the parable, and how the most common one in traditional Christianity, i.e., "the Prodigal Son," emphasizes the bad behavior of the younger son and the father's forgiveness.

At the literal level and in the human realm, the parable is about an untried youth, unaware of how good he has it, deciding to go out into the world, seeking his own way. Sure enough, the younger son discovers life is hard out on his own, and he decides to go back home. He works out what he must say so that his father will take him back, "I was wrong; you were right; I don't deserve it but please let me come home." We hear him rehearse it as he travels, but before he has a chance to deliver his rehearsed line, his father welcomes him without question. The older brother, who stayed home and worked, becomes angry at the father, resentful of the special treatment his wastrel brother undeservedly receives.

Those who identify with the younger son are reassured when the father welcomes him home. Parents may identify with the loving father, though for some—even if we are told he represents God—the father seems too eager, too undignified in his joy; he goes overboard in welcoming back his wayward son; he lets the boy off too easily. Some traditional interpretations label him as "too fond." A father who gives such a son his inheritance (money & goods) on demand, without question or condition, is perceived as a bit of a fool.[2] Easiest of all for us to understand is the older son's reaction. We sympathize with his sense of being treated unfairly and his perception that the father shows favoritism. We can understand why he sulks and stays home from the celebration.

This parable is based on certain expectations in the human realm. (1) Youth is not to be trusted with inherited wealth; (2) if a child leaves home, the parent should set boundaries and conditions before letting them come back; (3) someone who makes a mistake ("sins") must make amends ("repent") before being accepted again; (4) "I did more, so I deserve more," i.e., someone who follows rules/works harder deserves more than someone who does not follow rules/or work hard.

---

2. Such is the plot of Shakespeare's play, *King Lear.*

These "rules" may be helpful/necessary for society to function in the human realm. But Jesus taught about a different place altogether—the Kingdom of God—and in the parable about the prodigal son human-realm expectations don't apply and are overturned.

Two Lost Sons

The younger son is "lost" to the father because he chooses to go away. He loses himself from the father, but he also "finds" himself and returns to the father. Before he even knows why his younger son returns, the father is overjoyed at the mere sight of him. Before the son has a chance to say anything, the father welcomes him exuberantly. The father does not demand an apology or place conditions on his son's return. Forgiveness is part and parcel of his unconditional love. What we see in the father is the manifestation of abundant, joyful love, the kind Jesus has been telling us about all along, the kind that rules the Kingdom of God.

In what is essentially a second parable, the older brother, seeing how much his father loves his brother, becomes jealous and resentful. He considers himself more deserving of love than his brother, and in his anger, he "leaves the father" emotionally. He is unable to recognize the abundance and equality of the father's love, which is more than enough for both sons. Unfortunately, this way of being "lost" from God is common in the human realm. Consider all the kind, hard-working, churchgoing "older sons" convinced theirs is the only way to please and be loved by God. They deny God's love for people who disagree with them or who do things differently from them. Those who are jealous and possessive of God's love are the *most lost* because they don't know they are.

What's Fair in Families?

Given what Jesus talked about in all his teachings, let's consider that he told the parable as a metaphor for love and the Kingdom of God, with an emphasis on the loving/forgiving father. In his commentary on this parable, and citing other biblical scholars who agree with him, Arland J. Hultgren asserts that "the central figure is not the younger son but the father of the two sons," and that the parable "clearly portrays the love and forgiveness of God as unconditional and prevenient (= coming before human readiness to ask for them)."[3]

Hultgren also suggests that, besides illustrating "the loving character of God," Jesus told this story with another relationship in mind: the one between the older brother and the younger brother, between the "saved" and the "sinner," the righteous and the unrighteous, the Pharisees and the tax collectors.

> . . . of immense importance in this parable is the accent on the father's rejoicing and then his telling his elder son how necessary that is. Those who assert their own claims of righteousness ("never have I ever disobeyed your command") find it most difficult to rejoice when those who cannot do the same are considered equal to them. It is hard to recognize the work of God in and through such persons. Yet that is what is at stake in the parable.[4]

Here Hultgren essentially describes the divisive nature of traditional Christianity and perhaps all religions: believing one's own faith and/or practice is the only one acceptable to God and passing judgment on those with a different faith and/or practice. This continues to manifest, not only in harsh relations between Christians and Muslims, Buddhists, Jews, Hindus, etc., but between different Christian denominations. Indeed, between *members of the same denomination*. When it comes to belief about what will please God/the father, traditional Christianity tends to be the older brother, sure he is right and deserving and equally sure that his younger brother, who does things differently, is wrong and undeserving. Implicit in this reaction, of course, is that it is unfair of the father/God to accept and love him.

Regarding this tendency to judge each other in relation to different ways of perceiving or interacting with God, no one has expressed it better than Isaac Penington did in 1660. He points out it is not the way we worship or what we believe that causes problems but *judging* each other in that regard.

> Even in the apostles' days, Christians were too apt to strive after a wrong unity and uniformity in outward practices and observations, and to judge one another unrighteously in these things.
>
> This was the apostle's rule, for everyone to perform singly to the Lord what he did, and not for one to meddle with the light

---

3. Hultgren, *Parables of Jesus*, 72.
4. Hultgren, *Parables of Jesus*, 86–87.

of conscience of another (undervaluing his brother or judging him because his light and practices differed from his) but everyone to keep close to their own measure of light, even to that proportion of faith and knowledge, which God of his mercy hath bestowed on them.

And here is the true unity in the Spirit, in the inward life, and not in an outward uniformity.[5]

What's Fair in Faith?

Many kind and wonderful people are convinced there is only one way to be righteous in the eyes of God, which is the way they have found. With the best intentions, they feel compelled to convert others to their own understanding of God, Jesus, and ultimate Truth. Too often these well-intentioned people are judgmental (either gently or harshly) of those who follow different paths.

The website Grace Thru Faith: The Bible Made Clear and Simple[6] offers a contemporary glimpse of the righteous older-brother mentality. Among the beliefs listed on the Grace Thru Faith site is the following statement about being "saved": "We believe that our salvation is laid up in heaven, free for the asking, granted to everyone without condition or prejudice, out of the incomparable riches of God's grace." But the two listed beliefs that follow indicate there is only one way to be saved. Not even "the incomparable riches of God's grace" are enough.

- We believe that each human can, and indeed must, individually seek this salvation by choosing a personal relationship with the Lord Jesus.
- It is our Father's will that all who look to His Son and believe in Him will be saved.[7]

Below is a response to a question from the website's "Ask a Bible Teacher" page about mistakenly thinking you're saved when you're not.

> There are many people who identify themselves as Christians but have been taught a different path to salvation than the Bible

---

5. Penington, "Examination of The Grounds or Causes . . ."

6. The website was started it in 1996 by Jack Kelly. Before his death in 2015, Kelly had published over nine thousand Bible Study resources.

7. "About Our Beliefs," Grace Thru Faith.com.

teaches. Some believe it takes a combination of faith plus human works to be saved. Others have been taught you have to join a particular church and obey its requirements. Still others say all it takes is to join a church and try to live a good life. And there are those who believe that it doesn't matter what religion a person follows. As long as they are sincere they will find a path to salvation.

The response lays out all the ways Christians may fool themselves into thinking they are saved. Though not said directly, the implication is that such Christians are mistaken, unsaved, lost. The summary of how some Christians might come to such a mistaken conclusion is followed by a flat statement that "Jesus said He is the only way" and a description of exactly what that way entails.

> Jesus said He is the only way to the Father (John 14:6) and no one who isn't born again will enter God's Kingdom (John 3:3). Being born again means you believe you are a sinner, that Jesus died for your sins and rose again on the third day (1 Cor. 15:3–4), and you have asked Him to save you from your sins (Matt. 7:7–8).[8]

Such comments assert that only "being born again"—according to a very specific definition—guarantees one is saved. Certainty of one's own righteousness reflects the older-brother attitude which makes it difficult (even impossible) to rejoice in the possibility that one who follows a different path may also be "saved."

In contrast, early Friend Isaac Penington expresses the joy he finds in recognizing a variety of "believers," including "several forms of Christians," who can—each and all—learn, serve, grow, and love in their own ways.

> And oh! how sweet and pleasant is it to the truly spiritual eye, to see several sorts of believers, several forms of Christians in the school of Christ, every one learning their own lesson, performing their own peculiar service, and knowing, owning, and loving one another in their several places, and different performances to their Master, to whom they are to give an account, and not to quarrel with one another about their different practices!
>
> For this is the true ground of love and unity, not that such a man walks and does just as I do, but because I feel the same Spirit and

---

8. Kelly, "Thinking You Are Saved But Aren't?"

life in him, and in that he walks in his rank, in his own order, in his proper way and place of subjection to that. And this is far more pleasing to me, than if he walked just in that rank wherein I walk . . .[9]

Love as Key to The Prodigal Son

Love in the Kingdom of God is abundant, infinite, and unconditional. Love allows freedom to learn and grow. The God of Love loves freely, lavishly, without constraint. If a beloved child decides to go exploring and asks for their inheritance—which is Love—they receive it abundantly. After being away for a while, they may discover they'd rather be a servant in the Kingdom of God than a landowner in the human kingdom. Having traveled in the human kingdom for a while, though, the beloved child may pick up values and expectations characteristic of that kingdom. The beloved child fears his father won't let him come back unless he says the right thing, makes amends for his actions, etc. Once the child turns toward the Kingdom of Love, however, they find complete acceptance and welcome. Returning to Love, the child is greeted with unabated joy.

The child's sibling, who has always worked hard, who has always said and done what they thought was required to please the father, discovers that indeed, they would have been loved just as much if they had not worked so hard or followed all the rules! Instead of rejoicing, however, the sibling is jealous and angry.

The father is mystified that his older child believes love, which is infinite, can be portioned out, can be deserved, or not deserved. "My child," the father says, "all that is mine [abundant Love] is yours."

Each son has *all the Love there is*—neither has more than the other.

The Lost Son/Older Brother in Real Life

The older-brother-certainty-of-righteousness attitude that those-who-don't-follow-certain-rules-are-lost pervades all denominations, not only conservative and Evangelical churches with people's eternal souls at stake, but in more liberal or progressive congregations, including my own beloved denomination. The following true story of a Quaker

---

9. Penington, "Examination of The Grounds or Causes."

meeting in conflict happened more than forty years ago.[10] Each party in the conflict considered itself right. Depending on how we understand "Christian" behavior, either side might be the younger son veering off on the wrong track; either side might be the older brother, staying home and being responsible. As you read, consider, too, the loving father apparently unconcerned about what either son did or did not do, loving both unconditionally.

What Would You Have Me Do?

One evening Ray Braddock, the pastor at Pine Creek Friends Meeting, received a phone call from Beverly Perkins. When Ray answered the phone, Beverly reminded him they had served together on the local welfare advisory board. She was calling him, she explained, because she worked with Joann Morgan, who owned a foster home for children with disabilities, and Joann's aunt, who attended Pine Creek Friends, had only good things to say about it. She had something important to ask him; Ray said he had time to talk now if she did.

Beverly talked about what an extraordinary person Joann was and talked about the children. She explained that Joann and her husband, who had long been emotionally estranged, were in the process of separating, and then, tentatively, she said, "Now here is the tricky part, Ray." Over the past couple of years, working side-by-side, she and Joann had fallen in love. They finally decided they did not want to have to hide it anymore. Naively, Joann had confided in the pastor at the Methodist church where she took the children each Sunday, the church she had attended all her life, where she felt loved and accepted. To her pain and surprise, the pastor told her the church had held a "funeral" for her, essentially declaring her dead to them. Anxious that the children be able to attend church and Sunday school, Joann had thought of Pine Creek Friends Meeting because of what her aunt had told her about Quakers. Since Beverly knew the pastor, Ray Braddock, she agreed to contact him.

Beverly had called to ask Ray if he thought the Quakers at Pine Creek Friends would let Joann and her attend Meeting for Worship together, openly, as a couple, with the children. He responded that they and the children would be welcome. Later, when some in the Meeting

---

10. Details like names and locations have been changed to preserve individual privacy.

voiced concern, Ray asked, "When someone wants to know if they can attend our Meeting for Worship, what can I say but yes? What would you have me say?"

A few weeks later, Beverly and Joann began attending worship services at Pine Creek Friends, bringing with them each week as many as twelve children of varying ages and abilities, including some in wheelchairs.

In October, when Harold Morgan filed for divorce and custody of his and Joann's natural children on the grounds that she was an unfit mother, Ray Braddock was called to testify.[11] As their pastor, Ray had been to visit Joann and Beverly at the big farmhouse where they cared for a dozen children, including seven with disabilities, and he knew the environment in which the children lived. What he saw, and what he testified to, was a sprawling, tidy home in which every child was loved and his or her unique needs addressed with warm dedication.

During questioning, however, Harold Morgan's attorney pressed Ray on the issue of Joann's relationship with Beverly. Finally, he asked Ray, "Mr. Braddock, you're a pastor in a Christian church. Do you, or do you not, believe that homosexuality is a sin?"

"It depends on what you call sin. . . ."

Pressing Ray to respond, the attorney said, "Don't you think that folks like this should be burned at the stake?"

At this point, the judge interrupted, "Please just answer the question, yes or no, Mr. Braddock."

"Then no," Ray said, "I do not believe homosexuality in and of itself is sin."

That same night, a Thursday, Ray received a phone call from Dean Hanson, a member of Pine Creek Meeting and descendant of a founding family. Dean said several people were concerned about Ray's handling of the situation and they wanted a meeting with him. Ray agreed to meet them at Dean's home late Saturday afternoon. When he entered the Hanson farmhouse that Saturday, in the few pleasantries exchanged, Ray could sense anxiety and hostility. Several of the most dedicated members and supporters of the Meeting were there, seated around the dining room table with Dean and his wife, Lillian. Ray felt a sinking in the pit of his stomach—these were people he liked and admired, people who loved and were loved by Pine Creek Friends.

---

11. A few years earlier, Joann been named both county and state "Mother of the Year."

Ray sat down at the table and the discussion began right away. Someone read a transcript of the trial, and Dean put to him the question, "I ask you again, do you, or do you not, believe that homosexuality is a sin?"

"No," Ray answered, "No. I don't believe it's a sin."

Virtually everyone there disagreed with Ray, though a few said even if it wasn't a sin, it was just wrong. Among the concerns raised was "What will people think about us? People in town, in the other churches, in other Friends' meetings?" The rest of the afternoon was not pleasant.

The following morning, Ray Braddock's sermon was on Mark 1:40–45, the passage in which a leper begged Jesus, "If you choose, you can make me clean." Jesus, moved by pity, "stretched out his hand and touched him and said to him, 'I do choose. Be made clean!'" Jesus warned the man to "say nothing to anyone," but the man went out and told everyone who would listen, "so that Jesus could no longer go into a town openly...."

In those days, Ray said, anyone who touched lepers risked contamination; they were the untouchables. "Who are the untouchables now?" Ray Braddock asked his congregation. "And are we afraid we will be contaminated if we touch them? Are we afraid we will be guilty by association? What then shall we do? Shall we do as Jesus did and reach out in love to touch these people who already suffer? Or shall we turn away?"

In the next few days, Dean Hanson made phone calls and visited members of the congregation. He approached everyone with the copy of the trial transcript, reporting Ray's answer to the central question, as Dean saw it, and lobbying for Ray Braddock's dismissal as pastor. Some listened to Dean and agreed with him. Others were angered by his message and his approach.

Meanwhile weeks passed and life went on in the Meeting. An emergency meeting was called to discuss a dispute between the Lakota tribe and the U.S. government over eight hundred acres in the Black Hills. Valuable minerals had been discovered there recently, and the government was trying to renege on a treaty. Pine Creek Meeting approved a letter supporting the claims of the Lakota tribe and urging the government to honor a nineteenth-century agreement giving the land to them. Eventually it was time again for the annual discussion of the pastor's contract and its renewal. The minutes gave no indication that the meeting lasted five hours.

The financial report, a topic that usually dominated meeting minutes, was summarized in one sentence: "Discussed and approved." There followed a brief announcement about the Meeting history compiled for its one-hundred-fiftieth anniversary and approval of donating $500 to help youngsters in the Meeting attend Quaker summer camp. The Clerk of Ministry and Membership recommended the addition of two people to the membership roll, and "They were heartily approved." Then the Ministry and Membership clerk reported that the committee had agreed, except one member, to the re-hiring of Ray Braddock for another year. A lengthy discussion (almost four hours) followed on the pros and cons of doing so, but in the end, the Meeting approved re-hiring Ray.

The minutes report that the Superintendent of the Yearly Meeting[12] was in attendance. Though not a member of Pine Creek, he spoke up, saying he sensed he wasn't wanted there, but "absolutely out of love for the people and Ray," he had come. He and the yearly meeting were concerned about homosexuals attending Pine Creek Friends Meeting; among other things, he said it was a sin for which they needed to be forgiven. But the Meeting stuck by its decision to support Ray and accept Beverly and Joann.

About one-fourth of the members of Pine Creek Friends Meeting withdrew from the Meeting within the year. Others withdrew from the Meeting who were not members but active and involved attenders. Some who stopped attending Meeting couldn't bring themselves to have their names taken off the membership register. That same year, however, five adults and nine youths requested to be added to active membership in Pine Creek Friends Meeting. Joann Morgan, her five natural children and two foster children were among that number. Those who joined the meeting then and afterward embraced the Meeting for its adherence to the central tenet of Quakerism: "There is that of God in everyone."

Those who remained in the Meeting still mourn, decades later, the absence of friends and family members who left the congregation. Many of those who left also mourn, like Dana Hutchins who had attended Pine Creek since childhood. "It was "a living death, " she said,

---

12. Though Quakers meet every week for worship, individual meetings are referred to as "monthly meetings" because they meet once a month to conduct the business of the congregation. A "yearly meeting" is like a diocese or convention or synod. For Quakers, it is both an annual event and a collection of monthly meetings under one umbrella.

and wept as she recalled leaving Pine Creek Meeting over twenty years ago to attend another church.

In his sermon about Jesus healing the leper, Ray Braddock had shown a sad prescience; Pine Creek Friends experienced the effects of having "contaminated" themselves when they touched the "untouchables." For decades, Pine Creek Meeting has been scorned by some of the local townspeople, including other churches, and referred to by other Quakers in the Yearly Meeting as "that gay church." One Pine Creek member remarked that at area or regional gatherings of Quakers, "Whenever you rose to speak and announced you were from Pine Creek, people knew where you stood," and the tenor of discourse changed.

Incidents like this have played out in congregations in every denomination over the past few decades. One side acts from judgment; one side acts from compassion. One side acts from the teachings of the Church; one side acts from the teachings of Jesus. One side acts from righteousness and certainty that homosexuality is a sin condemned by God. The other side acts from faith that all have "that of God within," and that in the Kingdom of God all are equal, all are equally loved, and all are welcomed and forgiven, even before they ask.

9

The Pharisee and The Tax Collector

> Even in the apostles' days, Christians were too apt to strive after a wrong unity and uniformity in outward practices and observations, and to judge one another unrighteously in these things.
>
> ISAAC PENINGTON[1]

> Two men went up to the temple to pray, one a Pharisee and the other a tax collector. The Pharisee, standing by himself, was praying thus, 'God, I thank you that I am not like other people: thieves, rogues, adulterers, or even like this tax collector. I fast twice a week; I give a tenth of all my income.' But the tax collector, standing far off, would not even lift up his eyes to heaven but was beating his breast and saying, 'God, be merciful to me, a sinner!' I tell you, this man went down to his home justified rather than the other, for all who exalt themselves will be humbled, but all who humble themselves will be exalted" (Luke 18:10–14a).

BECAUSE IN JESUS' AUTHENTIC teachings he doesn't include an explanation or "moral of the story," the first part of the last sentence in this parable: "I tell you, this man went down to his home justified rather than the other," may contain interpretation from a common source used in Matt 23:12 and Luke 14:11. The last part of the sentence—"all who exalt themselves will be humbled, but all who humble themselves will be exalted"—echoes Jesus' teaching throughout the synoptic gospels that

---

1. Penington, "Examination of The Grounds or Causes..."

"many who are first will be last, and the last will be first" (Mark 10:31; Matt 19:30, 20:16; Luke 13:30).

Like the Parable of the Good Samaritan and the Parable of the Prodigal Son, the Parable of the Pharisee and the Tax Collector appears only in the Gospel of Luke. In all three of these parables, Jesus contrasts the behavior of those considered "righteous"—the Pharisees, the Levite, the older brother—with the behavior of those barely considered at all—a foreigner (the Samaritan), a tax collector, a wayward son. Though the situations are different, each parable teaches the same lesson, as Hultgren phrased it:

> Those who are righteous—or think they are—are still loved by God; the difficulty is to get them to realize that others are as well. Equally difficult—perhaps even more difficult—is to get them to realize that God's grace, not their own imagined righteousness, is the basis for their own salvation as well. A moralistic view of the divine/human relationship stands in the way of one's own fellowship with God, and it impedes the imagination in regard to God's relationship with others.[2]

The Pharisee in this parable is a religious lay leader. Unlike the elite Sadducees (priests), Pharisees were commoners, "pious laymen,"[3] who kept a watchful eye on Jesus, frequently challenging his teaching and behavior. Jesus expresses irritation with their pious insistence on the "letter of the law" and disapproval of their self-important self-righteousness, regularly cautioning his followers against the hypocrisy of the "scribes and Pharisees."

Tax collectors in Jesus' time were despised for several reasons: (1) they collected taxes for the Roman Empire *and* for Jewish temple authorities; (2) some of them were corrupt and dishonest; (3) they made a living from the hardships of others; and (4) tax collectors, who did the "dirty work" of the Empire and the Temple, were considered unclean, insignificant, and undeserving.

Both characters in the Parable of the Pharisee and the Tax Collector believe what society and religion have taught them about who counts and who does not. The Pharisee may not be as high on the status ladder as a Sadducee, but he is pious, certain of his beliefs, does all the right things like tithing and fasting. He has a high opinion of himself, certain he is superior to the wretched tax collector. In contrast, the humble tax

---

2. Hultgren, *Parables of Jesus*, 86–87.
3. Jeremias, *Jesus and the Message of the New Testament*, Loc. 522–23.

collector stays in the back of the temple, keeps his eyes downcast, and prays for mercy for his mistakes and imperfections.

Love as Key to The Pharisee and The Tax Collector

In the Kingdom of God, there is no hierarchy. Jesus makes this point repeatedly in his most direct teachings in the synoptic gospels and Thomas: "The last will be first, and the first last" (Matt 20:16; Mark 10:31; Luke 13:30; Thom 4:2). Consider his actions; consider who he spends time with; consider how he shocks the Pharisees and others of high status when he prefers the company of those they look down on as unclean and insignificant: tax collectors, prostitutes, beggars, widows, orphans, the sick, poor, and crippled. Consider his followers; the simple working men we know as his disciples according to the gospel writers; and the women barely mentioned by the gospel writers, but mentioned by critics of early Christianity who dismissed it as a cult of women, children, and servants.[4]

Imagine a place where there is only love, where all are loved and loved equally. If we were able to live in that place all the time, there would be no cruelty, no dishonesty, no poverty, no fear, no inequality, no injustice: these things simply do not exist in that place where there is only love. Forgiveness is not necessary there. For those entering the Kingdom of God from the earthly realm, who may wish for forgiveness for themselves, it is *for*-given, given beforehand, before it is asked for.

The Pharisee and the Tax Collector in Real Life

> *The following is a fictional account of attitudes found even among non-theistic Friends. Such attitudes have more to do with the "right" way to be a Quaker than with worshiping God (who, according to Jesus, doesn't really care how we do it).*

Early one Sunday, before anyone else arrived, two people entered a Quaker Meeting room and took their seats in silence. One of them was Dale, a member of the Meeting who attended regularly and who usually came early each week to "warm up the room," spiritually speaking, in good

---

4. "Celsus, Christianity's most persistent critic, pointed to the involvement of women as a cause for derision: '[Christians] show they want and are able to convince only the foolish, dishonorable, and stupid, only slaves, women, and little children'" (*Cels.* 3.44). Quoted in Krueger, "Early Christianity Was Mocked for Welcoming Women."

Quaker fashion. The other was Sylvia, who attended meeting for worship only occasionally, maybe once every few months.

Dale took being a Friend seriously, living as much as possible according to his understanding of Quaker testimonies: simplicity, equality, peace, integrity, community, and service. In Dale's thinking, simplicity included living sustainably, so he and his wife and two kids lived in a small three-bedroom house, furnished sparsely. He gave away what he didn't use and refused to buy things for his kids just because they were "cool" or fashionable. Dale and his wife shared one fuel-efficient car (think Prius) that had several bumper stickers with slogans like "War Is Not the Answer," "Live Simply so That Others May Simply Live," and "Co-Exist." He regularly donated money to good causes like Quaker Earthcare Witness, the American Friends Service Committee, and the local food bank. He served on two committees at his Meeting, was clerk on one of them, and regularly participated in larger events, like workshops or Building & Grounds Clean-Up Day. He accepted the Quaker notion that there is "that of God in everyone," and was super-conscious to treat everyone as equals, including those of different racial and socio-economic groups. Through the years, Dale had organized and participated in various demonstrations for peace or against dangers to the environment and had even traveled to other cities to support Quakers there who were demonstrating. He was gratified when anyone called him a "weighty Friend," meaning that he thoroughly understood Quaker process and could function slowly and deliberately through any meeting.

Though he wasn't sure there was a God, Dale believed that everyone has equal access to whatever God there might be, so ministers were unnecessary, as were planned or "programmed" worship services. He appreciated the opportunity to sit in silence, empty his mind, and meditate, as he had done when he practiced Zen years ago.

That Sunday morning, sitting in silence as others arrived, Dale was conscious when Sylvia sat down on the bench behind him. He tried to settle into meditation, but within minutes, it seemed, she squirmed and coughed and flipped pages of a book. He was very glad he was not like "Sometimes Sylvia," who seemed to get nothing out of the silence and had probably never experienced what Friends called "a gathered meeting." That thought made him a little uncomfortable though, since he wasn't sure he had experienced one, so he dismissed it and tried to focus.

Sylvia was uncomfortable as she sat in silence on the hard bench. She really liked the nice soft cushions at her sister's church. And the quiet room made her uncomfortable—what was one supposed to do with silence anyway? She knew she didn't get it, would never get it. But something had called her here to this Quaker meeting house a few months ago when she read about a class they offered called "Quakerism 101." She attended the class, did most of the reading, and admired people in the class who spoke so knowingly about "the Light," "George Fox," "SPICES" (which she learned stood for the Quaker "testimonies" of simplicity, peace, integrity, community, equality, and sustainability).

She respected the Quaker testimonies, but really, how was a person supposed to live like that? Take simplicity. She and Ralph still lived in their six-bedroom house, even now that the kids were grown and gone, because they often came back with the grandchildren. All the closets were full; the garage was full, and Ralph had rented a storage unit for stuff the kids left when they moved out. Sylvia still had a cleaning lady, and she knew she should raise the woman's salary, but Ralph wouldn't hear of it. Sylvia couldn't imagine having one car that she would have to share with Ralph—they didn't even like to go the same places. She still remembered the looks on Q101 faces when, during the discussion of the peace testimony, she mentioned the gun she kept in the drawer of her bedside table.

As for the Quaker view of God, as far as she could understand it, everyone had some of it inside them. The trick was to find "that of God within." She attended Meeting for Worship on Sundays and tried hard to pray or something during the silence, but she never "heard" the "still, small voice within" that Quakers talked about. *What am I doing here this morning?* Sylvia wondered as she watched dust motes in a shaft of sunlight. *I really don't belong here. I'd like a little music—or maybe a lot of music. I'd like to hear someone talk or say something inspiring. I'd love hearing God speak out of the silence. But why would he speak to me?* Her thoughts drifted, and she almost dozed off, but gradually she became conscious of resting in a deep, quiet place. It was so peaceful, she just wanted to stay there, and so quiet . . .

After Meeting for Worship, Dale got coffee, pastry, and some fruit, which he ate while musing aloud to others at the table about the need for composting at the meetinghouse. Sylvia felt a need to be alone and didn't stay for Fellowship time. Driving home, she saw some clouds so beautiful they brought her to tears. She pulled over and got out to stand by her car and watch the dark gray clouds outlined against the sun, then streaked with shafts of sunlight as they drifted. "Thank you, thank you, thank you . . . " she murmured. It was silly to think so, she knew, but the privilege of being present for such beauty felt like something Holy was speaking to her.

10

The Vineyard Workers

"For the kingdom of heaven is like a landowner who went out early in the morning to hire laborers for his vineyard. After agreeing with the laborers for a denarius for the day, he sent them into his vineyard. When he went out about nine o'clock, he saw others standing idle in the marketplace, and he said to them, 'You also go into the vineyard, and I will pay you whatever is right.' So they went. When he went out again about noon and about three o'clock, he did the same. And about five o'clock he went out and found others standing around, and he said to them, 'Why are you standing here idle all day?' They said to him, 'Because no one has hired us.' He said to them, 'You also go into the vineyard.' When evening came, the owner of the vineyard said to his manager, 'Call the laborers and give them their pay, beginning with the last and then going to the first.' When those hired about five o'clock came, each of them received a denarius. Now when the first came, they thought they would receive more; but each of them also received a denarius. And when they received it, they grumbled against the landowner, saying, 'These last worked only one hour, and you have made them equal to us who have borne the burden of the day and the scorching heat.' But he replied to one of them, 'Friend, I am doing you no wrong; did you not agree with me for a denarius? Take what belongs to you and go; I choose to give to this last the same as I give to you. Am I not allowed to do what I choose with what belongs to me? Or are you envious because I am generous?'" (Matt 20:1–15).

What's Fair in the Vineyard?

THIS PARABLE IS PARTICULARLY difficult for most readers because it upsets our expectations of fairness.

Humans are hard-wired to be concerned about fairness. Fairness demands equal distribution of resources, which is necessary for the cooperation that makes survival possible. Even children make sure everyone has an equal share of the candy, an equal number of equally-sized pieces. But that's because we live in a finite world and all resources are limited. Landowners who hire workers in the human realm have only so much money to pay the workers; the money is distributed according to which workers are most valuable in terms of earning the landowner more money, like those working longer hours. Simple economics.

In this parable when the first-hired workers complain to the owner that "you have made them equal to us who have borne the burden of the day and the scorching heat," the Vineyard Owner replies, "Friend, I am doing you no wrong; did you not agree with me for a denarius? Take what belongs to you and go . . . are you envious because I am generous?" At the end of the day, the first-hired workers have lost *nothing* because the other workers receive the same payment as they do. Early in the day circumstances permitted them to be hired, and they were, for what they accepted as a normal daily wage. They have what they agreed to earlier. At later times during the day, circumstances were different, such that others were hired "for whatever is right," as the owner says. The Greek word *dikaios* goes a bit beyond what "right" suggests in English. *Dikaios* means, "equitable (in character or act); by implication, innocent, holy (absolutely or relatively)."[1] The connotation is equity but at a divine level, as in the Kingdom of God.

If we read and interpret this parable as happening in the human realm, we understand the outrage of the workers hired first, and we find the actions of the vineyard owner puzzling. Paying everyone the same amount is not fair. Not in the material world of humans.

Why would Jesus tell a story about unfairness? Some say the parable is not about unfairness to the workers, it's not about the workers at all, but about the mystifying generosity of the vineyard owner.

---

1. "G1342 - *dikaios* - Strong's Greek Lexicon (kjv)," Blue Letter Bible.

What If It's Not About Money?

In May 2022 President Biden considered putting in place policies to forgive student loans. The possibility evoked a response reminiscent of the workers' outrage in the vineyard parable. Senator Mitch McConnell called it "student loan *socialism*" and described it as "a giant slap in the face to every family who sacrificed to save for college, to every graduate who paid their debt, to every worker who made a different career choice so they could stay debt-free." Many people agreed with McConnell, such as the man who wrote a letter to the editor, published later that month in the *New York Times*.

> Why should I pay for your student loans? Are you going to pay my mortgage? If we really want to wipe out debt, let's give tax amnesty to anyone who owes more than $10,000. I'd vote for that!
>
> We saved and paid for our son to go to a state college, and he graduated with no debt. The tuition was about an eighth of the tuition at the big-name private university where I was teaching. And he got a great education and was recruited for a good job. I took some of the best classes I ever had at a practically free community college.
>
> Why should I now have to pay for the people who knew perfectly well that they were going deep into avoidable debt? I know it's politically valuable to tell millions of people you are going to forgive their debt, but it's not right.[2]

This is the outrage we feel when someone gets something we don't think is fair. The letter writer probably pays many taxes he either doesn't know about or approve of, but that is beside the point. Student loan forgiveness seems much more personal than taxes that go toward paying down the national debt or repairing roads and bridges in parts of the country where he may never travel. It feels to him like the government paying off other people's student loans will come straight out of his bank account.

In McConnell's voice and the voice of the letter writer, we hear the anger of the first-hired vineyard workers and of the older brother in the Parable of the Prodigal Son who feel they deserve more because they worked longer or more diligently.

---

2. Letters to the Editor, "Debate Over Canceling Student Debt," *New York Times*.

If we read this parable as though it happened in the Kingdom of God, however, with the rules and values of the God of the Good News, it's an entirely different story, and the one Jesus wanted his listeners to hear.

Unlike the human realm, the realm of God is infinite, unbounded by time or space. In the Kingdom of God, the currency is not *denarii* or any other money, but Love. The crop or harvest or product is Love. Wages earned are counted in Love. There is no earlier or later in eternity, so all who work for God are equally valued no matter when they work; there is also no "when" in eternity—just the eternal now. In this realm, Love is abundant and infinite. There is more than enough for everyone, and everyone "deserves" boundless love. We can scarcely imagine such a place. But that is what Jesus asks us to do in the parable. Imagine a vineyard where the generous owner rewards (loves) everyone in equal measure, no matter what they have done or not done, and no one minds.

The sad thing is that we don't want God to be like that. Like the older brother in the Prodigal Son, we want God/the father to reward "good" behavior (however we define it) and to punish "bad" behavior (however we define it). *That* we can understand. That's fair. Loving everyone equally is just not fair . . . The first-hired workers deserve more because they worked longer, and "deserving more" in the human realm usually means more money and/or goods.

"Deserving" in the realm of God, however, has no meaning; all are loved unconditionally. Period.

The Parable of the Vineyard Workers in Real Life

It is difficult to find examples in real life of radical equity motivated by love such as that displayed by the owner of the vineyard in this parable. In our contemporary Christian nation, such actions are threatening and elicit labels like "socialism" or "communism," or "cult" if they have a religious element.

Yet in the years following Jesus' death, early Christians, influenced by his apostles, established communities based on this ideal of radically loving equality and equity. Acts 2:44–47 describes one such early Christian community: "All who believed were together and had all things in common; they would sell their possessions and goods and distribute the proceeds to all, as any had need. Day by day, as they spent much time together in the temple, they broke bread at home and ate their food with glad and generous hearts, praising God and having the goodwill of all the people."

In 197 CE, Tertullian, a Roman theologian from Carthage, described the Christian community there as "a body knit together as such by a common religious profession, by unity of discipline, and by the bond of a common hope."

> We meet together [he wrote] in an assembly and congregation that we may besiege God like a marshalled corps with our prayers....
>
> Certain approved elders preside who have obtained this honor not by purchase but by testimony; for no divine privilege is obtainable by money. Even the kind of treasury which we have is not filled up with sums paid under a sense of obligation, as if they were the price of religion [i.e., not like the Jewish temple tax]; but each one places there a small contribution on a certain day of the month, or when he wishes, provided only he is both willing and able,—for the offerings are not compulsory but voluntary. These are, as it were, the deposits of piety. For afterwards they [are spent] in supporting and burying the needy, and in relieving destitute orphan boys and girls, and infirm old men, or shipwrecked sufferers, and any who may be in the mines, or islands, or prisons, provided it is for the cause of God's religion, who thus become pensioners of their own confession. But even the putting into practice of so great a love as this brands us with a mark of censure in the opinion of some. 'See,' say they, 'how they love each other!'—for they themselves hate each other; and 'how ready they are to die for each other!'—for they are more ready to kill each other.[3]

Over the centuries, the hopeful re-creation of such equitable communal living has been tried again and again in different parts of the world, to greater or lesser success. Many exist today in the U.S. and elsewhere. These communities are not perfect; most seem to fail because of flawed leaders or friction between individuals. Few if any achieve the radical equity of the vineyard in the Kingdom of God, but at least they give it a try.

One such community that has so far been successful is in an older suburb of Cincinnati, Ohio. Now known as the Madison Place Community, the original Gladstone community was founded in 2007 and modeled on Acts 2–44: "All the believers were together and had everything in

---

3. Bindley, trans., *Apology of Tertullian*, Chapter 39.

common." The following comes from an excellent article by Justin Williams in *Cincinnati Magazine*.

> Members of the community live together in "common purse," meaning they share all of their income, contributing everything to a single account. Each adult is doled out only enough to pay his or her bills plus a small, uniform stipend. They hold everything in common—clothing, cars, personal possessions—purposely limiting themselves in an effort to give everything they have as an offering to God. This includes living and worshipping in a communal sense . . .[4]

Members share housing and work full-time; some in one of the community's businesses, others work outside the community. "Among the members are lawyers, nurses, engineers, janitors, and baristas."[5]

I recently had lunch with a friend at the Madison Place coffee shop (rated 4.8/5 on Yelp) which is owned and staffed by community members. In an old building remodeled by members of the community, the coffee shop is spacious and oddly peaceful. Nothing jangles—not the décor nor the music nor the quietly efficient staff and baristas.

In addition to the coffee shop, the Madison Place Community has a successful home improvement business that offers remodeling, handyman repair, landscaping, lawn care and housecleaning services. Its website has excellent reviews from satisfied customers and photographs of beautifully landscaped yards and remodeled homes.

Not surprisingly, the Madison Place Community has its detractors and critics, dissatisfied former members; people who think it's a cult; some aghast at the idea of "common purse" living, sure that it is communism, pure and simple. In contrast to the passion and anxiety in posted warnings and rumors on Facebook and other social media (even on the town's website), the Madison Place Community website, like its businesses, emanates calm, harmony, and gentleness. A dropdown tab titled "On Common Purse" explains how those practicing that lifestyle see it as biblical. Another dropdown tab, "On Controversies," offers this:

> "Why We Don't Defend Ourselves"
>
> . . . while we are aware of some of the gossip and slander spread about our fellowship, we have made the decision together not to engage with it or spend time defending ourselves. . . .

---

4. Williams, "Houses of the Holy."
5. Williams, "Houses of the Holy."

> Of course, it is not easy to do this. There are many good reasons for self-defense. A damaged reputation makes it harder to do good to others, as they are suspicious of your motives. It adds needless tensions between members of a congregation and members of their families, who hear about or read accusations and believe them. And, to be honest, it is simply painful (and even embarrassing) to have people thinking such terrible things about you and people you love.
>
> The purpose of this writing is simply to explain to anyone who is looking for our "responses" to various gossip about our little Christian community why they will not find it. We want to set our eyes on the Lord, doing good to as many people as we can in this world, and we do not want to allow our lives to be embroiled in any meaningless strife.

Hard to find fault with the quiet dignity of this response.

While I could not live in the Madison Place Community nor do I agree with all their theology, I am impressed by the way their lives preach what *they* believe. It seems to me closer than most to being a community based on the radical equity of the vineyard where all are equally valued, and all have what they need.

11

Who's Welcome in The Kingdom?

> Our gracious Creator cares and provides for all his creatures. His tender mercies are over all his works, and so far as true love influences our minds, so far we become interested in his workmanship and feel a desire to make use of every opportunity to lessen the distresses of the afflicted and increase the happiness of the creation. Here we have a prospect of one common interest from which our own is inseparable, so that to turn all we possess into the channel of universal love becomes the business of our lives.
>
> —JOHN WOOLMAN

Three Versions of a Banquet

ONE DIFFICULTY FOR THE reader trying to understand Jesus' parables is that they are preserved in different versions. For instance, a parable about a great meal appears in Thom 64:1–12, Matt 22:1–14, and Luke 14:16–24, but not in Mark. Matthew and Luke may have found the story in Q,[1] a common source known to each of them. The Fellows of the Jesus Seminar believe the Parable of the Feast to be authentic to Jesus, but Matthew's and Luke's have been heavily edited. Below are all three

---

1. To explain "the striking agreements between Matthew and Luke, a German scholar hypothesized that there once existed a source document, which he referred to as a Quelle, which in German means "source." The abbreviation 'Q' was later adopted as its name." Funk and Hoover, *Five Gospels*, 12.

versions for comparison, along with traditional interpretations of each, beginning with Thom 64:1–12.

The Non-Canonical Gospel of Thomas

The Gospel of Thomas was discovered in 1945 among writings preserved on scrolls in a cave at Nag Hammadi, Egypt. Scrolls of writings considered heretical by the early Church were probably hidden in the third century to keep them from being destroyed. Among the scrolls are remnants of ancient "sayings" gospels, like the Gospel of Thomas, which were attempts to preserve in writing what Jesus taught in parables, proverbs, and aphorisms. These "sayings gospels" contain little if any interpretation or commentary, but within a few decades, these remembered words of Jesus no longer matched the theology promoted by the early Church in the narrative gospels (Matthew, Mark, and Luke), and so were banned as heresy.

Similarities of materials that appear in those three gospels, however, suggest to biblical scholars that their common source ("Q") was also a "sayings" gospel like Thomas. Although experts believe that Thomas is not Q, the two are markedly similar in content. For instance, thirteen of the sixteen parables in Thomas also occur in the synoptic gospels whose writers supposedly used Q as their source.

Some biblical scholars suggest that the Gospel of John,[2] written around 90–100 CE, was a refutation of the theology in the "sayings" gospel of Thomas. An example of theological differences between the writer of Thomas and the writer of John is highlighted in an interview with Elaine Pagels, author of *Beyond Belief*:

> The Gospel of Thomas says, "The kingdom is inside of you and outside of you. When you come to know who you are, then you will know that you are the children of the living God." The secret of knowing who you are is not about the ordinary self, but about the part of us that comes from the divine source.

In contrast, according to Pagel,

> John says, yes, Jesus comes from the light from the beginning of time when the Word came into the world. But the good

---

2. The Gospel of John uses parables of his own creation, none of which appear in the other gospels.

news is not that you are the light. No, you are not. Jesus is the light, and he alone.

You can begin to see that the author of the Gospel of John knew the teaching in the Gospel of Thomas and opposed it. He says Jesus is the Son of God. He is the light of the world. You and I are not. We live in darkness. We live in sin. The message [in John] is Jesus is the light, but only Jesus.[3]

Thomas records parables, aphorisms, and proverbs of Jesus the teacher; John writes poetry about the risen Christ. John's poetic interpretation of Jesus' life and death became more important than the teachings of Jesus while he was alive. As Christianity evolved, Thomas' gospel was refuted and banned by the early Church fathers, while John's gospel was embraced and became part of the New Testament canon. Thus, for over two thousand years, traditional Christianity has focused on the finger pointing at the moon rather than on the moon itself.[4]

An early Quaker version of this ancient Buddhist teaching appears in Barclay's Third Proposition: "Concerning the Scriptures": "because [the scriptures] are only a declaration of the fountain, and not the fountain itself, therefore they are not to be esteemed the principal ground of all Truth and knowledge."[5] While the first Friends valued scripture, they understood the primary source for truth must be the "Spirit of God" that inspired Jesus, the prophets, and writers of scripture. What is written on the heart by the Spirit is to be trusted more than what is written on the page by human beings.[6]

3. Elaine Pagels, "What is the Gospel of Thomas."

4. "The Buddha told Ananda, 'You and others like you still listen to the Dharma with the conditioned mind, and so the Dharma becomes conditioned as well, and you do not obtain the Dharma-nature. This is similar to a person pointing his finger at the moon to show it to someone else. Guided by the finger, the other person should see the moon. If he looks at the finger instead and mistakes it for the moon, he loses not only the moon but the finger also. Why? Because he mistakes the pointing finger for the bright moon. Not only does he lose the finger, but he also fails to recognize light and darkness. Why? He mistakes the solid matter of the finger for the bright nature of the moon, and so he does not understand the two natures of light and darkness. The same is true of you.'"

5. Barclay, *Apology*, Third Proposition: "Concerning the Scriptures."

6. Expressed beautifully by Paul in 2 Cor 3:2–3. 6, this metaphor was often used by the early Friends: "You yourselves are our letter, written on our hearts, known and read by all, and you show that you are a letter of Christ, prepared by us, written not with ink but with the Spirit of the living God, not on tablets of stone but on tablets that are human hearts. . . . our qualification is from God, who has made us qualified to be ministers of a new covenant, not of letter but of spirit, for the letter kills, but the

Thomas' Version: The Parable of the Dinner Party

Thomas 64:1–12: The Parable of The Dinner Party

Someone was planning on having guests. When dinner was ready, they sent their servant to call the visitors.

The servant went to the first and said, 'My master invites you."

They said, 'Some merchants owe me money. They're coming tonight. I need to go and give them instructions. Excuse me from the dinner.'

The servant went to another one and said, 'My master invites you.'

They said, "I've just bought a house and am needed for the day. I won't have time."

The servant went to another one and said, 'My master invites you."

They said, 'My friend is getting married and I'm going to make dinner. I can't come. Excuse me from the dinner."

The servant went to another one and said, 'My master invites you."

They said, "I've just bought a farm and am going to collect the rent. I can't come. Excuse me."

The servant went back and told the master, 'The ones you've invited to the dinner have excused themselves."

The master said to their servant, "Go out to the roads and bring whomever you find so that they can have dinner."

"Buyers and merchants won't [enter] the places of my Father."[7]

Thomas' version makes no mention of the master becoming upset or angry, but simply remains persistent in issuing his invitation. The last sentence about "buyers and merchants" not entering the Kingdom "of my Father," would seem to have been said by Jesus, but because it contradicts Jesus' message of inclusive love, it was probably Thomas' comment. Threatening punishment or exclusion is something humans do to control others. How can threats, which induce fear, be part of unconditional

---

Spirit gives life."

7. Mattison, trans., *Gospel of Thomas*, 64:1–12.

love? The God Jesus teaches us about issues endless invitations for us to be loved but leaves it to us to accept or avoid.

The dinner party parable, the way Jesus told it, teaches that people may find all sorts of excuses to avoid the unconditional love God offers, but God persists in offering it anyway. Everyone is welcome at the table and the invitation is unending.

Luke's and Matthew's Versions: The Parable of the Feast/Banquet

Luke 14:15–24: The Parable of the Feast

> One of the dinner guests, on hearing this, said to him, "Blessed is anyone who will eat bread in the kingdom of God!" Then Jesus said to him, "Someone gave a great dinner and invited many. At the time for the dinner, he sent his slave to say to those who had been invited, 'Come, for everything is ready now.' But they all alike began to make excuses. The first said to him, 'I have bought a piece of land, and I must go out and see it; please accept my regrets.' Another said, 'I have bought five yoke of oxen, and I am going to try them out; please accept my regrets.' Another said, 'I have just been married, and therefore I cannot come.' So the slave returned and reported this to his master. Then the owner of the house became angry and said to his slave, 'Go out at once into the streets and lanes of the town and bring in the poor, the crippled, the blind, and the lame.' And the slave said, 'Sir, what you ordered has been done, and there is still room.' Then the master said to the slave, 'Go out into the roads and lanes, and compel people to come in, so that my house may be filled. For I tell you, none of those who were invited will taste my dinner.'"

In Luke's version of the parable, the "owner of the house" sends invitations first to people of higher economic and social status, such as owners of land and oxen, and a newlywed wealthy enough to anticipate time off for a honeymoon. When these refuse his invitation, the owner angrily goes to the other extreme and has his slave invite those of the lowest social status. Notice this is done out of anger, not compassion. Luke also adds the owner's desire to "compel" acceptance of his invitation. Such human reactions do not appear in the simpler version of the story from Thomas (except in the last line which is more likely to be Thomas than Jesus), and they don't gel with the unconditionally loving God we know from Jesus' teachings.

Luke adds to the story a lesson implicit in other teachings of Jesus, i.e., the idea that "the first will be last and the last will be first." This disturbing "first/last/first" idea appears in teachings of Jesus which turn every human condition upside down: the grieving will rejoice; the meek/weak will overcome, etc. Jesus shows our fears to be unwarranted and our hierarchies to be without merit in the Kingdom of God.[8] In another dinner scene, the Last Supper (which occurs only in the Gospel of Luke), Jesus is quoted as saying: "the greatest among you must become like the youngest and the leader like one who serves. For who is greater, the one who is at the table or the one who serves? Is it not the one at the table? But I am among you as one who serves" (Luke 22:26–27).

> Matt 22:1–14: The Parable of The Wedding Banquet
>
> Once more Jesus spoke to them in parables, saying: "The kingdom of heaven may be compared to a king who gave a wedding banquet for his son. He sent his slaves to call those who had been invited to the wedding banquet, but they would not come. Again he sent other slaves, saying, 'Tell those who have been invited: Look, I have prepared my dinner, my oxen and my fat calves have been slaughtered, and everything is ready; come to the wedding banquet.' But they made light of it and went away, one to his farm, another to his business, while the rest seized his slaves, mistreated them, and killed them. The king was enraged. He sent his troops, destroyed those murderers, and burned their city. Then he said to his slaves, 'The wedding is ready, but those invited were not worthy. Go therefore into the main streets and invite everyone you find to the wedding banquet.' Those slaves went out into the streets and gathered all whom they found, both good and bad, so the wedding hall was filled with guests.
>
> But when the king came in to see the guests, he noticed a man there who was not wearing a wedding robe, and he said to him, 'Friend, how did you get in here without a wedding robe?' And he was speechless. Then the king said to the attendants, 'Bind him hand and foot, and throw him into the outer darkness, where there will be weeping and gnashing of teeth.' For many are called, but few are chosen."

Matthew and Thomas recount a similar situation in their parables about a banquet, but the details couldn't be more different. In fact, Matthew's

---

8. There are no hierarchies in Love, the Kingdom of God. See Mark 10:31; Matt 19:30, 20:6; and Luke 13:30. Also, in Matthew's "Parable of the Vineyard Workers," "first" and "last" have no meaning in terms of reward.

version is so different even from Luke's that scholars question whether it comes from the common source ("Q") the two used for other parables, proverbs, and aphorisms.

Listen to Matthew's word choice in the parable: "slaughtered," "seized," "mistreated," "killed," "enraged," "sent troops," "destroyed those murderers, and burned their city," "not worthy," "Bind him hand and foot, and throw him into the outer darkness" "weeping and gnashing of teeth." According to biblical scholars in the Jesus Seminar, Matthew's "thoroughly Christianized" version "has virtually lost touch with Jesus," and become an "allegory of the history of salvation."[9]

Love as Key to the Dinner Party/Feast/Banquet

Let's go back to the Kingdom of God that Jesus talked about.

In the Kingdom of God, Love rules.

In the Kingdom of God, Love is power; Love is the currency and only measure of value.

Love is unconditional, infinite, abundant, and eternal.

As discussed in Chapter 7, Jesus' parables show us what happens during interactions between the Kingdom of God and the human realm. In the Good Samaritan, for instance, the Pharisee and the Levite operate in the human realm while the Samaritan acts from the Kingdom of God. Something like this is happening in the Parable of the Dinner/Feast/Banquet.

The Source of Love (God) invites everyone to a joyous banquet in the Kingdom of Love, but a surprising number of his friends decline the invitation. They give various reasons: property to manage or maintain; businesses or shops to run; family relationships or love affairs that consume time, energy, and attention; some have busy social lives. They send regrets, saying, "Thank you, God, but I just can't get away right now." These are people so caught up in the material realm, they pass up opportunities to participate in the spiritual realm of love.

Though many of his "friends" do not accept his invitation, the undeterred host sends out more invitations, including to those "out on the roads," strangers, passersby. This gathering in love is open to strangers as well as friends (think Gentile as well as Jew, Muslim as well as Christian, etc.), and these strangers don't have to do anything to be

---

9. Funk and Hoover, *Five Gospels*, 235.

invited. The point is that *all* are invited to the banquet; there is more than enough love for everyone. All are loved. All are welcome in the Kingdom of God. Without exception.

What a different message Jesus teaches than the Church does!

The Parable of the Banquet in Real Life

No Questions Asked

Good Plates Eatery, near the campus of the University of Cincinnati, opened its doors in August 2020 during the pandemic when more restaurants were closing than opening. Andrew and Jamie, the young couple who own it, had long dreamed of having their own restaurant, and (in a series of events that Quakers might call "Way opening") that dream became possible in an impossible time.

Inspired by the hope evident in the endeavor, several local news outlets ran stories about it. In *Cincinnati Magazine*, Jamie shared an underlying goal for their new restaurant.

> The hope is to create a place for students to feel at home. When Jamie went away to school, she remembers feeling uneasy about all the changes and living in a new setting. "I didn't feel like there was anywhere on campus that felt comfortable for me," she says. "I want kids, anyone, to feel comfortable and like they can come in any day. Even if they're far from home, they're safe and can eat and hang out [at the restaurant].... There's just something homey about grilled cheese and tomato soup.... I basically want to be the campus mom."[10]

In November 2023, the following story appeared in local news sources including this version from *CityBeat* magazine.

> For the fourth year in a row, Good Plates Eatery will pass out free Thanksgiving and Christmas meals to anyone interested, no questions asked.
>
> "There is no charge, no questions, no reason needed. Just show up, let us know how many meals you need, and you'll be on your way."
>
> Good Plates will be passing out the meals at their restaurant on Wednesday, Nov. 22 starting at noon . . . Each meal comes with

---

10. Garver, "Couple Started Their Own Eatery."

roasted chicken, mashed potatoes, gravy, green beans, stuffing, and bread.[11]

According to the article, Andrew and Jamie began doing this during the pandemic in their first year of business, a dark time for most of us. As Andrew explained, "When COVID was still going strong during the holiday season of 2020, we wanted somewhere for people that couldn't travel home, or didn't want to cook, or just needed a meal. We didn't really know what to expect. I think we passed out around thirty meals during Thanksgiving and another fifty during Christmas."

This compassionate practice has grown (like the mustard seed) and this year (2023), with support from other local businesses and suppliers, Good Plates Eatery "plans to serve 2,000 meals for Thanksgiving and another 2,000 for Christmas but will increase the number for Christmas if needed." Good Plates packs individual meal items in microwaveable containers, then bags them together as a takeout meal. Meals are also served warm if someone wishes to eat right away.

No mention of religion, faith, or Christianity appears in stories about the Good Plates Eatery and its owners. But their compassionate practice of caring for strangers and welcoming all to the table is as "Kingdom of God" as it gets.

"Convicted" of Being Christian

A second example of the Parable of the Banquet in real life occurred a few years ago when I taught an Introduction to Quakerism class at Wilmington College (Ohio). Most of the students were not Quakers and took the class only to fulfill a humanities requirement, but many became interested in knowing more about the Religious Society of Friends who founded the college in 1870.

In discussing the early Friends' approach to Christianity, i.e., "let your life preach," we read a parable by Peter Rollins, a young Irish theologian. Based on a bumper sticker Rollins saw—"If Christianity were illegal would there be enough evidence to convict you?"—the story takes place in a courtroom which could have been almost anywhere, almost any time in the past two thousand years. "You" are being tried for "following Christ," who brought the message to humanity that God wants us to love one another, be merciful, seek justice, and care for the widows, orphans, and

---

11. Barrier, "Clifton Heights' Good Plates Eatery."

strangers among us. In the world of Rollins' parable, however, Christianity is "a subversive and illegal activity." Evidence presented to prove you are "guilty" of being a Christian includes your regular church attendance, faithful tithing, fervent praying, etc. In the end, however, such evidence is unconvincing, and you are found "Not Guilty" of following Christ.[12]

The following week in a conversation before class, one of my students told me about his mother, who "is not religious and doesn't go to church." After hearing Mike's story about her, I told him she might have trouble proving she was "not guilty" of following the teachings of Jesus. He shrugged and said, "People do what they do."

The conversation began when Mike mentioned to me that he was engaged to be married to a girl he'd known most of his life, and they were looking for a house. He was looking forward to moving into a house with his bride, in part because there were twelve people in the house where he currently lived.

"Twelve!" I exclaimed. "Are you sharing a house with other students?"

"No," he replied, explaining that the twelve people included himself, his mother, his grandparents, and eight foster kids.

"Eight foster kids!" I exclaimed again.

"Yeah," he said, "Right now that's how many we have. Over the years, we've had more than fifty."

I asked him how his family came to take in foster kids, and he told this story.

Mike's father died when he was five, so for most of his life, it was just Mike and his mom, a pre-school and kindergarten teacher. When Mike was about twelve, she talked with him about the awful circumstances of some children and asked how he would feel about her becoming a foster parent. They talked it over, and with his agreement, they both went through "foster family" training to offer a home to a series of lost and abused kids.

"My mom will take only the hard cases that no one else wants," Mike said. He spoke warmly of these kids, who had all sorts of mental and emotional problems, some quite severe; some violent. For instance, he was hospitalized a few years ago when a boy broke some of his ribs. Another time, a different boy twisted his mother's arm so badly that it severed all the tendons. But that boy, paranoid and schizophrenic,

---

12. Peter Rollins, *Orthodox Heretic*, 4–9.

stayed with them until he "aged out" of foster care. Mike and his mom were still in contact with him—he was now institutionalized in Toledo—and they visited him when they could. Mike said he and his fiancée had talked about taking in foster kids. He would like to, but he's afraid she's too easily "attached," and wouldn't be able to handle it when kids were sent back to abusive homes.

I knew from earlier conversations with Mike that he didn't believe in God, much less Christ as the Son of God. I didn't know what Mike's mother believed, but I did know she was "guilty of Christianity" and had influenced her son to be the same way. I was particularly moved by Mike's statement that his mother would "only take the hard cases that no one else wants."

Sort of like the God in Jesus' parable who welcomes everyone to the banquet, even (or especially) the hard cases.

12

How the Kingdom Grows

The Mustard Seed

> He put before them another parable: "The kingdom of heaven is like a mustard seed that someone took and sowed in his field; it is the smallest of all the seeds, but when it has grown it is the greatest of shrubs and becomes a tree, so that the birds of the air come and make nests in its branches" (Matt 13:31–32).
>
> He also said, "With what can we compare the kingdom of God, or what parable will we use for it? It is like a mustard seed, which, when sown upon the ground, is the smallest of all the seeds on earth, yet when it is sown it grows up and becomes the greatest of all shrubs and puts forth large branches, so that the birds of the air can make nests in its shade" (Mark 4:30–32).
>
> He said therefore, "What is the kingdom of God like? And to what should I compare it? It is like a mustard seed that someone took and sowed in the garden; it grew and became a tree, and the birds of the air made nests in its branches" (Luke 13:18–19).

JESUS REFERS TO A kind of mustard seed being *purposely* sown in this parable. Those of us who live in Europe or North America may picture yellow fields of wild mustard, a nuisance to farmers and gardeners. This mustard species, *Sinapis arvensis,* is native to the Mediterranean area, but it grows wild and spreads prolifically, so would probably not be sown on purpose, and its plants grow only up to a meter (thirty-nine inches) or so tall. If Jesus refers to the seed of this plant, we must imagine the unnatural event of it growing to be tree-size.

One type of mustard plant native to the Middle East, however, *can* grow to be thirty feet in height— *salvadora persica*, the mustard bush or mustard tree.[1] In the parable, Jesus says the tiny mustard seed is *sown* in a field or in a garden and grows big enough for birds to build nests in its branches, something that naturally happens with *salvadora persica*. His point becomes that the Kingdom of God grows from seemingly insignificant things, like tiny seeds, into great things, like tall spreading trees. Imagine a forest of such trees, each one, year after year, producing thousands more tiny seeds. This image of the Kingdom of God suggests exponential growth, a concept that also occurs in the Parable of the Leaven and The Parable of the Talents.

Leaven

> He told them another parable: "The kingdom of heaven is like yeast that a woman took and mixed in with three measures of flour until all of it was leavened" (Matt 13:33).

This simple one-sentence parable communicates more about the Kingdom of God than many of Jesus' longer parables. Leaven or yeast is a powerful fermenting agent that causes bread to rise. Here are some things most twenty-first century readers won't know about leaven. (1) It is "a member of the fungus kingdom"; (2) it is "microscopic in size and a single oval yeast cell is considered an organism"; (3) "all yeast cells are identical to each other"; and yeast "requires an organic host to survive."[2]

Two qualities common to the tiny mustard seed and the even tinier leaven are (a) the miniscule size and (b) the incomprehensible exponential growth of each. One "tiniest-of-all-seeds" can become a large tree with branches large enough for birds to nest in. As for leaven, "two days can turn 100 yeast cells into 400 billion. . . . a yeast's work rate on glucose is the equivalent of a 200-pound person chopping 2 million pounds of wood in two days."[3]

---

1. *Salvadora persica*. Also called the "Toothbrush Tree," it has been used for centuries as a natural antiseptic, astringent, and toothbrush.
2. "Mold vs. Yeast," Moldbusters.com.
3. Cassidy, "Who Figured Out How to Make Leavened Bread?"

Jesus' first listeners probably did not know this precise math about leaven, but they witnessed its action daily and knew at a deeper level its expansive power. For Jesus to say the Kingdom of God is like yeast is to suggest a realm whose potential to increase is exponential.

Love as Key to the Mustard Seed and the Leaven

"With what can we compare the kingdom of God?" Jesus begins, then answers his own question: "It is like a "mustard seed, the smallest of all the seeds on earth." This must have caused some confusion among his first listeners. Surely the Kingdom of God would be huge, powerful, rich, greater than any human kingdom. Jesus goes on to say it can be as tiny as a mustard seed, which, after it takes root, may grow to be larger and greater than all other shrubs, even a tree with branches large enough for birds to nest in.

Then he adds another surprising comparison: "The Kingdom of God is like leaven that a woman took and mixed in with flour . . ." Not only is he *not* describing the Kingdom of God as full of power and wealth, but he claims it is as simple, familiar, and accessible (even to women) as the yeast particles in air and flour that they use to make their daily bread.

Such humble images must have made his followers realize Jesus was asking them to re-imagine what a kingdom or realm could be. In the Kingdom of God as Jesus describes it, the only thing of value is love, priceless and beyond measure. Love is infinite, which means in effect, size has no meaning. Infinity goes both ways, infinitely small as well as infinitely large. In the Kingdom of God, love begets love—each loving smile, each kindness, each act of compassion—adds to the whole of love and contributes to the spreading of love. In such a way, human participation in the Kingdom of God may spread and grow.

The Mustard Seed and Leaven in Real Life

Small acts of compassion or kindness stay with us, whether we give them or receive them; such acts are reciprocal in some way. Tiny, unimportant-to-anyone-else exchanges can leave an image and feeling that lingers for years. For instance, I can still see in my mind's eye the smile from a rough-looking fellow when I unexpectedly waved him to go ahead across the intersection as I waited in my car. That's all. Just eye contact, his nod of gratitude, and a warm recognition of each other's existence; a brief and simple connection in the Kingdom of God.

Tiny seeds of the kingdom even grow from *telling stories* of acts of compassion. When someone shares with us how a "random act of kindness" happened, it warms our hearts and, because stories are natural to humans, we remember them and like to tell them.

A Tiny Seed on the Street

The following story comes from a young Quaker minister writing about a member of her congregation, a contractor we'll call Hank.

> [Hank]was at a worksite when he noticed two young men across the street arguing. The more that they argued, the more escalated the situation became. Fearing that something violent was going to happen, another person from the worksite went over to talk to them. Unfortunately, his intervention only made things worse, at which point Hank decided to go over there.
>
> When Hank told me this story, he said that he had no idea what he was going to do when he got to the young men. He just knew that he felt compelled to help, and to his own surprise, when he approached the angriest young man, the words, "Do you need a hug?" came out of his mouth. The young man (who had been the main instigator of the fight) fell into Hank's arms and burst into tears.

Hank not only planted a seed of the Kingdom (i.e., love] in the angry young man and in the hearts of those watching the encounter, he planted a seed in the heart of the young minister, who planted a seed in the hearts of those who read her account of what happened. And now, Hank's compassionate act told in the young minister's words has planted seeds of loving kindness in all those who may read this. Thus, the Kingdom grows exponentially.

A Tiny Seed in Macy's Shoe Department

Some years ago, I served as minister and Public Friend for Cincinnati Friends Meeting, a progressive, semi-programmed Quaker meeting in Ohio.[4]

---

4. "Semi-programmed" meant that the minister could speak ten to twelve minutes,

One year in late summer, a young woman named Jamie began attending our Sunday Meeting for Worship, and she signed up for the fall Quakerism 101 class. At the first class, I asked people to introduce themselves and tell us what had brought them to Quakerism 101.

When it was Jamie's turn, she said, "I'm here because about six months ago, a woman came into Macy's shoe department where I work. She was a Quaker minister looking for some good walking shoes because she was going to Kenya."

I knew most of the Quakers in the area and knew no other women ministers in Cincinnati, so I asked, "Do you know where she was from?"

"She was from here. From Cincinnati," Jamie said.

Strange, I thought, mentally running through the names of those in southwestern Ohio who, like me, had attended the spring FWCC World Gathering in Nakuru, Kenya. No other women from Cincinnati had been there and I could remember only one man from our entire yearly meeting.

"She said she was going to teach a Quakerism class at a college there."

In April, I had gone to Kenya to teach a short course at Friends Theological College before attending the FWCC gathering. But she couldn't be referring to me. For one thing, I didn't shop at Macy's, and for another, I had no memory of the conversation she described. Yet no one else fit the description she gave and I realized she must be talking about me.

"I'm here," Jamie continued, "because she was the only person who was kind to me all week. And I decided I wanted to know more about Quakers."

I was at a loss for words. How could I not remember this? I felt awful, worried that it had hurt her feelings. and apologized to Jamie for not remembering our conversation. (In hindsight I can imagine myself cruising through Macy's on my way out of the mall, stopping briefly to browse the expensive shoes and being chatty with the young clerk waiting on me because, knowing I wouldn't buy anything, I felt bad for her.)

It's difficult to express how humbling it was — and still is — to realize that something I didn't remember saying or doing could have such an effect on a stranger. A tiny seed I didn't even know was planted took root. Jaimie found her way to Quakerism, and years later, the seed is still spreading as you read this story of the way the Kingdom of God

---

but the rest of our weekly worship service was silent, waiting, Quaker worship.

grows among us, here and now, in every small act of kindness, even if done unconsciously.

A Leavening in Kenya

After teaching the short course at Friends Theological College for two weeks, I was to take a bus from the small village of Kaimosi in Western Kenya to Nakuru in central Kenya, site of the World Gathering of Friends (Quakers). I had read warnings in Kenya travel guides about traveling overland in Kenya, especially alone, but there was no other way to get where I needed to go.

Very early in the morning, I waited with others outside the brightly painted concrete block bus depot. I watched the baggage loaded into the bus's undercarriage compartment (noting where mine was), along with various boxes, including one cardboard box containing a live chicken, its head sticking out between the flaps.

When I boarded the bus I sat down next to a Kenyan woman wearing a white kerchief. The woman and I nodded and acknowledged each other, but didn't speak for the first couple of hours. I dozed and watched the scenery. Finally, I asked if she knew how much farther it was to Nakuru. She did; she made the trip regularly by bus from Kaimosi to Nairobi and knew about what time we should arrive. She asked what I was doing in Kaimosi, and we discovered we were both Quakers![5] Her name was Mary and she taught at a Quaker school for girls in the area. She knew a woman from Ohio not far from where I lived in Cincinnati, a nurse who worked for many years at the Friends Hospital in Kaimosi. The bus ride passed more quickly after we began talking.

As we drove through the Molo Hills, west and slightly north of Nakuru, Mary pointed out places where the worst violence had occurred after the 2007–2008 elections—we were passing through the place where it had been the worst. People killing their neighbors, running them off their land. "There are still displaced people camps in Nakuru," she told me, "People afraid to go back to their land."

When we finally arrived at the bus station, she asked me if I needed to use the bathroom—after five hours over bumpy Kenyan roads, of course I did. "Come on," she said. "Let's go."

---

5. Her white kerchief should have given me a clue. Members of the United Society of Friends Women (USFW) in Kenya often wear such scarfs.

"But shouldn't I get my bag first?" I was concerned about it disappearing.

"No. Let's go to the bathroom first and then we'll get it."

Mary and I were the first ones off the bus, and she led me straight to the ladies' toilets. There, we had to pay ten pence to use the facilities, and while I was searching through my bag, she said, "I've already paid it for you. Come on." I didn't know why, but she clearly wanted me to hurry.

By the time we came out of the bathroom stalls, there was a line of women out the door and into the hallway. Mary led me back to the bus and told the driver to get my bag. He unlocked the compartment, but my bag wasn't there! Mary persisted—had him open another compartment. It wasn't there either. She started talking to him in Swahili until he thought *maybe* it was in a compartment on the other side of the bus ... and it was, oddly enough, the only bag there.

She wanted to know who was meeting me. I told her I would be picked up by a taxi driver sent by the B&B where I was to stay for a few days before the conference began. She nodded when she heard the name of the B&B, apparently satisfied it was reputable. She steered me toward the bus station restaurant and showed me how to use the telephone there and how to order food at the counter. I offered to buy her lunch, but she had a connecting bus and had to go. I thanked her for her help and assured her I would be fine, but still she left reluctantly. In a little while, though, she came back to the restaurant to check on me one last time. I was afraid she would miss her bus, and I think she might have, but after I told her I had called the B&B, they were expecting me, and their driver was on his way, she seemed willing to leave me.

Only in hindsight did I realize how carefully she had watched over me, a stranger, protecting me from my own naïve ignorance in a vulnerable situation. I will always remember her kindness, and I tell the story whenever I can.

13

The Parable of the Talents

Money makes money. And the money that money makes, makes money.

—Benjamin Franklin

"For it is as if a man, going on a journey, summoned his slaves and entrusted his property to them; to one he gave five talents, to another two, to another one, to each according to his ability. Then he went away. At once the one who had received the five talents went off and traded them and made five more talents. In the same way, the one who had the two talents made two more talents. But the one who had received the one talent went off and dug a hole in the ground and hid his master's money. After a long time, the master of those slaves came and settled accounts with them. Then the one who had received the five talents came forward, bringing five more talents, saying, 'Master, you handed over to me five talents; see, I have made five more talents.' His master said to him, 'Well done, good and trustworthy slave; you have been trustworthy in a few things; I will put you in charge of many things; enter into the joy of your master.' And the one with the two talents also came forward, saying, 'Master, you handed over to me two talents; see, I have made two more talents.' His master said to him, 'Well done, good and trustworthy slave; you have been trustworthy in a few things; I will put you in charge of many things; enter into the joy of your master.' Then the one who had received the one talent also came forward, saying, 'Master, I knew that you were a harsh man, reaping where you did not sow and gathering where you did not scatter, so I was afraid, and I went and hid your talent in the ground. Here you have what is yours.' But his master replied, 'You wicked and lazy slave! You knew, did you, that I reap where I did not sow and gather where I did not scatter? Then you ought to have invested my money with the bankers, and on my return I would have received what was my own with interest. So take the talent from him and give it to the one with the ten talents" (Matt 25:14–28, also in Luke 19:13, 15–24).

THIS MEANING OF THIS story is considerably more difficult to grasp than the meaning in "easy" parables like the Good Samaritan. The Parable of the Talents *seems* to be about money and resources, about getting a good return on an investment, and most traditional interpretations focus on what God expects humans to do with the gifts/resources they are given.

Note that the part of the parable considered to be in the authentic words of Jesus ends with the master simply saying, "So take the talent from him and give it to the one with the ten talents," a completely unexpected and puzzling outcome. So puzzling that the gospel writers of Matthew and Luke continue the story past this point, adding elements contradictory to Jesus' other teachings, i.e., the master is ruthless, violent, and cruel; he shames the fearful servant, calls him "lazy" and "wicked," then punishes him. In Matt 25:28, he says, "As for this worthless slave, throw him into the outer darkness, where there will be weeping and gnashing of teeth." In Luke 19:27, he says, "But as for these enemies of mine who did not want me to rule over them—bring them here and slaughter them in my presence," which seems to have nothing to do with the parable of the talents. Probably because of this angry and punishing reaction of the master, traditional Christian interpretation often associates the parable with what will happen when Christ returns "to judge the quick and the dead."

Such fury and cruelty on the part of the master contradicts everything else in Jesus' teachings about the Kingdom of God.

The Love That Love Makes

Most readers find this parable unsettling, particularly the seeming unfairness of the master taking away what little the fearful investor has and giving it to the most successful investor. But this echoes a similar disturbing teaching of Jesus found in Matt 13:12: "For to those who have, more will be given, and they will have an abundance, but from those who have nothing, even what they have will be taken away."[1] Both Matthew and Luke include the saying in the Parable of the Talents, adding it after the master's comment when he takes the one talent away from the fearful investor and gives it to the most successful investor.

There doesn't seem to be any way to reconcile this and make it okay in the human realm.

If, however, we look at this "hard" teaching as a lesson about love in the Kingdom of God, it makes sense. The context of Matt 13:12 is Jesus telling his disciples that they have been told the secrets of the Kingdom of Heaven. To those who already know this secret he says, "more will be given in abundance." But from those who reject or know nothing of these mysteries, "even what they have will be taken away." The context of Mark 4:25 is "Pay attention to what you hear; the measure you give will be the measure you get, and it will be added to you." In other words, listen to what I'm telling you about *love in the Kingdom of God: the more you love, the more love you will have.* The context of Luke 8:18 is, once again, pay attention to what you've been taught, "for nothing is hidden that will not be disclosed, nor is anything secret that will not become known and come to light." This knowledge of love in the Kingdom of God *will be disclosed and brought to light. Listen well, lest you lose what understanding you have gained of the Kingdom of God.*

> Robert Barclay (1678):
>
> ... he that had two talents was accepted as well as he that had five because he used them to his master's profit. And he that had one might have done so: his talent was of the same nature with the rest, it was as capable to have proportionably brought forth its interest as the rest. And so though there be not a like proportion of grace given to all, ... yet there is given to all that which is sufficient, and no more is required than according to that which is given: "For unto whomsoever much is given, from him shall much be required..."[2]

Here, early Friend Robert Barclay points out the Parable of the Talents is not about *how much* you have, but what you *do* with what you have. Even though the three servants are given different quantities, each has what is

---

1. Also Mark 4:25 and Luke 8:18; 19:26.
2. Barclay, QBI, "Matthew 25:14–30."

sufficient for him. And *all have the same currency* (love in the Kingdom of God), which has the same power, proportionately, to earn interest.

The message in the Parable of the Talents is that love begets love, and God is pleased when we have enough faith to risk all for love and compassion. As Bishop Barron put it, the talents represent "a share in the mercy of God, a participation in the weightiness of the divine love."[3] Jesus teaches that all can participate in love, a/k/a "the Kingdom of God," and we are encouraged to imitate God by holding nothing back in the way of love, by acknowledging love wherever it exists, and by sharing it freely. This is the way it is in the Kingdom of God. All love, all the time, to everyone.

In the actions of fearful servant, Jesus shows us how not to behave in the Kingdom of God. Do not be afraid. (He says this often.) Do not be afraid to invest in love. Do not fear how God will react if you spend love on others. Do not fear there is not enough. Do not hide or hoard love, keeping it safely put away where only you know the location and can get to it. Do not lock away love or reserve it for those you think deserve it. Don't try to return it to God untouched. Love increases exponentially when it is spent, shared, and given away.

Love as Key to the Talents

Imagine a priest or preacher, who has read the Church's complicated explications, trying to explain this parable to his congregation. Consider, on the other hand, Jesus telling the parable to his listeners and not explaining it at all, but letting those who could, hear the parable as related to the Kingdom of God, not human economics.

The Parable of the Talents begins, as most of Jesus' parables do, with a reference to "this is what it's like in the Kingdom of God/Heaven," the spiritual realm different from the earthly realm. In the rest of his teachings, Jesus consistently stresses that only two commandments are essential: "Love God and love one another."

In the Kingdom of God, the owner/master has abundant "wealth," i.e., love (indeed, limitless), which he entrusts to those who serve him. Because he knows them well, he gives them responsibility for differing amounts, "to each according to his ability." Again, think in terms of compassionate love, not financial investment skills. Some workers in the

---

3. Bishop Barron, "Deeper Meaning."

Kingdom of God are faithful, loving, and compassionate; others are capable of love and compassion, perhaps not so thoroughly tested in faith, but growing; and some find it challenging to be loving and compassionate, and/or they doubt that God is so.

An emphasis on the number of talents invested and increased seems natural in the human realm, but in the Kingdom of God, the quantity risked and invested is not significant so long as nothing is held back (5 x infinite love = infinite love; 2 x infinite love = infinite love; 1 x infinite love = infinite love). Workers who are faithfully loving and compassionate—or those who have deep faith that God is—understand that the nature of love is to compound itself. Such a worker has confidence that love is meant to be spent, to be invested and put to work. The second kind of worker, still growing in love and compassion and/ or with a growing faith, also recognizes that "love begets love" and thus puts it to work. Both these servants/workers receive approval and the invitation to "enter the joy of the Master."

The worker given only one talent finds it difficult to feel love and compassion for others, or doubts/misunderstands the love of God and tries to protect what little love he has been given, which he constantly fears losing. Thus, he buries it and keeps it from being used, erring on the side of caution when God would have him err on the side of love and compassion.

The servant's explanation for why he does what he does describes the way some people perceive God, i.e., as harsh and demanding. To his dismay, the servant observes that the Master reaps crops he doesn't sow from places where he doesn't scatter seed. Apparently, the fearful servant sees such actions as at least a trifle unethical, and perhaps ruthless. In the parable, God/the Master acknowledges this is so; he *does* reap where he does not sow and gather where he does not scatter seed. What are we to make of this? In the Kingdom of God, it seems, love grows not only in cultivated fields where it is intentionally planted (like a synagogue or church), but in other "untended" places as well! Love (like weeds) may grow anywhere; all harvests of Love are welcome—wherever, however, or by whomever planted.

The Parable of the Talents in Real Life

Because in this parable Jesus uses the context of investing money, which is so important in our earthly existence, we have difficulty separating money from the message.

The meaning in the Parable of the Talents, however, is related to the message in the Parables of the Mustard Seed, the Leaven, and in the short Parable of the Seed.[4]

In the leaven parable, both seed parables, and the talents parable Jesus uses images from the material realm as examples of the exponential growth of love in the Kingdom of God. We scatter seeds which sprout and grow though we don't know how. From the tiniest seeds great trees may grow. As for the talents, the more money is invested and used, the greater the return. In the Kingdom of God, love grows exponentially, like the spread of seeds, like leaven, like money invested at compound interest. To paraphrase Ben Franklin, *love makes love. And the love that love makes, makes love.*

The "Magic Penny" in the Kingdom

Financial consultant Shahar Ziv teaches a lesson about compounding interest in a personal finance workshop. At the first session, he begins by asking participants: "Which Would You Pick: $1,000,000 Or A Magical Penny?" and gives them the following scenario:

> Wandering on the street one day, you notice a shiny penny on the sidewalk. When you pick it up you learn that this isn't an ordinary penny, but a magical one.[5] The power of this penny is that it doubles in value each day for a month. In other words, when you wake up the next day, you miraculously have two pennies; on day three, four pennies; on day four eight pennies, and so forth.

He asks participants to estimate how much an investment in the magic penny will be worth after a month and which they would choose, the magic penny or a million dollars. Most people pick the million dollars and

---

4. Mark 4:26–27: "He also said, 'The kingdom of God is as if someone would scatter seed on the ground and would sleep and rise night and day, and the seed would sprout and grow, he does not know how.'"

5. The song "Magic Penny" by Malvina Reynolds makes this concept simple enough for children to understand.

are surprised when he tells them that, after thirty-one days of compounding interest, the magic penny will be worth over $10 million dollars![6] He reminds attendees that there are, of course, no such "magic pennies."

According to Jesus, love functions as Ziv describes the "power" of the magic penny: it increases each time it is given, lent, invested, or shared. If each day, one person gives love to one other person, you have double the love. If each day one person simply passes love on to one more person, love increases incrementally. If, on the other hand, the first person *and* the second person each pass love on to another person, we suddenly have four people receiving and spreading love; by the second round, we have eight people receiving and spreading love, and so on. When love is reciprocated each time it is given, it increases exponentially. This is the kind of investment that interests the God of Love Jesus teaches about. This is what is at stake in the Parable of the Talents.

The Fearful Investors of Clovis, New Mexico

In the Chapter 7 discussion of the Parable of the Good Samaritan, I mentioned that in May 2006, the group called CrossWalk America stayed a few days in my hometown, Clovis, New Mexico, on its journey to promote Jesus' message of love as they walked from Arizona to Washington, D.C.

In Clovis, the walkers were refused hospitality by all the churches in town. Except one. The one church that did respond with open hearts was the tiny Llano Estacado MCC,[7] which welcomed the walkers and provided them hospitality during their time in Clovis.

Here's part of the story as reported a day or so later in a front-page article of the local newspaper.

> [Cross]Walk co-president Eric Elnes said the team relies on the hospitality of local churches along the route to provide warm beds and meals. But when CrossWalk officials approached the Clovis Ministerial Alliance via e-mail, Elnes said the response was less than welcoming. Clovis Christian Ministerial Alliance Chairman Lance Clemmons, a Presbyterian minister, was the recipient of the CrossWalk e-mail.

---

6. Ziv, "$1,000,000 Or A Magical Penny?"

7. Metropolitan Community Church (MCC). An international Protestant denomination with a specific outreach to members of the LGBTQ community.

In return correspondence, Clemmons thanked the group for the invitation to assist the project but said he was unaware of any churches in the Clovis area that followed "progressive theology." Clemmons wished them well and directed them to seek assistance in another community. In a telephone interview on Thursday, Clemmons told the *Clovis News Journal* the Ministerial Alliance chose not to support the walkers because of their affirmations.

"I agree with some of the points," Clemmons said, "but when it comes to excusing behavior that God has clearly condemned as sin, I must agree to disagree."

... Frank Sherman, pastor of Westminster Presbyterian Church, said he is a member of the Ministerial Alliance but rarely attends meetings since he is nearing retirement as a minister. Sherman said his congregation might have offered hospitality if asked.

"I can't find anything in the Bible to support the gay lifestyle," he said, "but I wouldn't condemn them for their beliefs."

Efforts to contact other leaders with the Ministerial Alliance on Thursday were not successful.

The nondenominational Llano Estacado Metropolitan Community Church of Clovis has welcomed the group. MCC includes gay, lesbian, bisexual and transgender members. Clovis' Llano Estacado MCC member Tino Cordova said his church plans to provide meals for the walkers and has invited them to preach the sermon for Sunday morning's worship service.[8]

Like the "fearful investor" in the parable, Evangelical Christians represented by the Clovis Ministerial Alliance held on to the love they received from God, afraid to risk loving too broadly, to invest love too widely, and to give love to those they fear God disapproves of, such as progressive Christians and LGBTQ folks.

The irony of this behavior by local churches was not lost on other citizens in Clovis. The citizens of Clovis who were not churchgoers, as well as many churchgoing folks, saw the hypocrisy of the "good Christians" in the response of the Ministerial Alliance. Once word got around, several things happened, and other "investors" stepped forward to respond with love. Two of the walkers were asked to speak to classes at a public school on the topic of commitment. A Baptist minister joined them for conversation at a local coffee shop. Two local radio stations (including

---

8. Garner, "Progressive Christians."

KIJN Jesus Radio) interviewed walkers and promoted their mission, and a local minister preached a sermon about CrossWalk America on KIJN. The story of their reception, written by a staff writer for the *Clovis News Journal*, appeared on the front page of the paper. People driving through Clovis heard the story on the radio, and afterward, as the walkers continued their journey, people passing them on the highway showed support with friendly honks and waves. (Among those who heard the KIJN interview was a profoundly moved truckdriver from Bovina, Texas, where the walkers spent the night after leaving Clovis.)[9]

Fearful investors in the Kingdom of God lock away what little love they have, so it doesn't benefit them or anyone else; it doesn't grow or expand, just stays safely hidden away. But hoarding is not a profitable use of any asset. Only by using love joyfully and unapologetically (as those who opened their hearts and doors to the CrossWalkers did) can we realize a profit and increase the overall supply. According to the teachings of Jesus, the God of Love gives us all the love we can possibly hold and more, and according to the Parable of the Talents, he prefers that we take risks with love and compassion, investing them fearlessly.

Through the Valley of The Kwai by Ernest Gordon

The most powerful example in real life of Jesus' message in the parables of the Talents, the Mustard Seed, and the Leaven comes from the memoir of Ernest Gordon, *Through the Valley of the Kwai*.

During WWII, Gordon, a Scotsman, served in the Far East as company commander of the 2nd Battalion, Argyll and Sutherland Highlander Regiment of the British Army. In 1942, he was captured and spent three-and-one-half years as a Japanese prisoner-of-war. He was among the thousands of POWs and Southeast Asian civilians forced to build the Thai-Burma Railway, which required construction of many railway bridges across jungle rivers, including the River Kwai.

Gordon survived the war, and by 1957 when the popular movie *Bridge Over the River Kwai* came out, he was dean of the chapel at Princeton University. Gordon wrote his memoir, in part as a corrective about what happened during the building of that railway and bridge. More than that, however, his memoir is an account of what the reader must finally understand as Christianity the way Jesus taught it (though of course, Jesus

---

9. Elnes, *Asphalt Jesus*, 58–65.

did not call it Christianity). Among other things, it exemplifies the parable of the mustard seed through the slow change in the POW camp, one small act of kindness at a time; individual seeds of compassion grow to create a "tree" greater than the sum of its parts. Beyond that, it dramatizes the parables of the Leaven and the Talents in the exponential return on the "investment" of compassionate love by two or three men.

The quotations that follow cannot do justice to the impact of reading all two-hundred-and-eleven pages of Gordon's book, but they provide a few compelling examples of humans living out Jesus' teachings, specifically "love your neighbor as yourself" and "love your enemies," until the darkest most hopeless place imaginable—hell, if you will—becomes the Kingdom of God.

The first hundred pages or so detail the prisoners' descent into the hell of a brutal Japanese POW camp. The men were forced to work, daylight to dark, seven days a week, and survive on a diet of rice three times a day. Gordon says the men might have survived on rice, but the four-hundred-and-twenty grams a day officially allotted was decreased by Japanese soldiers "dipping into the supply line" so that "far less was left by the time the rice reached" the POWs. No rice was allotted for the sick; only for those who could work. Gordon writes:

> Death called to us from every direction. It was in the air we breathed—it was the chief topic of our conversation.... As conditions steadily worsened, as starvation, exhaustion and disease took an ever-growing toll, the atmosphere in which we lived was increasingly poisoned by selfishness, hatred, and fear. We were slipping rapidly down the scale of degradation.... Existence had become so miserable, the odds so heavy against us, that nothing mattered except to survive. We lived by the rule of the jungle, "red in tooth and claw"—the evolutionary law of the survival of the fittest.... The weak were trampled underfoot, the sick ignored or resented, the dead forgotten.... When a man lay dying we had no word of mercy. When he cried for help, we averted our heads. Men cursed the Japanese, their neighbors, themselves, and God.... Everyone was his own keeper. It was free enterprise at its worst, with all the restraints of morality gone.... Little acts of meanness, suspicion, and favoritism permeated our daily lives. Even the drawing of our meager ration was a humiliating experience.[10]

---

10. Gordon, *Through the Valley of the Kwai*, 73–77.

The catalog of horrific details continues, and hopelessness pervades the camp. Gordon, an atheist at the time, offers this comment on religion:

> At Changi, many had turned to religion as a crutch. But the crutch had not supported them; so they had thrown it away. Many had prayed, but only for themselves. Nothing happened. They had sought personal miracles from the Bible—and none had come. They had appealed to God as an expedient. But God apparently had refused to be treated as one.[11]

The "hospital" was for those POWs who could survive a wound or any of many illnesses—amoebic dysentery, cholera, malaria, diphtheria—but for the dying, there was a large hut the men called "The Death House," with the morgue located conveniently just outside it. After an appendectomy without anesthesia followed by contracting diphtheria, malaria, typhoid, dysentery, and intestinal worms, Gordon was taken to the "Death House" where he lay for many days among the dying.

One day, a recently arrived POW, a fellow he had served with in one of the campaigns, came to find him in the Death House. He walked right by Gordon without recognizing him. Finally, Gordon was able to get his attention and the man talked while he listened, speech being very difficult for him. After he left, Gordon asked for a mirror and did not recognize himself, he was so thin, his skin waxy, eyes sunken. He writes: "The last shreds of my numbed sensibilities rebelled against my surroundings—against the bedbugs, the lice, the stenches, the blood-mucous-excrement-stained sleeping platforms, the dying and dead bedmates, the victory of corruption."[12] He begged one of the orderlies to take him out into the fresh air, even though the only place they could put him was at the "morgue," which was cleaner than where he was. He had to lie on the bare ground, but it was dry.

Another of his friends recently arrived at Chungkai came to see Gordon one night to tell him that he and some others were building a small hut for him that he could have all to himself. Unable to walk or care for himself in any way, he was moved to the hut, and a young Scotsman from his battalion, Dusty Miller, volunteered to care for him after his night job in the kitchens. A few days later, Dinty Moore, another fellow Scotsman that Gordon had known at school, stopped by to offer

---

11. Gordon, *Through the Valley of the Kwai*, 78.
12. Gordon, *Through the Valley of the Kwai*, 83.

his help. Under their care, and in a clean hut, Gordon began to recover and eventually could walk again.

> What I had experienced—namely, the turning to life away from death—was happening to the camp in general. We were coming through the valley. There was a movement, a stirring in our midst, a presence. . . . Stories of a different kind began to circulate around the camp, stories of self-sacrifice, heroism, faith, and love.[13]
>
> Our regeneration—sparked by conspicuous acts of self-sacrifice—had begun while [conditions were at their worst], when work on the railroad was in its most exhausting phase and we were at the very bottom of the abyss.[14]
>
> . . .
>
> Death was still with us—no doubt about that. But we were being slowly freed from its destructive grip. We were seeing for ourselves the sharp contrasts between the forces that make for life and those that make for death. Selfishness, hatred, jealousy, and greed were all anti-life. Love, self-sacrifice, mercy, and creative faith, on the other hand, were the essence of life, turning mere existence into living in its truest sense.[15]

By the time Gordon and the remaining POWs were rescued in 1945, the prisoners had taken on helping the sick—finding nutritious foods in duck eggs, fermented rice, and plants they grew in a garden beside the hospital. They gave blood. They respected the dead, seeing to it that each man had a separate grave and marker; they distributed his possessions to those closest to him in his unit.

The camp held regular "classes" taught by any POW with a particular knowledge or expertise; it had a lending library where books were freely passed from one to another. The men held Bible discussion groups and eventually a small chapel was built. The camp held an art show where more than forty sculptures and drawings were exhibited. Eventually the camp had an orchestra of handmade bamboo wind instruments, kettledrums made from oil barrels with hide stretched over them, cymbals from barrel lids, and six violins passed on by the Japanese from a YMCA shipment. Thanks to a gifted musician with a photographic

---

13. Gordon, *Through the Valley of the Kwai*, 101.
14. Gordon, *Through the Valley of the Kwai*, 106.
15. Gordon, *Through the Valley of the Kwai*, 109.

memory who wrote out all the parts, the orchestra played selections like Beethoven's Fifth symphony and the Mikado. Then the men built a stage and put on plays written by one of the POWs.

The second half of Gordon's memoir recounts anecdotes and examples of how the "mustard seed" of faith and love sown in the POW camps continued to grow and spread, even after the war ended and the men went back to civilian life. In the last chapter, Gordon writes about his decision "to study theology in preparation for the ministry."

> In many ways it was not an easy choice to make, for it necessitated adjustment to an entirely different environment, language, and attitude. After my return I had gone to church every Sunday, but what I saw and heard depressed me. The sermons belong to a different age. They suggested Victorian parlors, elderly people dressed in black, horsehair chairs and antimacassars. We had seen a vision of far horizons and caught a glimpse of the City of God in all its beauty.

This "glimpse of the City of God" was more powerful than his disappointment in church, however, and Gordon persevered in his decision to prepare for the ministry; this was "not unusual among former POW's," he says, adding that for years he heard of "other alumni of the hell camps" who entered the ministry.[16]

Consider the parable of tiny mustard seed producing a great tree and the parable of invested money that compounds exponentially. Consider the return on the "investment" of compassionate love by two or three men in that Japanese prison camp, spread through decades, exponentially stirring faith in the power of love and compassion for all who read this story.

---

16. Gordon, *Through the Valley of the Kwai*, 251.

14

The Unmerciful Servant

"For this reason the kingdom of heaven may be compared to a king who wished to settle accounts with his slaves. When he began the reckoning, one who owed him ten thousand talents was brought to him, and, as he could not pay, the lord ordered him to be sold, together with his wife and children and all his possessions and payment to be made. So the slave fell on his knees before him, saying, 'Have patience with me, and I will pay you everything.' And out of pity for him, the lord of that slave released him and forgave him the debt. But that same slave, as he went out, came upon one of his fellow slaves who owed him a hundred denarii, and seizing him by the throat he said, 'Pay what you owe.' Then his fellow slave fell down and pleaded with him, 'Have patience with me, and I will pay you.' But he refused; then he went and threw him into prison until he would pay the debt.

When his fellow slaves saw what had happened, they were greatly distressed, and they went and reported to their lord all that had taken place. Then his lord summoned him and said to him, 'You wicked slave! I forgave you all that debt because you pleaded with me. Should you not have had mercy on your fellow slave, as I had mercy on you?' And in anger his lord handed him over to be tortured until he would pay his entire debt (Matt 18:23–34).

Whose Parable?

THIS PARABLE OCCURS ONLY in Matthew's gospel.

By a vote of sixty-five to thirty-five, biblical scholars in the Jesus Seminar classified it as an authentic Jesus parable. Two-thirds of the scholars ranked the parable as "authentic" to Jesus because it has the "marks of both oral tradition and exaggeration that are typical of Jesus' stories."[1] But these same scholars have identified elsewhere other important markers of an authentic parable, including this "rule of evidence": "Jesus' sayings and parables surprise and shock: they characteristically call for a reversal of roles or frustrate ordinary, everyday expectations."[2] In the parable of the unmerciful servant as Matthew tells it, there is no surprise or shock. We are appalled but not terribly surprised by the actions of the unmerciful servant. And what's worse, the king responds to those actions with anger and punishment, just the way we would *expect* a king to react. Where is the "surprising twist" we are accustomed to in Jesus' stories?

Another characteristic of the authentic parables identified by the Jesus Seminar is that "the parable has no conclusion. It always teases the hearer with its possible application. . . . Jesus himself never explicitly tells us how he meant them to be understood."[3] There is a very definite conclusion in this parable, but perhaps it was added by the gospel writer: a servant who gives no mercy receives no mercy, but does receive retaliation, judgment, and punishment. The king's response contradicts all Jesus' authentic teachings about the God of Love; indeed, he displays a perfectly *predictable human* response to the actions of the Unforgiving Servant. In what sounds like an early version of hell, the servant is not only thrown in prison, but sent there to be tortured until he pays back his debt!

From the beginning line about a king who wants to "settle accounts," we seem to be talking about a different king from the one who rules the Kingdom of God/Heaven, the one Jesus describes as "your Father in heaven," and encourages his listeners to emulate:

> But I say to you: Love your enemies and pray for those who persecute you, so that you may be children of your Father in heaven, for he makes his sun rise on the evil and on the good and sends rain on the righteous and on the unrighteous. For if you love those who love you, what reward do you have? . . .

---

1. Funk and Hoover, *Five Gospels*, 218.
2. Funk and Hoover, *Five Gospels*, 31.
3. Funk, et al., *Parables of Jesus*, 16–17.

Be perfect therefore, as your heavenly Father is perfect (Matt 5:43, 45–46, 48).

The word translated from the Greek as "perfect" meant, even in English when it was first used, "complete" or "comprehensive." Notice that Jesus has been talking about love just before he says, "Be perfect" as God is. How is God "perfect" or "complete"? He loves comprehensively, loving all, whether they are good or evil, righteous, or unrighteous. And the Kingdom of this God is characterized by unconditional, boundless love, mercy, and forgiveness.

Parable of Jesus?

If any part of the parable of the Unmerciful Servant is authentic to Jesus, the writer of Matthew's gospel has heavily edited it to fit his own agenda, perhaps of organizing an early Christian community and keeping its members in line. Let's consider the part of the parable that *might* fit with the other teachings of Jesus regarding Love and the Kingdom of God/Heaven.

The situation in the parable, stripped to its essential story is this: A slave could not repay ten thousand talents (an enormous debt, equivalent to millions of dollars) he owed the king, so he begged his master saying, "Have patience with me, and I will repay you everything." The king pitied him and forgave all the debt. Later, the forgiven slave encountered one who owed him 100 denarii (a small debt), and said to him, "Pay me what you owe." When his fellow slave pleaded, 'Have patience with me, and I will pay you," the forgiven slave refused and had him thrown into prison until he could pay the debt. Since the king forgave an enormous amount, listeners/readers expect the one who received such mercy to be humbled by it and extend it to his fellow slave. Instead, the debt-forgiven slave has his debtor thrown in prison for a piddling amount.

It would be more like an authentic Jesus' parable if it ended here, *with no further conclusion or explanation*, leaving the generosity and mercy of the king to stand in stark contrast to the hypocrisy and pettiness of the unmerciful slave, unwilling to extend to another the forgiveness he received.

The last few verses of the parable, however, move it squarely back into the kingdom of humans.

> When his fellow slaves saw what had happened, they were greatly distressed, and they went and reported to their lord all that had taken place. Then his lord summoned him and said to him, 'You wicked slave! I forgave you all that debt because you pleaded with me. Should you not have had mercy on your fellow slave, as I had mercy on you?' And in anger his lord handed him over to be tortured until he would pay his entire debt.

Recognizing how inconsistent those verses are with Jesus' other teachings, let's consider only the first part of the parable as possibly being authentic to Jesus, and see if we can find in it his lesson about the Kingdom of God.

Trying Love as a key to unlock its meaning, we know that first, it's not about money; the item of highest value in the Kingdom of God is Love, which is abundant, universal, and eternal. The unforgiving slave, like each of us, has been "loaned" or given all the love possible. Though he accepts God's love, he does not extend it to a fellow slave. Like the king at the beginning of the parable, God freely gives love (forgiveness, mercy) without demanding anything in return, without expecting repayment. The unmerciful slave, however, does demand repayment of love he "loaned" to a someone else; he expects to get it back. When the love is not "repaid," he demands punishment. The contrast here, the message here, is that while humans may be stingy with love and only love those who love them back, God's love is freely given to all, even without reciprocation.

The Unmerciful Servant in Real Life

Admittedly, countless individuals and groups have done great works under the auspices of Christian churches, but the Church as an institution has done at least as much harm as good in the world. In fact, the Church itself is a prime example of an "unmerciful servant." How else, for instance, would we classify the Catholic Church during the Inquisition? Its intentional annihilation of the Cathars in the eleventh through thirteenth centuries?[4] How else can we understand evangelical churches in the United States sentencing to hell any who oppose their beliefs? The "love" of such "Christian" institutions extends only to those who "repay" them with absolute obedience and acceptance of specific creeds and doctrines.

In the parables and other teachings of Jesus, we find a God of Love whose realm is characterized by unconditional love with unlimited

---

4. Crawford, "Cathars."

mercy, kindness, forgiveness. Instead of focusing on this understanding of Jesus' God, however, the Church (or what is called "Christianity") has focused on the death of Jesus, a death demanded by a judgmental Father/God who requires "payment" in blood for the errors of humankind. This God of the Church is characterized by *conditional* love and *conditional* mercy, kindness, and forgiveness, available only to those who abide by the "rules" established by a particular denomination and based on its unique interpretation of the gospels.

As a contemporary example, the Westboro Baptist Church in Topeka, Kansas, epitomizes the Unmerciful Servant in real life. Though professing to be a Christian church, its beliefs and actions are based on the jealous, vengeful God of the Old Testament rather than on the teachings of Jesus. The church is known for its hateful actions against any group that makes space for LGBTQA people. This includes picketing the funerals of slain soldiers because the U.S. military permits LGBTQA people to enlist and serve. Westboro also demonstrates against other religions, including Judaism and Islam; it condones horrific tragedies, from school shootings to tsunamis, as God's punishment for the iniquity of the world.

In Megan Phelps-Roper's memoir, *Unfollow*,[5] she recounts her life growing up as the granddaughter of Westboro Baptist Church founder and pastor, Fred Phelps, who:

> would load up his red pick-up with homemade signs, representing what he believed was the "scriptural position on homosexuality": "Militant gays spread aids," "Gays are worthy of death," and—what would become the Church's most infamous message—"God hates fags." Phelps would set off to spread what he believed was God's message, and the rest of the congregation—consisting almost entirely of Megan's aunts, uncles, cousins, siblings, and parents—would follow in a caravan of vehicles. Rain or shine, without fail, they stood on the roadside with their placards.[6]

In 2006, Westboro Baptist Church picketed a Marine's funeral in Maryland, carrying signs like "Thank God for dead soldiers" and "Semper Fi Fags." The Marine's father filed a civil lawsuit against the church for, among other things, invasion of privacy and the intention to inflict

---

5. Now a BBC Radio4 podcast/audiobook read by the author. Listen to it here: https://www.bbc.co.uk/programmes/p07wp2zt.

6. Phelps-Roper, "How I Escaped the Notorious Westboro Baptist Church."

emotional distress. Fred Phelps called a meeting of the Westboro congregation to decide what to do. Below is a passage from *Unfollow*:

> Gramps spoke matter-of-factly into the strained silence. "The Lord could just kill them, you know." And thus we began to pray for the Lord to kill the father of the Marine and his accomplices.
>
> We were the representatives of the Most-High God, and we prayed that he would show himself strong on our behalf. Our requests were made in the spirit of King David's imprecatory prayers—prayers of cursing, invocations of the wrath of God. When King David was being pursued by his enemy, he prayed that the Lord would "let his days be few and let another take his office. Let his children be fatherless and his wife, a widow."
>
> It is disconcerting, shamefully, unimaginably so, to look back and accept that my fellow church members and I were collectively engaging in the most egregious display of logical blindness that I have ever witnessed. . . . The partition between the piece of my mind that confessed love for my neighbors and the piece that asked God to dash the young men to pieces was vast, opaque, and impenetrable.[7]

For more than two millennia, such "logical blindness" has persisted in the Church as an institution and in individual denominations to greater or lesser degrees. Like the Unmerciful Servant, the Church never grasped, or forgot, or ignored, the mercy offered by the God of Love that Jesus knew. The Parable of the Unmerciful Servant shows remarkable prescience about what eventually happened to the message of unconditional love that Jesus brought to the world. And yet, in that message, we must believe that even the worst of us, even those who, like the Westboro Baptist Church, promote hatred instead of love, even these are loved and receive mercy from the God in Jesus' teachings.

---

7. Phelps-Roper, *Unfollow*, Episode 2: "Something is Wrong."

15

The Dishonest Manager

Then Jesus said to the disciples, "There was a rich man who had a manager, and charges were brought to him that this man was squandering his property. So he summoned him and said to him, 'What is this that I hear about you? Give me an accounting of your management because you cannot be my manager any longer.' Then the manager said to himself, 'What will I do, now that my master is taking the position away from me? I am not strong enough to dig, and I am ashamed to beg. I have decided what to do so that, when I am dismissed as manager, people may welcome me into their homes.' So, summoning his master's debtors one by one, he asked the first, 'How much do you owe my master?' He answered, 'A hundred jugs of olive oil.' He said to him, 'Take your bill, sit down quickly, and make it fifty.' Then he asked another, 'And how much do you owe?' He replied, 'A hundred containers of wheat.' He said to him, 'Take your bill and make it eighty.' And his master commended the dishonest manager because he had acted shrewdly,[1] for the children of this age are more shrewd in dealing with their own generation than are the children of light (Luke 16:1–8a).

JESUS SEMINAR SCHOLARS AGREE that this strange and difficult parable almost certainly originated with Jesus, and that he ended with the statement in the first half of verse 8: "And his master commended the dishonest manager because he had acted shrewdly." The rest of verse 8 and all of

---

1. "Phronimos," s.v., *Strong's and Thayer's*, Blue Letter Bible. Elsewhere in the Bible, *phronimos* is translated as "wisely, prudently." Translating it as "shrewdly" implies the steward is self-serving and perhaps not entirely honest.

verse 9 seem to be comments added by Luke (or a member of a Christian community before him) attempting to explain the shocking statement that the master "commended the dishonest manager." This ending, however, when read with the Kingdom of God in mind, is consistent with the characteristics of an authentic Jesus parable:

- They surprise and shock: cut against the social and religious grain; call for a reversal of roles or frustrate ordinary, everyday expectations.
- They are characterized by exaggeration, humor, and paradox.
- They use concrete and vivid language and images.
- They are customarily metaphorical and without explicit application or explanation.[2]

Once again, we have a parable that seems to be about money. Arland J. Hultgren offers some useful insights into the nature of the manager's responsibilities in this parable. For instance, "the manager has authority to carry out the business of the estate. He can make sales and loans, and he can collect, forgive, and pay off debts for his master. . . . In this particular case the manager deals with debtors of his master." We need not know precisely what the debts entail, Hultgren says. "What is important to observe is that the manager can deal directly with persons who are indebted to his master."[3]

The Parable of the Dishonest Manager is known by other titles, such as the Parable of the Unjust Steward, the Parable of the Penitent Steward, the Parable of the Shrewd Manager, each reflecting a different emphasis on the character of the manager. The Greek word translated as "dishonest" or "unjust" can, in one sense, connote acting wrongly, breaking a law, or perhaps, going against precedent.[4] Perhaps "Unconventional Manager" would be a better title for the parable than "Dishonest" or "Unrighteous" Manager.

This parable occurs only in Luke, which also includes another much simpler parable attributed to Jesus about someone forgiving debts that has some parallels with the Dishonest Manager. Luke inserts it into an

---

2. Funk and Hoover, *Five Gospels*, 30–32.
3. Hultgren, *Parables of Jesus*, 148–49.
4. "G93 - *adikia* - Strong's Greek Lexicon (rsv)," Blue Letter Bible.

account of the woman anointing Jesus, a story found in all three synoptic gospels.

> [Jesus said] 'A certain moneylender had two debtors; one owed five hundred denarii, and the other fifty. When they could not pay, he canceled the debts for both of them. Now which of them will love him more?" Simon answered, 'I suppose the one for whom he canceled the greater debt.' And Jesus said to him, 'You have judged rightly'" (Luke 7:41–43).

In the context of a woman washing Jesus' feet with her hair and tears and anointing them with myrrh, Luke's insertion of the moneylender parable seems contrived to make a point to Simon the Pharisee. Adding this parable to a conversation with a Pharisee gives Luke the chance to show Jesus puncturing Simon's certainty of righteousness. After he tells the moneylender parable, Jesus points to the woman and says, in Luke 7:47: "her many sins have been forgiven; hence she has shown great love. But the one to whom little is forgiven loves little." (In other words, if you are very good, you don't need much forgiving, right? So you probably won't be as grateful or loving as someone who has sinned and received forgiveness.)

The real question is, who told the moneylender parable: Jesus or Luke? The Jesus Seminar does not include it among the authentic words of Jesus, but if we consider the moneylender alongside the dishonest manager, there are interesting similarities.

In both parables, the one who cancels debts is morally questionable, a moneylender and a "dishonest" manager. The moneylender cancels the debts of two men: one who owes him a large sum and the other who owes a small sum. (This little parable must have offended those who could not accept a *moneylender* as the figure traditionally representing God.) The "dishonest manager" cancels portions of debts owed to his Master, who when he discovers it, *approves* of the manager's unconventional solution.

And Again, What If It's Not About Money, But Love?

To hear the Parable of the Dishonest Manager in a way consistent with the rest of Jesus' teachings, we must step out of the human-realm preoccupation with material wealth and step into the Kingdom of God where the only wealth/currency/value is love and the unconditional mercy and forgiveness that goes with it.

In the Kingdom of God there is no shortage of love, which exists abundantly, outside time, size, and space. God's love is eternal and infinite; it cannot be limited, divided, or hoarded (though it can be multiplied; see the Parables of the Leaven, Mustard Seed, and Talents).

In Jesus' parables, owners, rich men, kings, masters, etc., usually represent God. In this parable, the rich man would represent God, who is rich in Love, and the manager is someone entrusted with the master's wealth. This implies that the manager represents someone who "manages" love; who counsels and ministers to people, a religious leader, a priest, or a teacher—like Jesus. His job is to collect from people the love they owe God. Perhaps the "debtors" owe love to God for times when, in the human realm, they have been unloving; angry or hateful; jealous or resentful; times they have acted unwisely and missed the mark. Some of them are deeply indebted and can never repay all they owe God. Laboring under a heavy burden of guilt, they berate themselves like the tax collector, hopeless of ever being forgiven.

Perhaps we should ask *why* the manager has not been collecting his master's debts. If the "debts" are sins, errors in judgment, behavior-unbecoming-a-child-of-God, maybe this manager is soft-hearted and reluctant to make the person pay! When his master asks him to account for his inaction, the manager realizes he has been remiss in collecting love owed to God.

Then he has an epiphany: he doesn't have to collect ALL that each debtor owes. Who could possibly pay God back for all they owe him? But they may be able to pay a percentage. And in the Kingdom of God, where Love is infinite, fifty percent of infinite love is the same as one hundred percent of infinite love! His solution recirculates love and alleviates anxiety for those weighed down with what they believe is unforgiven debt.

The manager calls the debtors one by one, asking each "How much debt do you owe?" i.e., "How much do you owe the God of Love?" Whatever the person responds, the manager assures them a lesser amount is acceptable and the rest will be forgiven (i.e., wiped out and forgotten) by the master. In allowing them to have portions of their debts (sins, mistakes, etc.) forgiven, the manager assures that the debtors love the master *even more* than before.

When the master, the God of Love, hears what the manager has done, he commends him for acting wisely. Love is repaid, debts forgiven, and more love generated.

The Parable of the Unconventional Manager in Real Life

While writing this analysis of the "dishonest manager" parable, I realized it could be Jesus talking about himself, irregular prophet and unconventional teacher that he was. (*He* did not title the parable; that was done by those who interpreted it and homed in on the fact that the manager broke rules and did not do what was expected of him.) Jesus was always in trouble for what and who and how he taught about the Kingdom of God. He broke the rules; he did it wrong. He healed people on the sabbath because that's when they needed healing, and he was available. He wore simple clothes and sandals like other poor people. He spent time with Samaritans, Roman centurions, tax collectors, prostitutes, and other "sinners." He wasted his time talking with women and children. As someone entrusted with his employer's most valued asset (love), he couldn't harangue and hassle those who "owed debts" to his master; he wasn't that kind of debt collector. Complaints were made about him, and someone reported him as "wasting" the riches of his master.

We take everything in the Bible and New Testament so seriously, yet scholars assure us that Jesus had a sense of humor. Humor does not translate well from language to language, culture to culture, century to century, or religion to religion. If this *is* a parable authentic to Jesus, maybe he told it with a smile, explaining to his disciples that if he required sinlessness from people, he might lose his job opening the world to love. The verses in the parable about the manager's concern for what will happen to him if he loses his job are unusual. Unlike other parables with dire consequences, the manager shows no fear of his master having him thrown in jail or tortured; he's just worried about how people will accept him into their homes if he no longer has this job. The lines about not being "strong enough to dig" and "ashamed to beg" could be Jesus joking about himself. We just don't get the joke.

Jesus was radically unconventional in teaching his followers that they were beloved citizens in the Kingdom of a God who loved the least of them as much or more than those with wealth and power. A God who loved and forgave them no matter what they may have done. Outrageous! Jesus was *so* radical and outside our boundaries, we still can't handle his Truth.

One contemporary real-life minister with an outrageously-unconventional profile comes to mind. You may have heard of her.

> Nadia Bolz-Weber bounds into the University United Methodist Church sanctuary like a superhero from Planet Alternative

> Christian. Her 6-foot-1 frame is plastered with tattoos, her arms are sculpted by competitive weightlifting and, to show it all off, this pastor is wearing a tight tank top and jeans.
>
> . . .
>
> In her body and her theology, Bolz-Weber represents a new, muscular form of liberal Christianity, one that merges the passion and life-changing fervor of evangelicalism with the commitment to inclusiveness and social justice of mainline Protestantism. She's a tatted-up, foul-mouthed champion to people sick of being belittled as not Christian enough for the right or too Jesus-y for the left.[5]

Raised in a strict Christian fundamentalist home, Bolz-Weber left religion as a young woman. She was the prodigal daughter. She did all the things she wasn't supposed to do. She didn't make it through college; she worked in restaurants and eventually in comedy clubs. She became a stand-up comic and an alcoholic. She got sober, met her husband, was drawn back to Christianity and to the Lutheran faith. She was called to become a minister to "her people" and enrolled in seminary. While still a student there, she was led to start a church for people who were not welcome in regular churches: addicts and homeless people. LGBTQ and transgender people. People with spiky hair and tattoos.

In her book, *Pastrix: The Cranky, Beautiful Faith of a Sinner and Saint,* Nadia Bolz-Weber tells the story of how she was called to ministry. As the only religious one in her group of friends, she was asked to do the funeral service for a friend who had committed suicide. This is how she tells it:

> The memorial service took place on a crisp fall day at the Comedy Works club in downtown Denver, with a full house. The alcoholic rowing team and the Denver comics, the comedy club staff, and the academics: These were my people. Giving PJ's eulogy, I realized that perhaps I was supposed to be their pastor.
>
> It's not that I felt pious and nurturing. It's that there, in that underground room filled with the smell of stale beer and bad jokes, I looked around and saw more pain and questions and loss than anyone, including myself, knew what to do with. And I saw God. God, right there with the comics standing along the walls with crossed arms, as if their snarky remarks to each other would keep those embarrassing emotions away. God, right there with the woman climbing down the stage stairs after sharing a

---

5. Boorstein, "Bolz-Weber's Liberal, Foulmouthed Articulation."

little too much about PJ being a "hot date." God, among the cynics and alcoholics and queers.

. . . It was here in the midst of my own community of underside dwellers that I couldn't help but begin to see the Gospel, the life-changing reality that God is not far off, but here among the brokenness of our lives.[6]

Bolz-Weber, too, could be the manager in the parable, unconventional in every sense, working for God's Kingdom in unexpected ways, loving God's people who are not welcome at "respectable" churches, bringing them back to the Kingdom of God by letting them know they are worthy, loved, and already forgiven.

In 2019, Bolz-Weber delivered an unconventional benediction at the funeral of her friend, another unconventional Christian who challenged traditional evangelical views, Rachel Held Evans.[7] Below is an excerpt from that benediction.

> Blessed are the agnostics. Blessed are they who doubt. Blessed are those who have nothing to offer.
>
> Blessed are the preschoolers who cut in line at communion. Blessed are the poor in spirit. You are of heaven and Jesus blesses you.
>
> Blessed are those whom no one else notices. The kids who sit alone at middle-school lunch tables. The laundry guys at the hospital. The sex workers and the night-shift street sweepers. The closeted. The teens who have to figure out ways to hide the new cuts on their arms.
>
> Blessed are the meek. You are of heaven and Jesus blesses you.
>
> Blessed are they who have loved enough to know what loss feels like. Blessed are the mothers of the miscarried. Blessed are they who can't fall apart because they have to keep it together for everyone else.
>
> Blessed are those who "still aren't over it yet." Blessed are those who mourn. You are of heaven and Jesus blesses you.[8]

6. Bolz-Weber, *Pastrix*, 8–9.

7. Rachel Held-Evans wrote in a blog post in May 2016, "I thought I was called to challenge the atheists, but the atheists ended up challenging me. I thought God wanted to use me to show gay people how to be straight. Instead, God used gay people to show me how to be Christian." From May 2016 blog post, "Let the World Change You: A Commencement Address Do-Over."

8. Bolz-Weber, "Benediction."

BOOK III **THE CHURCH, THE QUAKERS, AND THE PARABLES**

16

George Fox and Experiential Christianity

> This I knew experimentally....
>
> —GEROGE FOX, *JOURNAL*

AS A RELIGIOUS SEEKER in seventeenth-century England, young George Fox studied scripture and sought instruction from priests, parsons, preachers, i.e., Church of England clergy, whom he naively expected to be experts in religious matters. Because of continued conflict between Protestants and Catholics, however, preparation and requirements for being a clergyman were uneven, and some of those Fox consulted were less educated and less thoughtful than he was.

Eventually Fox realized that none of the "experts" could answer his burning questions about scripture and faith. In his *Journal*, he recorded experiences that led him to understand true authority does not come from institutions like the Church, but from a higher source. For instance, he recounts one sabbath morning when he "received an opening from the Lord," the revelation "that to be bred [educated] at Oxford or Cambridge was not sufficient to fit a man to be a minister of Christ."[1] In other words, serving God requires more than human knowledge acquired from prestigious institutions. After that, he gave less credence to Church-trained clergy and was drawn to those who dissented from Church doctrine and practice. Eventually he realized that not even "those esteemed

---

1. Fox, *Journal*, 7–8.

the most experienced people" could address his "condition," his deep longing to understand scripture and know God.

> When all my hopes in them and in all men were gone, so that I had nothing outwardly to help me, nor could I tell what to do, then, oh, then, I heard a voice which said, "There is one, even Christ Jesus,[2] that can speak to thy condition"; and when I heard it, my heart did leap for joy.[3]

Rather than receiving information about the divine second-hand through the Church or religious authorities, in the voice and its instruction, Fox, in his words "knew experimentally," i.e., knew the divine through experiencing it. He was directed from a higher source to seek truth from Jesus himself rather than from human understanding.

A Third Kind of Christianity

According to Quaker historian Howard Brinton, seventeenth-century Friends felt their approach to Christianity was significantly different from Catholicism and Protestantism to constitute a third form of Christianity, an idea promoted by Barclay in his *Apology*.[4] Brinton identifies the three main types of Christianity as "Catholic, Protestant, and Quaker; the altar-centered, the sermon-centered and, at least in intention, the prophetic. That which is most prominent in Catholicism is the priestly sacramental ministry, in Protestantism the ministry which expounds God's plan of salvation as delineated in the sacred Book, and in Quakerism the prophetic ministry arising spontaneously and unpredictably under a sense of Divine urgency, while the worshiper waits silently upon God."[5]

Below, Brinton explains these three approaches to Christianity using the metaphor of different teaching and learning styles.

> As a former teacher of physics, I may be permitted to compare the three types of ministry to three ways of teaching science, the lecture demonstration method, the lecture method, and the laboratory method. The lecture demonstration method in which the lecture is illustrated by experiments [conducted by the teacher] corresponds to those rituals in which the

2. ". . . even Christ Jesus," that is, Jesus Christ himself.
3. Fox, *Journal*, 11.
4. Brinton, Introduction, *Friends for 350 Years*, xvii.
5. Brinton, *Prophetic Ministry*, Pendle Hill pamphlet.

> congregation observes, hears and spiritually participates in acts performed by the priest; the lecture method can be compared to the preaching of the pastor expounding the Word of God revealed in Scripture; and, finally, the laboratory method is not unlike the Quaker meeting in which direct experience is sought and where words are used from time to time as they arise from, or lead to, direct experience. In scientific instruction the three methods are used at different times and usually in different places. The same holds true in religion.[6]

Those in education know too that different students have different learning styles; what works for one student doesn't work for another. Not every teaching style can reach every student. "The same holds true for religion."

Fox on the Church and Scripture

The active presence of God within each of us, a concept taught by Jesus and embraced by George Fox, is remarkably difficult for people to accept. From the beginning, what became Christianity could not grasp it and so ignored it, or reinterpreted it, often completely changing what Jesus said. Fox, who understood scripture at a spiritual level, was a fiery evangelist for the faith he learned from "Jesus, the opener of the door, with his heavenly key," who was understood among early Friends to be the Inner Christ/Inner Teacher. Fox was also a convincing critic of the Church and those who claimed to be Christian, but who did not "possess what they professed." Full of conviction that the Church had long ago fallen away from the truth and become corrupt, Fox was able to communicate the difficult concept of the Inner Christ/Inner Teacher/God Within clearly enough that thousands of people followed his teachings and became Quakers.[7]

Below is an example of his style, in 1654, rather shockingly accusing the Church of creating the scriptures in *its own image*.

> Now all you Priests and People that talk of these things without[8] you, from the Letter, this is a Parable to you, and you read the outside in the Letter: and from that you Imagine, and so set up a Form, or Likeness, or Image of these things; and here

---

6. Brinton, *Prophetic Ministry*.

7. In 1660, the population of Great Britain was about 5.27 million. Estimates of the Quaker population range from thirty-five to fifty thousand.

8. "Without you," i.e., external reality, outside yourself, as opposed to "within you."

> you Worship, and for this you contend, and would compel all to Worship your Image you have set up, and you go about to persecute and destroy all that will not bow to it with you: But it is but the Form you have, and not the Substance; And you put the Dead Letter for the Living Word, and your own meanings of it, arising from the brain, and first Wisdom, and natural Learning...[9]

Paraphrased into modern English:

> Now all you Priests and People who talk of things outside you, external reality, this is what you think a parable is when you read the Scriptures: you read in the words there what you know of things outside yourselves, the external, the material world. And from that reality you create models or images, and this is what you worship. These models you created are what you argue for. And what you compel all to worship: your own image that you have created. And you persecute and destroy all that will not bow to it with you. But what you have is only something that looks like the scriptures, and not the real meaning or higher truth in them. Using your own meanings that come from your brain, your instinct, and what you've learned about the world, you substitute material reality for spiritual truth...

Fox on the Blood of Christ

One of the most moving instances of Fox bringing the idea of the Inner Teacher/Inner Christ to professing Christians occurred in 1648 in Mansfield, "where there was a great meeting of professors and people."[10] They were talking about the blood of Christ, which in Christian tradition, represents the saving sacrifice demanded by God through the crucifixion. Fox experienced an on-the-spot epiphany of the true nature and meaning of "the blood of Christ." He described it this way:

> ...I saw, through the immediate opening of the invisible Spirit, the blood of Christ. And I cried out among them, and said, "Do ye not see the blood of Christ? See it in your hearts, to sprinkle your hearts and consciences [away] from dead works, to serve the living God"; for I saw it, the blood of the New Covenant, how it came into the heart.

---

9. Fox, *Word From the Lord*...
10. Fox, *Journal*, 90.

> This startled the professors, who would have the blood only without them and not in them.[11]

Loosely paraphrased, this is what happened. Fox suddenly saw the blood of Christ *within* each of the people in the group, "how it came into the heart." He tried to get them to see it too: Christ's lifeblood *sprinkled* in their hearts and consciences to lead them away from practices and beliefs that no longer had life in them, could lead them instead to serve the God of life, here and now. The New Covenant Jesus brought was to be written on their hearts. The professing Christians listening to him were shocked, for they could only think about Christ's blood in the context of an external event (the crucifixion) and could not imagine it living inside them.

If we don't know as much about the Bible as Fox did, we may not notice the connections he made. Several words and phrases he used to describe his "opening" about the blood of Christ show how his deep knowledge of scripture informed his vision. He read so much of it and absorbed so much of it that his own speech was peppered with words and phrases from the Bible translations he had access to, i.e., the King James Version (1611) and perhaps the Geneva Bible (1599). In the blood-of-Christ incident, we can trace in his word choice how the disturbing vision of Christ's-blood-within-us came together for him. (In the following sentences, all italics are mine, added for emphasis.)

First, Fox was listening to the discourse about "*the blood of Christ,*" a phrase associated with well-known verses in the synoptic gospels used by the Church for the communion ritual[12] which appears in the King James Version:

> And as they did eat, Jesus took bread, and blessed, and brake it, and gave to them, and said, Take, eat: this is my body. And he took the cup, and when he had given thanks, he gave it to them: and they all drank of it. And he said unto them, *This is my blood of the new testament*, which is shed for many (Mark 14:22–24 KJV).

Second, in the Old Testament book of Jeremiah, God announces through the prophet that he is going to make a *new covenant* with the Israelites which will be unlike the old covenant he made with them when Moses led them out of Egypt.

---

11. Fox, *Journal*, 90–91.

12. The idea of communion is pretty disturbing, i.e., eating Jesus' body and drinking his blood, even symbolically. The practice was responsible for rumors spread about early Christians that they practiced forms of cannibalism.

> The days are surely coming, says the Lord, when I will make a *new covenant* with the house of Israel and the house of Judah. . . . this is the covenant that I will make with the house of Israel after those days, says the Lord: *I will put my law within them*, and I will *write it on their hearts*, and I will be their God, and they shall be my people. No longer shall they teach one another or say to each other, "Know the Lord," for *they shall all know me, from the least of them to the greatest*, says the Lord, for I will forgive their iniquity and remember their sin no more (Jer 31:31–34, KJV).

In the King James Version of the Bible, "new covenant" occurs only in Jer 31:31 and in three verses from Hebrews, twice when Paul quotes from Jeremiah, and in the following verse when he connects "new covenant" with Jesus and blood: "And to Jesus the *mediator of the new covenant*, and to *the blood of sprinkling*, that speaketh better things than that of Abel" (Heb 12:24, KJV).

Note the words and phrases Fox used in his blood-of-Christ epiphany:

> I saw, through the immediate opening of the invisible Spirit, the *blood of Christ*. And I cried out among them, and said, "Do ye not see the *blood of Christ? See it in your hearts, to sprinkle your hearts* [away] from dead works, to serve the living God"; for I saw it, *the blood of the New Covenant, how it came into the heart*.

Fox made a connection between God's law and the "new covenant" written "on their hearts" in Jeremiah, the "new testament in my blood" in the communion passage, and the "blood of sprinkling" and "Jesus the mediator of the new covenant" in Hebrews.[13] Fox's knowledge of scripture informed his epiphany with its strange image that still shocks and disturbs us. Though his vision of Christ's blood *within* people is disturbing, it is strangely more affecting than thinking of his blood in a communion cup.

---

13. In the Jeremiah passage, God uses phrases like "I will put my law *within* them," "they shall all know me, from the least of them to the greatest" which reflect early Friends' understanding of our relationship with God.

17

Jesus Un-Churched

> The Church may distort Jesus into a white middle-class pillar of American respectability; it may pervert his image into that of a religious Babbitt pushing the cult of successfulness; it may distort and pervert his image, but the Church cannot forget Jesus. And in spite of its best efforts to domesticate that Jesus, the Church knows and frequently fears that his message will be rediscovered.
>
> —William Sloan Coffin, *Credo*

Locked in the Church

IN THE DAYS WHEN a Jew named Jesus gathered followers around his message of love and compassion, Christianity didn't yet exist, and Jesus was not a Christian. Christianity is a religion built on his death and resurrection, while his teachings are buried under centuries of rewritten, edited, and controlled theology.

The Church tells the story this way. On a day observed in the Church calendar as Palm Sunday, Jesus rode the colt of a donkey into Jerusalem, a symbolic act that reenacted a Jewish prophecy of the arrival of the Messiah, the anticipated savior of Israel. That day, with his followers spreading palms in the road before him as he entered a city, the crowd treated Jesus as they treated conquering generals. Within five days Jesus was arrested, tried as a traitor to Rome, and crucified. A day or so after that, according to the Church, he left his tomb and ascended into Heaven to sit on a throne at the right hand of God. At some future time, he will return "to judge the quick (i.e., living) and the dead," taking some to heaven and casting others into eternal hellfire.

Jesus' crucifixion had the opposite effect from what those in power wanted, which was to get rid of this troublesome Jew and his followers. The Christian Church began with that gruesome death and has lasted over two thousand years. Jesus' execution, observed each year on the day we call "Good" Friday, is central to its beliefs. In fact, the entire church calendar depends on when Easter falls and the whole liturgical year of worship is arranged around the compelling mixture of beauty and terror that is Holy Week: the hope of Palm Sunday, the irony and tragedy of "Good" Friday, the sorrow of Holy Saturday, and the strange, doubting wonder of Easter Sunday.

With its focus on the drama and tragedy of Jesus' death, what became the Church unwittingly provided a container for his *authentic* teachings which, though hidden or distorted, have survived in fragments in the New Testament. The blood-soaked story the Church tells about Jesus has held the interest of multitudes through centuries, and along the way, individuals have perceived his true teachings in the fragments that remain. As challenging as Jesus' simple message is, it might not have survived without the elaborate, violent packaging the Church provided.

While the Church and the New Testament—as written by those associated with the Church—may have helped preserve his teachings, Christianity the way it is widely practiced today has little or nothing to do with the authentic teachings of Jesus. The Church doesn't need Jesus; it has Christ, a superhero character created so people can believe they will escape hell because Christ suffered a horrible death and thereby "saved" them. Even worse, a growing number of "Christians" don't even *want* Jesus—they find him too "soft." They don't like all this love-stuff in the New Testament. In a 2023 National Public Radio interview with Russell Moore, a former leader in the Southern Baptist Convention, Moore spoke about why he believes Christianity is in crisis. It was, he said:

> the result of having multiple pastors tell me, essentially, the same story about quoting the Sermon on the Mount, parenthetically, in their preaching—"turn the other cheek"—[and] to have someone come up after to say, "Where did you get those liberal talking points?" And what was alarming to me is that in most of

these scenarios, when the pastor would say, "I'm literally quoting Jesus Christ," the response would not be, "I apologize." The response would be, "Yes, but that doesn't work anymore. That's weak." And when we get to the point where the teachings of Jesus himself are seen as subversive to us, then we're in a crisis.[1]

Christianity is also in crisis because an increasing number of people, especially the young, do not trust the Christian Church, especially denominations that cater to those who consider the teachings of Jesus too weak. The quotation below might explain why:

> [In 2011] Dieter Zander, the pastor of the first GenX church in America, spoke at an Evangelism Conference about reaching people in the age of relativism. He cited a Barna study that asked people to use single words to describe Jesus. They responded, "wise, accepting, compassionate, gracious, humble." Then he asked them to use single words to describe Christians, they said, "critical, exclusive, self-righteous, narrow and repressive."[2]

Organized vs. Disorganized Religion

Organized religion is ordered, controlled, manipulated, dictated, and mandated by humans. A spiritual experience is beyond the control of humans. Religion is built on man-made rules; faith emerges from encounters with the Divine. Jesus challenges organized religions in the most radical way possible: the one God he speaks of is *within all* and *available to all*. No need for all those rules and commandments; no need for priests and synagogues. Within decades of his death, however, an organized religion with limited understanding of what he said had formed around Jesus and his teachings.

Christian history is full of others who challenged organized religion, whatever it happened to look like in their time. For Jesus, it was "organized" Judaism; for Paul, myriad versions of early Christian communities; for the Cathars among others in the Middle Ages, and later, for Luther, the organized Catholic Church; for early Friends, it was the organized Anglican church and the organized Puritan challenge to it. It seems that no sooner does an individual or group challenge an organized religion than they begin organizing their own version of it.

1. Moore, "Christianity Is in Crisis."
2. Dalrymple, "Everything Counts All the Time."

This is not a newly recognized truth. In 1866, an influential "Particular Baptist" preacher named Charles Haddon Spurgeon, famous in his time for the power of his preaching and still a source for Christian devotionals, was asked to give a talk on the topic of George Fox to a large gathering of Friends. He began by saying that no matter what he did, it would probably be a sermon rather than a lecture.

> *"George Fox": An Address Delivered by Charles Haddon Spurgeon to the Society of Friends in the Devonshire House Meeting House, Bishopsgate Street, London, on Tuesday Evening, November 6th, 1866*[3]
>
> George Fox, it seems to me, was a blessing, not to you alone, but to the whole of Christendom. He was sent of God, not only with a view to this Society in after years, but to the Christian church at large of that time, and to the church of God in all times.
>
> I do believe that under God, directly or indirectly, perhaps more indirectly than directly, George Fox was the means of driving out from their nests those who were very willing to have feathered those nests well, and to have taken their rest. He stood up in the face of the Christian Church, and said to it, "No, thou shalt not do this! Thou shalt not conform thyself to the world; thou shalt not go into an unholy alliance with the State; there shall still be in the midst of thee a spiritual people who shall bear their protest that Christ's kingdom is not of this world, and that religion standeth not in forms and ceremonies, but is a matter connected with the inner man, and is the work of God's Spirit in the heart."
>
> You will judge, therefore, what my idea of Fox is when I have said that I look upon him as having been sent from our heavenly Father upon the important mission of saving the Christian church, at a particular juncture, when, through having obtained the possession of State power, and being much exercised with the brawls of rival creeds and contentions upon outward ceremonies, the inward power was declining, and the church was likely to become absorbed into the world, or to set up a dead formalism which is neither acceptable to God nor serviceable to man.[4]

---

3. Like many of Spurgeon's sermons, this "lecture" is still in print and available through Google Classic Books.

4. Spurgeon, "George Fox: An Address."

In the beginning of this book, I spoke of the influences on my writing it. One of the strongest was the conviction that Jesus spoke in a consistent voice, not contradicting himself even while upsetting human expectations. Anything inconsistent with Jesus' message about love and the Kingdom of God is not the voice of Jesus, but the voice of humanity. For centuries we have interpreted and re-interpreted what remains of Jesus' words until his teaching is obscured like a Rembrandt hidden under layers of paint applied by later less-gifted artists. It was affirming when I read the works of early Friends and understood they sought the same consistency, and like me, they did not find it in the Church, but found recognizable traces of it in scripture.

Early Friends often alluded to Paul's distinction between the letter of the law and the spirit of the law in 2 Cor 3:5-7:

> Not that we are qualified of ourselves to claim anything as coming from us; our qualification is from God, who has made us qualified to be ministers of a new covenant, not of letter but of spirit, for the letter kills, but the Spirit gives life.

For instance, below is a quotation from early Friend, John Naylor in 1653:

> And see yourselves the prodigal: when he saw himself what he had done, went home unto his father's house; and thou hast read of a prodigal in the scripture that fed among swine, but dost thou see thyself to be the prodigal feeding among the swine, feeding on husks? Is this opened to thee? Dost thou know what this husk is? . . . When thou art come to thy father's house thou wilt see that thou hast been feeding among the swine on the letter, the outside which profits not.[5]

Naylor says the Church essentially feeds its followers pig swill, i.e., the literal meaning ("the letter") of words in scripture. Such literal interpretations are empty shells, only husks, of the spiritual truth Jesus taught in metaphor and simile. If we return to the source (the "father's house," God, the Holy Spirit), we feed on substantial, nourishing, spiritual truth that exists within each of us.

Early Friends found a different message in the New Testament, and they questioned the validity of the Church's interpretation of all that happened to and through Jesus. Stories of his birth and death, narrated third hand, did not include the Spirit of Truth that his own words did when you could sift through and find them.

---

5. John Nayler, QBI, "Luke 15:16-20."

Setting Jesus Free

Early Friends believed that we didn't have to wait for a "second coming" to be with Jesus, that Jesus had already come back, in the Spirit, and all that he taught lives within each of us. Friends found this idea in John 15 and 16, where Jesus talks to his disciples the week or so before he will be arrested, preparing them for what lies ahead. While the Gospel of John differs substantially from the synoptic gospels and, according to biblical scholars, includes no recognizably authentic words of Jesus, it does seem to grasp the essence of those teachings. For instance, John is the gospel that says straight out, "God is Love," which is entirely consistent with what Jesus taught.

Below are some lines from the 1611 King James Version of the Bible, which early Friends would have read, and where they would find the Comforter, the Inner Christ, the Inner Teacher/the Spirit of Truth that Jesus said he would send to be with them, and within them, always.

> But the Comforter, which is the Holy Ghost, whom the Father will send in my name, he shall teach you all things, and bring all things to your remembrance, whatsoever I have said unto you (John 14:26).[6]

> ... when he, the Spirit of truth, is come, he will guide you into all truth: for he shall not speak of himself; but whatsoever he shall hear, that shall he speak: and he will shew you things to come. All things that the Father hath are mine: therefore said I, that he shall take of mine, and shall shew it unto you (John 16:13–15).

The Spirit of Truth "will take what is mine and declare it to you," Jesus says in the Gospel of John, a favorite of early Friends. The source of my teachings, Jesus says, is from the God of the Kingdom, which the Spirit of Truth will affirm to you. ("All that the Father has is mine" echoes what the father says in the Prodigal Son parable: 'Son, you are always with me, and all that is mine is yours.")

As George Fox said, "Christ has come to teach his people himself." Rather than focusing on his bodily death or resurrection, early Quakers embraced Jesus' promise as reported in the poetic words of John's gospel, to send a "Comforter" or "Spirit of Truth" so that the truth of his teachings will be with us and within us, always.

---

6. *Paraklētos*, the Greek word translated here as "Comforter" and "Spirit of Truth," can also be translated as Paraclete, advocate, helper, or counselor. "G3875—*paraklētos* – Strong's Greek Lexicon (kjv)," Blue Letter Bible.

It is time to let Jesus out of the Church that doesn't know him, understand him, or want him. Let him speak to people who don't want the Church the way it is or believe what it teaches. It is time to retrieve and revive the *pre-Christianity* message in his teachings. We may yet find—in his simple words—his Truth about abundant, eternal, unconditional Love, about God within each of us, and about living here and now in the Kingdom of God which we must *co-create* with the Creator.

18

Opening Parables: Discussion, Advices & Queries

An Inauthentic Parable

BELOW IS A PARABLE considered to be *inauthentic* to Jesus; in other words, it was told by someone else in an early Christian community. As you read it, note the essential "plot," i.e., what happens? Is there cruelty and violence in the story? Is anyone punished? Is there an unexpected twist in the story? Is anyone unexpectedly kind? Or cruel? Be watchful for the explanatory voice of the gospel writer or later editor. What elements suggest it is a parable told by early Christians, and not by Jesus?

> Someone planted a vineyard, leased it out to some farmers, and went abroad for an extended time. In due course he sent a slave to the farmers, so they could pay him his share of the vineyard's crop. But the farmers beat him and sent him away. He repeated his action by sending another slave; but they beat him up too, and humiliated him, and sent him away empty-handed. And he sent yet a third slave; but they injured him and threw him out.
>
> Then the owner of the vineyard asked himself, "What should I do now? I know, I will send my son, the apple of my eye. Perhaps they will show him some respect."
>
> But when the farmers recognized him, they talked it over and concluded: This fellow's the heir! Let's kill him so the inheritance will be ours! So they dragged him outside the vineyard and killed him.

What will the owner of the vineyard do to them as a consequence? He will come in person, do away with those farmers, and give the vineyard to someone else (Luke 20:9–15a).

(Read also in Mark 12:1–8, Matt 21:33–39; Th 65:1–7.)

Two Authentic Jesus Parables

Below are two parables believed to be authentic to Jesus.

> Luke 18:2–5: The Corrupt Judge
>
> "In a certain city there was a judge who neither feared God nor had respect for people. In that city there was a widow who kept coming to him and saying, 'Grant me justice against my accuser.' For a while he refused, but later he said to himself, 'Though I have no fear of God and no respect for anyone, yet because this widow keeps bothering me, I will grant her justice, so that she may not wear me out by continually coming.'"
>
> Mark 4:26–29: The Parable of the Growing Seed
>
> He also said, "The kingdom of God is as if someone would scatter seed on the ground and would sleep and rise night and day, and the seed would sprout and grow, he does not know how. The earth produces of itself first the stalk, then the head, then the full grain in the head. But when the grain is ripe, at once he goes in with his sickle because the harvest has come."

Does it seem to you the message in each parable is consistent with Jesus' teachings about love and the Kingdom of God? Discuss why or why not.

Try interpreting and rephrasing each parable with love as the central idea and message. Does it work?

Questions to consider when interpreting a parable attributed to Jesus:

1. What is the item of value in the material world, the earthly reality of the parable? What is it in the Kingdom of God?
2. How do characters in the parable respond to that item of value?
3. Is there a character who acts out of love or kindness?
4. If so, what is that character's attitude toward the item of value?
5. Are there characters who act from fear, jealousy, anger, greed, etc.?

6. If so, what is their attitude toward the item of value?

7. What is their attitude toward the character acting from love or kindness?

8. Is there a surprising twist in the parable, an unexpected thing that happens?

9. Does the parable have introductory details that may have been added by the gospel writer?

10. Does the parable have a conclusion that tells us what happened to the characters? (If so, it was probably added by the gospel writer.) Watch for the place where Jesus would stop, in the middle of the surprising twist so people must "tease out the meaning."

Keys to Meaning in Jesus' Parables

HUMAN REALM	ASPECT	KINGDOM OF GOD
Earth	REALM	Love
Linear/Hierarchy (Top Down)	STRUCTURE	Circular/Equality ("First shall be last / last shall be first")
King/Emperor	RULER	God (a.k.a Love)
Servants/Slaves/ Employees/Workers	CITIZENS	Beloveds of God ("beloved children")
Material/Physical The Body	QUALITY	Spiritual The Soul and Spirit
Many; Restrictive Judgment & Punishment	LAWS	One; Expansive Unconditional Forgiveness

HUMAN REALM	ASPECT	KINGDOM OF GOD
Fear Stern Father Stern King/Boss/ Owner Hireling Shepherd Stranger, Enemy	GOVERNED VIA	Love Loving Father Generous King/Boss Good Shepherd Neighbor, Brother/Sister
Power & Wealth Social Status Certainty	HIGHEST VALUES	Love Humility Faith
Coins, Gold, Silver, Property, Goods, etc.	CURRENCY	Compassion/Kindness
Scarcity Exclusion Stinginess Discord Violence Competition Selfishness "Me First" Strangers/Enemies	PREVAILING CONDITIONS	Abundance Inclusion Generosity Harmony Gentleness Cooperation Sharing All Are One Friends/Brothers/Sisters

Discussion Questions

1. Discuss the idea that we can find some words/teachings that are authentic to Jesus, meaning either he said this or something very like it. Does it seem possible or improbable? What difference would it make, if any?

2. Biblical scholars from an array of denominations identify certain passages in the parables as "authentic to Jesus" and other parts of the parables as additions or modifications by later writers. Why does it

matter whether the words are those of Jesus or those an early Christian gospel writer? If it doesn't matter, why not?

3. How do you react to the ambiguity in Jesus' parables? Explain why you believe his ambiguity was intentional or not intentional. How does the ambiguity affect your reading of the New Testament?

4. What do you think about the idea that Jesus was a "one-sermon preacher," i.e., that he had only one message which he expressed in different contexts?

5. If we interpret all Jesus' teachings as variations on the theme of love/compassion, does this affect your understanding of his life and purpose?

For Further Study

Below are the twelve Phoenix Affirmations. Discuss them in terms of Jesus' authentic teachings in the parables.

Christian Love of God includes:

1. Walking fully in the path of Jesus, without denying the legitimacy of other paths that God may provide humanity;

2. Listening for God's Word which comes through daily prayer and meditation, studying the ancient testimonies which we call scripture, and attending to God's present activity in the world;

3. Celebrating the God whose Spirit pervades and whose glory is reflected in all of God's Creation, including the earth and its ecosystems, the sacred and secular, the Christian and non-Christian, the human and non-human;

4. Expressing our love in worship that is as sincere, vibrant, and artful as it is scriptural.

Christian Love of Neighbors includes:

5. Engaging people authentically, as Jesus did, treating all as creations made in God's very image, regardless of race, gender, sexual orientation, age, physical or mental ability, nationality, or economic class;

6. Standing, as Jesus does, with the outcast and oppressed, the denigrated and afflicted, seeking peace and justice with or without the support of others;

7. Preserving religious freedom and the Church's ability to speak prophetically to government by resisting the commingling of Church and State;

8. Walking humbly with God, acknowledging our own shortcomings while honestly seeking to understand and call forth the best in others, including those who consider us their enemies;

Christian Love of Self includes:

9. Basing our lives on the faith that, in Christ, all things are made new, and that we, and all people, are loved beyond our wildest imagination—for eternity;

10. Claiming the sacredness of both our minds and our hearts, recognizing that faith and science, doubt and belief serve the pursuit of truth;

11. Caring for our bodies, and insisting on taking time to enjoy the benefits of prayer, reflection, worship and recreation in addition to work;

12. Acting on the faith that we are born with a meaning and purpose; a vocation and ministry that serves to strengthen and extend God's realm of love.[1]

---

1. "Phoenix Affirmations Summary Version 3.8."

Advices & Queries

Advices for Contemplation: The Kingdom of God
and How It Grows

> *Mark 4:26-27*
>
> He also said, "The kingdom of God is as if someone would scatter seed on the ground and would sleep and rise night and day, and the seed would sprout and grow, he does not know how."
>
> *Matt 13:31-33*
>
> He put before them another parable: "The kingdom of heaven is like a mustard seed that someone took and sowed in his field; it is the smallest of all the seeds, but when it has grown it is the greatest of shrubs and becomes a tree, so that the birds of the air come and make nests in its branches." He told them another parable: "The kingdom of heaven is like yeast that a woman took and mixed in with three measures of flour until all of it was leavened."
>
> *"Empowerment Grows Wild"*
>
> The Aramaic word for "parable" is derived from the word meaning to stretch out or extend a cover over something. The telling of a parable covers a process of transformation that can go on underneath its telling. . . .
>
> The parables of the mustard seed and the yeast both present us with a process that, once begun, works on its own as though in secret. . . .
>
> The Aramaic word for "mustard seed" . . . derives from a root that describes something spreading freely, like a wildfire. . . .
>
> The Aramaic word for "yeast" or "leaven" suggests from its roots something within a body that is hot and glowing and spreads its heat outwards.[2]
>
> *Robert Barclay, 1678*
>
> Though then this Seed be small in its appearance, so that Christ compares it to "a grain of mustard seed, which is the least of all seeds," and that it be hid in the earthly part of man's heart; yet therein is life and salvation towards the sons of men wrapped up, which comes to be revealed as they give way to it. And in

---

2. Douglas-Klotz, *Hidden Gospel*, 93–94.

this Seed in the hearts of all men is the Kingdom of God, as in capacity to be produced, or rather exhibited, according as it receives depth, and is nourished, and not choked.[3]

Queries: How the Kingdom Grows

Is it significant that the Kingdom of God is "hidden" or secret? Why or why not?

The Aramaic language of Jesus has connotations about mustard seeds and leaven that don't exist in modern English. What are some connotations that stand out to you? How does knowing these connotations affect your feelings about the Kingdom of God/Heaven within?

Have you ever had the sense of something working, in Douglas-Klotz's words, "on its own as though in secret" to transform you from within?

How do you respond to Barclay's statement that "the Seed in the hearts of all [humans] is the Kingdom of God"?

How do you respond to the idea that "therein is life and salvation [for humankind] . . . which comes to be revealed as they give way to it"?

Do you believe the hidden Seed, i.e., "that of God," is love/compassion? Could the Seed be consciousness? Or the life force itself? All of these? None of these?

Advices for Contemplation: Self-Emptying

> *Phil 2:3–8*
>
> Do nothing from selfish ambition or empty conceit, but in humility regard others as better than yourselves. Let each of you look not to your own interests but to the interests of others. Let the same mind be in you that was in Christ Jesus, who, though he existed in the form of God, did not regard equality with God as something to be grasped, but emptied himself, taking the form of a slave, assuming human likeness. And being found in

---

3. Barclay, QBI, "Matthew 13:33."

appearance as a human, he humbled himself and became obedient to the point of death—even death on a cross.

"Kenosis"

"In Christian theology, *Kenosis* is the concept of the 'self-emptying' of one's own will to become entirely receptive to God's perfect will."[4]

A Cup of Tea (Zen Parable)

Nan-in, a Japanese master during the Meiji era (1868–1912), received a university professor who came to inquire about Zen.

Nan-in served tea. He poured his visitor's cup full, and then kept on pouring.

The professor watched the overflow until he no longer could restrain himself. "It is overfull. No more will go in!"

"Like this cup," Nan-in said, "you are full of your own opinions and speculations. How can I show you Zen unless you first empty your cup?"

Queries: Self-Emptying

Do any of these advices "strike home" for you? If so, which ones and why?

Do you resist the idea of "emptying yourself"? What would happen if you did?

Have you had an experience in which you were receptive to "God's perfect will"?

Isaac Penington on the Parable of the Pearl

> Isaac Penington (1661)
>
> The pearl is exceeding rich, the treasure of life unutterable; and he that will possess it, must sell all for it; yea, all the riches of his nature (the best of his will, the best of his wisdom most refined); nay not only so, but all the riches of his spirit, all that he hath held, or can hold out of the life. Then, when he is poor in spirit,

---

4. *"Kenosis," New World Encyclopedia.*

and hath nothing in him but emptiness, . . . then alone is he fit to be comprehended and brought forth in the eternal spring.⁵

What, in your understanding, is this "exceeding rich" pearl in the passage above, and is it worth the price Penington describes?

Penington lists non-material elements of life as what must be "sold" or given up to purchase the "exceeding rich" pearl. How do you feel about being asked to give up "the best of [your] will, the best of [your] wisdom most refined and all the riches of [your] spirit"? Would this also involve giving up material wealth and possessions? Why or why not?

How do you respond to the possibility suggested in Penington's language that "poor in spirit" means "being humble" or "humbled"?

Have you experienced having "nothing in [you] but emptiness"? Would you use the phrase "in despair"? How is being humbled related to despair? How is it different? If you have had such an experience, how did it affect your spiritual life?

Robert Barclay on the Parable of the Talents

Robert Barclay (1678)

> . . . he that had two talents was accepted as well as he that had five because he used them to his master's profit. And he that had one might have done so: his talent was of the same nature with the rest, it was as capable to have proportionably brought forth its interest as the rest. And so though there be not a like proportion of grace given to all . . . yet there is given to all that which is sufficient, and no more is required than according to that which is given: "For unto whomsoever much is given, from him shall much be required. . . ".⁶

Barclay interprets the Parable of the Talents in terms of the distribution of grace. What does he mean by "grace" here?

---

5. Penington, QBI, "Matthew 13:33."
6. Barclay, QBI, "Matthew 25:14–30."

How do you understand Barclay's statement: "though there be not a like proportion of grace given to all . . . yet there is given to all that which is sufficient, and no more is required than according to that which is given"?

Have you ever felt obliged or called to "invest" your "portion of grace"? Explain.

APPENDIX

Traditional Interpretations Vs. Quaker Applications

Meditations for Every Day in The Year

AT THE TIME IT was published in Latin (the language of the Church) in 1639, *Meditations for Every Day in The Year: Collected from Different Spiritual Writers* was attributed to "N.B." who compiled "*Meditations*" from other writers not identified individually. "N.B." was later identified as Nathanial Bacon, Jesuit priest and bibliographer (1598–1676) who also used the pseudonym "Southwell." According to the *Catholic Answers* website, he was "the author of *A Journal of Meditations for Every Day in The Year*," and "On the same authority we learn that he was accounted by his religious brethren a model of virtue and sanctity."[1]

While George Fox and Early Friends were challenging the Church's understanding and use of scripture, *Meditations* was being widely shared in Latin among England's Catholic/Anglican community; it was published in English in 1669 and has remained in constant use and publication ever since.

In 1823, after being edited, revised, and updated by Rev. Roger Baxter, Jesuit missionary and prefect of studies at Georgetown College, *Meditations* was published in the United States. In 1884 it was republished by Father Pye Neale, who received a note (included in the 1884 edition) from Archbishop of Baltimore James Gibbons to the effect that "This precious

---

1. Spillane, "Nathanial Bacon."

book was . . . used by Challoner, Walmsly, and other Confessors of the Faith in times of persecution."[2] Now in the public domain, *Meditations* is available at theological institution libraries; freely accessible online at sites such as Open Library, World Cat, or Internet Archive (used by this writer); and it can be purchased from Walmart and Amazon.

Because it has been valued and consulted for centuries and is still used by Catholic and Protestant Christians alike, samples from *Meditations* will, for our purposes, represent traditional Christian interpretation of Jesus' teachings.[3]

Traditional Interpretation of Hidden Treasure & Pearl

From "*Meditations for Every Day in The Year*/Historical Narratives."

The Treasure Hidden in a Field.

I. "The kingdom of heaven is like to a treasure hidden in a field." (Matt. xiii. 44.) This treasure, says St. Gregory, is the desire of heaven, or the love of virtue and heavenly things, and it is said to be hidden in the field of this world, because all do not know its value. "Thou hast hid these things from the wise and prudent, and hast revealed them to the little ones." (Matt, xi. 25.) Hence most men abhor poverty and humility and consider them as curses. Entreat our Lord to open your eyes, that you may be able to discover this treasure.

II. Consider how this treasure is to be kept, "which when a man hath found, he hideth." We must conceal this treasure in our hearts, and cover it with the veil of humility, lest the praises of men or vain glory deprive us of it. Examine whether this be your conduct, or whether you do not rather on all occasions boast of the merits which you think you possess. Our road to heaven is infested with many thieves, "and he wishes to be robbed," observes St. Gregory, "who carries his treasure in open view on the road." Hide it, therefore, as much as you can, in order that you may preserve it.

III. This treasure can only be purchased by the sale not of one or more things, but of all that we have. "He goeth and selleth

---

2. Nathaniel Bacon, et al., *Meditations for every day in the year*.

3. Original spelling has been converted to American English except in passages quoted from the Bible or other source that include obsolete verb forms ("hast," " hideth," etc). Original punctuation and sentence structure in *Meditations* have not been changed, hence the plethora of commas.

all that he hath, and buyeth that field." Christ in another place pronounces, "Every one of you that doth not renounce all that he possesseth, cannot be My disciple." (Luke xiv. 33.) We must, therefore, leave all things in this world, at least in affection, to attain the perfect enjoyment of Christ, and we must consider that we have made a good exchange, for we gain a hundred-fold, a hundred times over what we have left.[4]

In paragraph II above, "We must conceal this treasure in our hearts" seems particularly wrong-headed and goes directly against other teachings of Jesus such as don't hide your light under a basket but let everyone see it (Matt 5:15; Luke 11:33). Quakers would be more inclined to say we must *search for, find and share* the treasure, which is the Kingdom of God within us.

The Pearl.

I. "The kingdom of heaven is like to a merchant seeking good pearls." (Matt. xiii. 45.) We are all merchants so long as we live in this world; hence, Christ in the parable of the talents said, "Trade till I come." (Luke xix. 13.) All men are in quest of pearls; that is, of the means of happiness; some place their happiness in temporal enjoyments, others in learning and science, and others in honors. They are, however, all mistaken; all these are false pearls; they have nothing to recommend them but their outward show. Hence the Apostle addresses the rich: "Your riches are putrefied, your gold and silver are rusted." (James v. 2.) Examine whether you be not employed in seeking such kind of pearls.

II. "When he had found one pearl of great value, he sold all that he had, and bought it." There is only one true and really valuable pearl, that is, Christ our Lord and the love of eternal things. "All gold in comparison to her is as a little sand, and silver in respect to her shall be counted as clay." (Wisdom, vii. 9.) There is no comparison between time and eternity, heaven and earth, nor is there any between Christ and all earthly goods whatever, and yet as often as you sin you prefer some temporal gratification to Christ.

III. Here we are told again that this precious pearl is not to be bought but by the sale of every thing else. "He went his way, and sold all that he had and bought it." "Happy is the man," says St. Gregory, "who with all his fortunes is able to purchase Christ." Hence, St. Paul writes: " For whom I have suffered the loss of all

---

4. *Meditations*, "Treasure Hidden in a Field" and "The Pearl."

things, and count them as dying, that I may gain Christ." (Phil. iii. 8.) Examine your conduct in this respect.

The *Meditations* writer says there is only one pearl, which is "Christ our Lord and the love of eternal things." He does not mention Jesus, but speaks only of Christ, a divinity, which Jesus himself did not do.[5] As in many other instances, this interpretation focuses on worship of a crucified, risen Christ and the "eternal life" promised for those who acknowledge him as savior. If this is a parable told by Jesus, this interpretation has him referring to himself as the precious pearl.

Early Quaker Application of Hidden Treasure & Pearl

Isaac Penington (1661):

The pearl is exceeding rich, the treasure of life unutterable; and he that will possess it, must sell all for it; yea, all the riches of his nature (the best of his will, the best of his wisdom most refined); nay not only so, but all the riches of his spirit, all that he hath held, or can hold out of the life. Then, when he is poor in spirit, and hath nothing in him but emptiness, . . . then alone is he fit to be comprehended and brought forth in the eternal spring.[6]

Isaac Penington (1667):

Is not this the pearl indeed, the precious pearl of price? Who would not buy it? Who would not sell all for it? Who would not dig in the field, where this treasure is hid, till he find it? The field is near thee, O man! which thou art to purchase and dig in, and must feel torn up by the plow of God in some measure, before this pearl or treasure appear to thee; thou must take up and bear the yoke and cross of Christ, until all be bowed down and crucified in thee which is contrary to its nature, before it be polished in thee, and thou come to behold and enjoy its riches and everlasting fulness.[7]

In these passages, Penington speaks rapturously of the pearl of great price which he identifies as "God's Truth." George Fox made the audacious claim that "the pearl" had been found in England among Quakers, and

---

5. "Jesus rarely makes pronouncements or speaks about himself in the first person. Jesus makes no claim to be the Anointed, the Messiah." Funk and Hoover, *The Five Gospels*, 30–32.

6. Penington, QBI, "Matt 13:44–46."

7. Penington, QBI, "Matt 13:44–46."

indeed, within everyone, though the Church couldn't see it. Early Friends perceived the Church's doctrine and dogma as misinterpretations of Jesus' teachings and a departure from the beliefs of the first Christians. They asserted the Church had fallen into centuries-long apostasy.[8]

Penington's understanding of the parable and its application is so clear and so close to the authentic teachings of Jesus about the Kingdom of God that it is worth sharing in its entirety. Note that the word "sin" occurs only twice in Penington's lengthy essay below, but it was a dominant focus in sermons of Puritan, Calvinist, and Anglican church services. Note, too, Penington says that God's Truth liberates humans from "unjust, erroneous deceit," and from all that "ensnares" us in "sin, misery and perdition" (which is a good description of the state of mind invoked by seventeenth-century Christianity). Penington's approach concerning "sin" is significantly more hopeful and enlightening than the Church's. (The reader is encouraged to read the following essay aloud, slowly. Spelling and punctuation have been modified for clarity. All italics are mine.)

> "OF THE PURE, CONSTANT, ETERNAL, UNCHANGEABLE NATURE OF GOD'S TRUTH"
>
> Truth is of God, and was with God, and in God, before anything else had a being.
>
> Truth was before error or deceit: for it was from the truth that the error was,
>
> and it was about truth that the deceit was.
>
> There was some[thing] which erred from truth and brought in deceit into the world; but truth remains the same that it was, keeping its pure, eternal, unchangeable nature; and is not, nor ever was, nor ever can be, defiled or tainted with any error or deceit; but testifies against it, reproves it, and condemns for it, draws out of it, and delivers from its bands and captivity all those that hearken and cleave to it, in the faith which is of [Truth's] nature and begetting.
>
> The Father, the fountain of truth, is the same.
>
> The Son, his express image (whom he fills with himself, and in whom he appears), is the same.
>
> The Spirit, the anointing (who is truth, and no lie), is still the same.

---

8. "Apostasy": "the total rejection of Christianity by a baptized person who, having at one time professed the Christian faith, publicly rejects it." *Encyclopedia Britannica*, s.v. "apostasy."

The principle or seed of truth is still the same.

The doctrine and way of truth is still the same; for it was the same truth which was preached in shadows under the law, the substance whereof appears, and is witnessed in the gospel:

and it was the same before the great apostasy, in the latter days from it, and all the time of the apostasy, and again after the apostasy.

It has the same nature still, the same properties, the same operations and effects, and gives forth the same testimony in the ears and hearts of all that are open to it. Indeed, the minds of men, and the states of men, may often change in relation to truth; but truth itself changes not, but is equal, fair, and just to all men upon the earth, in all ages and generations, always condemning that which is unjust, erroneous, and deceitful, and always justifying, what is pure, holy, and righteous.

Now is not this a pearl; Nay, is not this the pearl indeed, the precious pearl of price? Who would not buy it? Who would not sell all for it? Who would not dig in the field, where this treasure is hid, until he find it? The field is near thee, O man! which thou art to purchase and dig in, and must feel torn up by the plow of God in some measure, before this pearl or treasure appear to thee; and thou must take up and bear the yoke and cross of Christ, until all [which is contrary to its nature] be bowed down and crucified in thee, before [the pearl] be polished in thee, and thou come to behold and enjoy its riches and everlasting fulness.

Oh, happy are they that are begotten and born of it! happy are they that know its voice, and give up to it, to be gathered and redeemed by it, out of all deceits, out of all errors, out of all that entangles and ensnares the soul in sin, misery, and utter perdition; for destruction and misery everlasting is out of it, and life and salvation is alone to be found in it.

There is a witness in every heart, which knows these things, and will testify it to their faces, when the light of God is opened in them, and its tongue speaks therein to them. Oh, happy they that wait for, know, hear, and subject to the heavenly voice, while the day of their visitation and reclaiming lasts, wherein they may travel from sin to holiness, from death to life, by its help and guidance!

Oh! why should man perish? Why should man hearken to that which hates him, and seeks his destruction, and stop his ear against that which loves him, and warns him of his danger in the dearness of love, and in tenderness of [mercy] towards him?[9]

Indeed. Why should humans listen to the voice of a Church and its god which hate us and seek our destruction/damnation? Why do we stop up our ears so we can't hear the voice of the God who loves us and, out of love and mercy, warns us against listening to the other voice? Why for centuries have people listened to a Church telling them how bad they are and how unacceptable to God?

Jesus consistently said the opposite. We are deeply, completely, and unconditionally loved.

Traditional Interpretation of the Good Samaritan

The message of "the Good Samaritan" would seem difficult to misunderstand, but traditional Christianity adds layers of interpretation that obscure Jesus' message about unconditional love and compassion in the Kingdom of God.

The apparent simplicity of this parable may have inclined early church fathers to "elevate" it into complicated allegories to convince people they needed the Church to help them understand Jesus. For instance, Augustine interpreted it this way:

> ... the wounded man stands for Adam; Jerusalem, the heavenly city from which he has fallen; the thieves, the devil who deprives Adam of his immortality; the priest and Levite, the Old Testament Law which could save no one; the Samaritan who binds the man's wounds, Christ who forgives sin; the inn, the church; and the innkeeper, the apostle Paul.[10]

It's difficult to imagine Jesus had all this in mind as he told this parable to ordinary people, pre-Christianity.

Thirteen centuries later in the *Meditations* devotional, the good Samaritan parable is mentioned in a discussion of mercy.[11] The writer shows a grasp of the parable's main point, i.e., "be merciful as your heavenly father is merciful," but with no discussion of the parable itself, the writer begins with rules of church doctrine.

---

9. Penington, "Pure, Constant, Eternal, Unchangeable Nature of God's Truth."
10. Blomberg, *Interpreting the Parables*, 31.
11. *Meditations*, "Fifth Beatitude."

From "*Meditations for Every Day in The Year*/Beatitudes."

> I. "Blessed are the merciful." (Matt. v. 7.) There are seven acts of spiritual mercy, and seven works of mercy corporal. These are known to every one, who is acquainted with the elements of his religion.[12] These works of mercy, however, must be accompanied with three conditions to render them perfect and acceptable to God. 1. They must extend themselves to all without exception, even to our enemies. 2. We must take advantage of every occasion of doing good, in every species of distress, and exert ourselves to the extent of our abilities. 3. They must be accompanied with internal motives and internal devotion. Examine yourself on this subject, and remember, that a good intention alone, can sanctify an action, which might otherwise be only good.
>
> II. On this subject, as well as the other Beatitudes, Christ has given us the most perfect example. He addressed Himself to all mankind, when in His mercy He said, "Come to Me, all you that labor and are heavy laden, and I will refresh you." (Matt. xi. 28.) He took advantage of every occasion of doing good, therefore, "He was teaching daily in the temple." (Luke, xix. 47.) And "He went about doing good, and healing all, that were oppressed by the devil." (Acts, x. 38.) He performed all these works of mercy with the most tender affection, for He acted like the good Samaritan, "who bound up the wounds, of him that fell among robbers." (Luke x. 30.) Therefore "go thou and do in like manner."

The Section II paragraph above includes passages of scripture showing Christ being merciful (notice that it is Christ, not Jesus) including the only mention of the Good Samaritan. But the imposition beforehand of a numbered structure listing the "rules" of mercy (in Section I) buries Jesus' simple parable under the weight of organized religion, which adds even more church structure (like the seven deadly sins, the seven Christian virtues, rules of confessions, etc.) and more church control. Apparently, mercy only counts if done according to the rules.

---

12. "Corporal and Spiritual Works of Mercy," *The Catholic Encyclopedia*: "The traditional enumeration of the corporal works of mercy is as follows: To feed the hungry; To give drink to the thirsty; To clothe the naked; To harbour the harbourless; To visit the sick; To ransom the captive; To bury the dead. The spiritual works of mercy are: To instruct the ignorant; To counsel the doubtful; To admonish sinners; To bear wrongs patiently; To forgive offences willingly; To comfort the afflicted; To pray for the living and the dead."

Early Quaker Application of The Good Samaritan

William Penn (1736):

> Whilst men were perpetually wrangling and brawling about some ... opinion of religion, the most important points of faith and life were little regarded, unity broken, amity destroyed, and those wounds made that were never closed but with the extinction of one party: not a good Samaritan being to be found to heal and close them.[13]

Penn's description of a disagreement about religion so dire it can only end when one party is eliminated resonates today as Christian denominations argue, split and separate. Penn suggests the lesson in the parable of the Good Samaritan, i.e., that God would have us show mercy even to our enemies or opponents, might "heal and close" spiritual wounds caused (ironically) by rancorous arguments about religion. Among those arguing at the time, Penn says, none were able to manifest the mercy called for by the faith they claimed. This is too often still true.

John Woolman (1772):

> .... when we love God with all our heart and all our strength, then in this love we love our neighbors as ourselves, and a tenderness of heart is felt toward all people, even such who, as to outward circumstances, may be to us as the Jews were to the Samaritans.[14]

A few years before he wrote the sentence quoted above, Woolman was very ill and close to death. In a feverish dream, he found himself "part of a mass of matter of a dull gloomy color between the south and the east." In the dream, he was "informed that this mass was human beings in as great misery as they could be, and live, and that [he] was mixed in with them, and henceforth might not consider [him]self as a distinct or separate being." This dream shows Woolman's powerful identification with the suffering of those held as slaves in the American South. He understood that loving as comprehensively as God does erases all lines of separation among people.

Woolman applies the Good Samaritan parable to the love that Jesus says exists in the Kingdom of God, a love that includes all, those

---

13. Penn, QBI, "Luke 10:30–35."
14. Woolman, *Journal of John Woolman*.

we perceive as enemies as well as those who consider us to be their enemies; those who, Woolman says, "may be to us as the Jews were to the Samaritans."

In Jesus' parable, the Samaritan, a person disdained by Jews, unexpectedly shows mercy to a stranger when two Jews, the priest and the Levite, experts in the "laws" of their religion, do not. The Torah law about "loving one's neighbor," however, is limited to other Israelites, so technically they have not violated Hebrew law. In other teachings about "loving your enemy," Jesus says "If you love those who love you, what credit is that to you? For even sinners love those who love them." In this parable, Jesus uses the story of the good Samaritan to contrast the letter of the law in Torah with the spirit of the law in the Kingdom of God.[15] Woolman's dream exemplifies Jesus' point that all of us are of "one tribe," and the spirit of God's law requires us to love universally.

Traditional Interpretation of The Prodigal Son

"The Prodigal Son" warrants two entries in *Meditations* in the section titled "Historical Narrations & Parables of the Redeemer."[16]

> The Prodigal Son.—I.
>
> I. "A certain man had two sons, and the younger of them said to his father, give me the portion of substance that falleth to me." (Luke xv. 11.) God has two sons, the just and the wicked; the just are the elder, for "God made man right" (Eccles. vii. 30) in the beginning. The just always remain in God's house, and never wish to leave it, but the wicked estrange themselves from God, abuse the gifts both of nature and grace, and live riotously and perversely. Whoever leaves God, travels into a foreign land; he leaves "the way, the truth, and the life," and becomes a sinner. Of these David says, "Salvation is far from sinners." (Ps. cxviii. 155.)
>
> II. As soon as this young prodigal had left his father's house he fell into misfortunes. "He began to be in want." Thus sinners who estrange themselves from the sacraments, from exhortation,

---

15. Perhaps this is what Matt 5:17 refers to, i.e., Jesus says he came, "not to break the law [i.e., the Torah], but to fulfill it." The Greek word *plēróō*, translated here as "to fulfill," can also be translated as "to complete," "to carry out," "to realize, to bring to realization." Expanding our understanding of God's love to include all would seem a step toward completing, carrying out, realizing the "law" of God.

16. *Meditations*, "Prodigal Son."

and the company of the virtuous, soon begin to be in want of spiritual subsistence. "He joined himself to one of the citizens of that country," as a servant. Every sinner is a slave to the Devil; and as the citizen employed the prodigal youth in feeding swine, so the Devil employs his followers in gratifying their own sensual appetites, which brutalize human nature. The prodigal attempted to satisfy his hunger, by feeding on the husks of swine, but he did not succeed: neither can the sinner succeed in filling the capacity of his immortal soul by earthly gratifications.

III. "And returning to himself." When pressed by famine, he begins to recollect himself. "Vexation alone," says the Prophet to sinners, "shall make you understand." (Is. xxviii. 19.) Misfortune and distress make sinners feel how foolishly they have acted in leaving eternal things for such as quickly pass away. "How many hired servants in my father's house have plenty of bread, and I here perish with hunger!" Hence, he is moved to repentance; "I will arise," he says, " and will go to my father." How often have you followed this young prodigal in wandering from God! Follow his example in returning to your father.

The Prodigal Son.—II.

I. "And when he was yet a great way off, his father saw him, and was moved with compassion." (Luke xv. 20.) Thus Almighty God looks on sinners with eyes of mercy, whilst they are yet at a great distance from Him. He invites them by His exciting grace: "Return," he says, "O ye revolted children, — and I will bring you into Sion." (Jer. iii. 14.) This good father meets his revolted son on his return, and falling on his neck embraces him. "He put a ring on his hand and shoes on his feet." Thus God acts with returning sinners. "He enables their hands to do good works, and prevents their feet from being defiled by the ways of the world." O God, how is it possible that you should love man, who is formed of clay, in such a manner! He has a thousand times preferred the torments of hell to your service.

II. The elder brother, hearing of his father's joy and festivity, murmured through a spirit of envy. Ponder how easy it is, even among virtuous persons, to be touched with a spirit of envy, when another is commended or preferred to them. Learn, hence, to be particularly on your guard against this bad spirit. You ought rather to wish with Moses, that all might praise and honor God in the most exalted manner. "O that all the people might prophesy, and the Lord would give them His spirit." (Num. xi. 29.)

III. The father answers mildly and endeavors to reclaim him from his error. "Son," he says, "thou art always with me, and all I have is thine." O what a happiness it is for the just to have God always with them! How rich must he be, who has everything in common with God! Learn to rejoice, when your brother is brought back to Christ, and endeavor yourself to bring as many as you can to Him.

Notice the focus on sin, depravity, hell, not attending church, offending God, etc. Even when the love of God is acknowledged, the focus is on the depravity of humans: "O God, how is it possible that you should love man, who . . . has a thousand times preferred the torments of hell to your service." The *Meditations* interpretation of the prodigal son parable ends with an exhortation to proselytize, to "bring as many as you can" to Christ, i.e., the Church.

Early Quaker Application of The Prodigal Son

James Nayler (1653):

And see yourselves the prodigal: when he saw himself what he had done, went home unto his father's house; and thou hast read of a prodigal in the scripture that fed among swine, but dost thou see thyself to be the prodigal feeding among the swine, feeding on husks? Is this opened to thee? Dost thou know what this husk is? . . . When thou art come to thy father's house thou wilt see that thou hast been feeding among the swine on the letter, the outside which profits not.[17]

The prodigal son is reduced to eating only the husks of grain commonly fed to pigs, not the good and nourishing grain kernel itself. Naylor applies this to those fed (by the Church) only "husks" of scripture, only the "letter," only the words, not the nutritious spiritual truth of Jesus' teaching about love and the Kingdom of God.

Isaac Penington, 1663:

If [the Lord] please to kill the fatted calf, and set it before his prodigal son, let none that have walked faithfully with him in any dispensation be offended thereat; but rather let all (in whom

---

17. Nayler, *Discovery of Faith*.

is life) stand ready to shout at the issuings forth of love and mercy, in the varieties of the dispensations thereof, according to the need and capacity of every sort of vessels, prepared by the Lord to receive it.[18]

Penington directly addresses the jealousy of the older son in the parable, who is angered by his father's joyous reception of the younger son's return. Penington admonishes those who have "walked faithfully" with God "in any dispensation" to celebrate when anyone—no matter who or when or what "sort of vessel"—receives God's love and mercy.

"In any dispensation" has a double meaning here. Penington's use of the phrase includes the image of God dispensing love and mercy into vessels (read "humans") of different shapes and sizes, according to how much each vessel needs and has the capacity to hold. This is related to the early Friends' understanding that each of us has within "a measure of the Light of [God's] own Son, a measure of grace, or a measure of the Spirit,"[19] and that Jesus had the "full measure" of God's light, grace, and spirit.

"Dispensation" is also a term used by theologians to refer to "a divinely appointed order or age" [20] in God's timeline from creation to the present. Beginning with the early church fathers, theologians divided biblical time into various dispensations; for instance, the age or period between creation and the fall of Adam and Eve; the period leading up to God's "re-ordering" through the Flood and the covenant with Noah; the age of God's covenants with Moses and Abraham; and the age of the new covenant through Christ. Different theologians came up with different dispensations; some found four; others found seven or more.

In the quotation above, Penington implies that in every age or dispensation, some people "walked faithfully" with God, even if they did not live during the Christian dispensation, i.e., even if they were not Christian. This understanding that God's love pervades all ages and circumstances was common among early Friends. The highly respected Robert Barclay wrote in his 1678 *Apology for the True Christian Divinity: as professed by the people called Quakers*:

> The church [is] no other thing but the society, gathering or company of such as God hath called out of the world and worldly spirit to walk in his light and life . . . . Under this

---

18. Penington, "Some Deep Considerations Concerning the State of Israel."
19. Barclay, *Apology*, Sixth Proposition.
20. Dictionary.com, s.v. "Dispensation."

church ... are comprehended [included] all, and as many, of whatsoever nation, kindred, tongue, or people they be, though outwardly strangers and remote from those who profess Christ and Christianity in words and have the benefit of the Scriptures, as become obedient to the holy light and testimony of God in their hearts ... There may be members therefore of this Catholic [i.e., universal] church both among heathens, Turks, Jews and all the several sorts of Christians, men and women of integrity and simplicity of heart, who ... are by the secret touches of this holy light in their souls enlivened and quickened, thereby secretly united to God ... [21]

Traditional Interpretation of The Lost Sheep

From "*Meditations for Every Day in The Year*/Historical Narratives."

The Lost Sheep.

I. "What man among you that hath a hundred sheep, and if he shall lose one of them, doth he not leave the ninety-nine in the desert and go after that which was lost?" (Luke xv. 4.) This man is Christ, the sheep are the faithful. Christ performs to the full extent all the offices of a good shepherd. He came down from heaven to feed them; He marks them for His own, with a divine and indelible character; He leads them by His example to all virtue; He cures their infirmities; He defends them from the wolves of hell; He provides them with the rich pastures of His doctrine and sacraments, and finally He gives them His own body and blood for their food and nourishment. The faithful hear His voice, obey His commands and follow Him wherever He leads the way; they delight in His pastures and surrender themselves entirely to Him: living and dying they are His.

II. The strayed sheep is a sinner, who leaving the society of the just, and disobeying the commands of the Shepherd, wanders wherever he pleases. He is a most foolish and wretched man, he does not understand the happiness, which he enjoyed under the Good Pastor; he is indifferent to the spiritual food which he once received; he prefers such as is pleasing to flesh and blood; he does not hear nor follow the call of the Shepherd; he considers the ways of mortification and the cross too hard and difficult, and prefers to wander through devious and dangerous paths of his own will, amidst rocks and precipices. "All we, like sheep," says

---

21. Barclay, "Friends and the Christian Church," 224.

> the Prophet, " have gone astray, every one hath turned aside into his own way." (Is. liii. 6.) Reflect how often you have done so.
>
> III. The goodness of the Shepherd induces him to seek for His strayed sheep. He sought them Himself in the first place, by His exemplary life and doctrine, during the thirty-three years, in which "He conversed with men." He now continually seeks them by holy inspirations, directors, pious books, and by the whole economy of His infallible Church. When He has found His lost sheep, He kindly and affectionately conducts it back again to His fold. O Lord, thus receive me, and conduct me into Thy sacred fold. "I have gone astray like a sheep that is lost, seek Thy servant because I have not forgotten Thy commandments" (Ps. cxviii. 179).

The *Meditations* writer's traditional interpretation of the lost sheep parable shows how thoroughly the Church identifies with the situation described in it: "This man/the Shepherd is Christ; the sheep are the faithful. . . . The strayed sheep is a sinner." Much of the interpretation focuses on the relationship between Christ and "His infallible Church," even to church ritual and sacraments: "He defends them from the wolves of hell; He provides them with the rich pastures of His doctrine and sacraments, and finally He gives them His own body and blood for their food and nourishment."

(It is telling that the lost coin parable is not mentioned at all in *Meditations*, perhaps because the imagery does not fit Church doctrine. If the shepherd searching for a lost sheep in the mountains represents Christ or God, by extension then, the woman searching for a lost coin in her house represents Christ or God. To most traditional Christians in the seventeenth century, and now, the idea of Christ identifying with a woman, or vice versa, is . . . just wrong. Yet Jesus taught the Parable of the Lost Coin with a woman as the main character.)

Early Quaker Application of The Lost Coin and Lost Sheep

> George Fox (1676):
>
> And the parable of Christ, concerning the woman that lost her piece of silver, who lighted a candle and swept her own house, and found it in her own house; and when she had found it, she rejoiced, and told her neighbors. And must not every woman light her own candle at the light of Christ Jesus, and sweep her

own house with the power of God, before she finds God's treasure? And then for joy that they have found it, go and declare it unto their friends and neighbors? And do not all those women that have found this, preach Christ to their friends and neighbors, and call them together?[22]

Fox's interpretation of the lost silver coin as "God's treasure" that the woman finds "in her own house," reflects the early Friends' understanding that God/Christ/The Light is within each of us; like the woman searching for the coin, we must search "within our own house" until we find it. Fox says that every woman "must light her own candle," "sweep her own house" to find "God's treasure" within herself, and then go "preach Christ to their friends and neighbors." This was a heresy at a time when women were not considered worthy or capable of preaching which Christian tradition had reserved for men only. But Fox was enlightened in many ways, including the way he perceived women as equals.

> George Fox (1669):
>
> And all ye believers in the heavenly light as Christ hath taught, you seek that which is lost and driven away, but the false prophets, false ministers, and teachers they did not seek that which was lost and driven away from God; they put no difference between the precious and the vile but mash all together, like the priests and prophets of our times. . . . Therefore, seek that which is lost, ye that believe in the light. . . you see all the prophets, how they sought that which was lost, and the apostles, and how Christ encouraged [us] to seek that which was lost. And when the lost sheep was found, what joy there was, more than of the ninety and nine.[23]

Fox applies this parable to religious strife in seventeenth-century England between those who perceived in Christ's teachings a "heavenly light," and those ("false prophets, false ministers and teachers," "the priests and prophets of our times") who sought to maintain the muddiness ("mash all together" the "precious and the vile") of Church hierarchy, doctrine, and tradition. Fox often advised his listeners/readers to follow the light; here he urges them to persist in seeking it in the truth of Jesus' teachings about love and the Kingdom of God, "how Christ encouraged us to seek that which was lost."

22. Fox, QBI, "Luke 15:8–10."
23. Fox, QBI, "Epistle 265."

Traditional Interpretation of The Mustard Seed

From "*Meditations for Every Day in The Year*/Historical Narratives."

> The Mustard Seed.
>
> I. "The kingdom of heaven is like to a grain of mustard seed." (Matt. xiii. 31.) A mustard seed is small and not remarkable either for its smell or outward appearance, but it contains within itself great natural heat[24], and manifests it, particularly when it is bruised. Thus, Christ in outward appearance was "a worm and no man, the reproach of men and the outcast of the people." (Ps. xxi. 7.) Nevertheless He is possessed of all "the treasures of wisdom and knowledge." (Col. ii. 3.) When He was bruised and buffeted, and suspended on His cross, He expressed and manifested the most unparalleled charity for mankind. Do you on your part suffer yourself to be inflamed with emanations of love, from this divine source.
>
> II. In this world the just bear a resemblance to the mustard seed. They are simple and contemptible in the eyes of the world, but they are high in the estimation of God and His angels. Of them, the wicked will say at the day of judgment: "We fools esteemed their life madness, and their end without honor. Behold, how they are numbered among the children of God." (Wis, v. 4.) Observe also that good men display their virtue most, when they are under the pressure of afflictions. Hence the Apostle writes, "When I am weak, I am powerful." (2 Cor. xii. 10.)
>
> III. When the mustard seed is sown, it grows into a large tree, "so that the birds of the air come and dwell in the branches thereof." Thus, Christ was perfectly mortified and dead on the cross, and in His branches, that is, in His doctrine and example, devout souls dwell by holy contemplation. "I sat down," says the spouse in the Canticle, "under His shadow whom I desired and His fruit was sweet to my palate." (Cant. ii. 3.)[25]

This traditional interpretation of the mustard seed begins with Jesus' words: "The kingdom of heaven is like to a grain of mustard seed," but the writer completely ignores the first half of the sentence: "the Kingdom of God/Heaven is like. . . " In all three versions of the parable, Jesus states

---

24. The mustard plant in this parable may not be the species that originated in Europe and West Asia i.e., the yellow-flowered plant whose seeds are used as a spice, but to the mustard bush or mustard tree native to the Middle East and India, which can reach up to thirty feet in height.

25. *Meditations*, "Mustard Seed."

at the beginning his intent to describe the kingdom of God. The writer of *Meditations* has his own intention, i.e., to see Jesus as the seed, the lowly Christ, battered, bruised, and crucified. He mentions that other good people are like the mustard seed, "simple and contemptible" in the human realm, but ranked high by God and his angels. Note this writer's references to "doctrine and example," "holy contemplation," mortification, and other elements related to the Church.

Early Quaker Application of The Mustard Seed

Isaac Penington (1663):

The seed of the promise, the seed of the kingdom, is the least of all seeds. Man easily overlooks it; or if he have a little glimmering of it, readily despises it, as unlikely ever to have that in it, or bring that to pass for the soul, which it desires and expects. Yet there is no other way to the kingdom, but by this seed of the kingdom opening and growing in the heart, and gathering the heart into itself . . .[26]

Robert Barclay (1678):

Though then this Seed be small in its appearance, so that Christ compares it to "a grain of mustard seed, which is the least of all seeds," and that it be hid in the earthly part of man's heart; yet therein is life and salvation towards the sons of men wrapped up, which comes to be revealed as they give way to it. And in this Seed in the hearts of all men is the Kingdom of God, as in capacity to be produced, or rather exhibited, according as it receives depth, and is nourished, and not choked . . .[27]

Penington and Barclay apply the mustard seed parable to the human tendency to ignore or dismiss whatever is small and to seek outside themselves for "salvation" (i.e., gaining heaven after death by obeying the demands of the Church). In *Gospel Truth Demonstrated*, Fox describes this tendency when he addresses "professors" of Christianity, saying: "heaven is within you (like unto a grain of mustard seed)" but you "have been gazing for it without you." In other words, you are

---

26. Penington, QBI, "Matt 13:31."
27. Barclay, QBI, "Mark 4:31 and Matt 13:31."

looking for something big and outside yourselves when all the time the kingdom of heaven is inside you.[28]

Traditional Interpretation of The Parable of The Talents

From "*Meditations for Every Day in The Year*/Historical Narratives."

The Parable of the Talents, Parts I and II.

The Talents.— I.

I. "A man going into a far country called his servants and delivered to them his goods." (Matt. xxv. 14.) God is the universal Lord of all things, and He distributes His goods among mankind; for whatever qualities of body or mind we possess, whatever we have, internal or external, natural or supernatural, all comes from God. O man, "what hast thou, that thou hast not received!" (1 Cor. iv. 7.) God distributes His talents or gifts, whether natural or supernatural, unequally; He gives more to one and less to another, but to all He addresses the words, "Trade till I come" (Luke xix. 13), in order that they may take advantage of what they receive. Examine how many talents you have received, in order that you may be the better able to give an account of them.

II. "He that had received the five talents went his way and traded with the same and gained other five." (Matt. xxv. 16.) "And in like manner, he that had received the two, gained other two." The industry of both was equal, though their talents were unequal, and therefore, in the same proportion, their rewards were equal. God does not consider the greatness of the gain," says St. Jerome, "but good will and exertion." Although, therefore, you may imagine that you have received few talents in comparison to others, you may notwithstanding be equal to them in reward, if you equal them in the improvement of your stock.

III. The motive of reward ought to induce us to labor with great diligence and assiduity: "Because thou hast been faithful over a few things, I will place thee over many things; enter thou into the joy of thy Lord." And what is this joy? That which "the eye hath not seen, nor ear heard." (1 Cor. ii. 9.) A joy without limit or measure, never to end or be abated. Be therefore faithful over the little which God has entrusted to your care and conduct; employ everything which He has given you, to His glory, and

28. Fox, *Gospel Truth*.

thus you will deserve to be "placed over many things," and "to enter into the joy of the Lord."

The Talents— II.

I. "But he that had received the one "talent" going his way, digged in the earth and hid his lord's money." (Matt. xxv. 18.) Thus many imagine that they cannot appear equal to others in virtue, knowledge or skill, and, falling into despair, surrender themselves at discretion to the world, and become slothful and careless in the service of God. "The slothful hideth his hand under his armpit and will not so much as bring it to his mouth." (Prov. xix. 24.) Such, however, are called fools by the Divine Spirit: "The fool foldeth his hands together, saying, Better is a handful with rest than both hands full with labor." (Eccles. iv. 5.) Examine your conduct on this subject.

II. Consider the excuse of the slothful servant: "Lord, I know that thou art a hard man, — and being afraid, I went and hid thy talent in the earth; behold, here thou hast that which is thine." (Matt. xxv. 24.) He tells a falsehood, in order to excuse himself; for our Lord is not hard but a mild and merciful master. It is the custom of all slothful Christians, "to make excuses in sins." (Ps. cxl. 4.) They fancy to themselves that hardships and dangers exist, where there are none. "There is a lion in the way, and a lioness in the roads." (Prov. xxvi. 13.) Such tepid souls often say, "I cannot," when nothing but the will is wanting. Beware of tepidity and sloth as your greatest enemies.

III. Consider the sentence pronounced against this idle servant: "Take ye away, therefore, the talent from him, and the unprofitable servant cast ye out into the exterior darkness. There shall be weeping and gnashing of teeth." "He is not condemned," observes St. Augustine, "because he lost his talent, but because he kept it without making any profit of it." Use every exertion therefore to employ those talents well, which God has entrusted to you. You cannot want employment for them, whatever be your state or calling in life. Your own spiritual good, the glory of God, and the advantage of your neighbor ought to be always before your eyes.[29]

Notice that the above interpretations make no mention of God's love. Instead, the emphasis in the first is on accepting God's unequal distribution of gifts, and the "motive of reward" inducing us to "labor with great

---

29. *Meditations*, "Parable of the Talents."

APPENDIX: TRADITIONAL INTERPRETATIONS VS. QUAKER APPLICATIONS

diligence and assiduity." Emphasis in the second is on failure, sin, and punishment. The line in the parable condemning the one who "made no profit" receives the bulk of attention.

For help understanding the Church's approach to this difficult parable, below is an excerpt from a lengthy interpretation by Cornelius Cornelii à Lapide (1567–1637), a Jesuit priest known for his exegesis of scripture. His commentary, while making some good points about God's grace and our good works, has a slightly threatening tone; the underlying assumption is the common one in traditional Christian dogma, i.e., that we will be judged and if found wanting, punished.

> From *The Great Biblical Commentary of Cornelius À Lapide:*
>
> Ver. 16. Then he . . . five talents, &c. To gain talents is to increase the gifts of God by using and increasing them, especially by means of good works, and helping our neighbor to increase and multiply the grace of God in ourselves and others. This parable intimates that everyone ought to cooperate with the grace of God with all his might. For example, he who has, as it were, five degrees of charity, ought to exercise charity in a corresponding degree of intensity. By this means he will gain from God five degrees more. Again, by exercising charity thus increased as ten degrees, in acts of corresponding intensity, he may gain other ten decrees, and possess, as it were, twenty degrees. And so on, marvelously doubling, and multiplying the gain of his talents, that is to say, the degrees of his charity. Let it be, therefore, that a man by his charity should gain few or none to Christ by preaching, yet will he have the same merit and reward of his charity and preaching as if he had converted multitudes. The conversion of others is not often in our power, but the merit of doing so is always in our power.
>
> And likewise he that had received two, &c. This man also, by diligently and correspondingly using his talent, that is, cooperating with grace, doubled it.
>
> Ver. 18. But he that had received one . . . hid his lord's money . . . To bury a talent is, through negligence and sloth, not to use or exercise the grace bestowed upon one. Here observe, that this burying of his talent is ascribed to him who only received one talent. This is not because others, who have received more, do not often do the same, but in order that we may understand that if he, who had only misused his one talent, was thus severely punished by his master, far sharper will be the Lord's

> censure and punishment of those who have misused more and greater talents....
>
> Let those who do not use genius, learning, prudence, or other gifts of God, for their own or others' benefits, on account of sloth, or fear of sinning, or for any similar reason, note this. For of them will Christ demand an exact account of these gifts in the Day of Judgment. Observe also, that those who have received few talents, often, through sloth, leave them idle, and, as it were, bury them; whilst those who have received more are stimulated by them, and either use them rightly and meritoriously, or else abuse them to vanity. And these last are punished not so much for letting their talents lie idle, as for misusing them! Thus we commonly see that those who have great powers of intellect, if they do not employ them for good purposes, do so for bad.[30]

This interpretation begins wonderfully, with the idea of people "cooperating with the grace of God" by using "with great intensity" however many "degrees of charity" they receive; however, Lapide equates "using" one's "degrees of charity" only with converting others to Christianity. By doing so, he says, a person multiplies "the degrees of his charity . . . and will have the same merit and reward . . . as if he had converted multitudes." So long as a person works very hard to convert others, he will be rewarded. When Lapide gets to the fearful investor who hid the money, he stresses the "Lord's censure and punishment" of those who haven't worked hard enough (presumably converting others) and says Christ will call them to account for their lack of industry on Judgment Day.

The following interpretation from St. Theophan the Recluse (1815–1894), a saint in the Russian Orthodox Church, continues the tradition of focusing on judgment, punishment, and reward, though it does include a nod to the "leveling" of "earthly states" on Judgment Day.

> The parable about the talents offers the thought that life is a time for trading.
>
> That means that it is necessary to hasten to use this time as a person would hurry to a market to bargain for what he can. Even if one has only brought bast shoes, or only bast, (very inexpensive, unsophisticated items) he does not sit with his arms folded but contrives to call over buyers to sell what he has and then buy for himself what he needs.

---

30. Lapide, *Great Biblical Commentary*.

No one who has received life from the Lord can say that he does not have a single talent—everyone has something, and not just one thing; everyone, therefore, has something with which to trade and make a profit.

Do not look around and calculate what others have received but take a good look at yourself and determine more precisely what lies in you and what you can gain for that which you have, and then act according to this plan without laziness.

At the Judgment you will not be asked why you did not gain ten talents if you had only one, and you will not even be asked why you gained only one talent on your one, but you will be told that you gained a talent, half a talent or a tenth of its worth.

And the reward will not be because you received the talents, but because you gained.

There will be nothing with which to justify yourself—not with nobleness, nor poverty, nor lack of education. When this is not given, there will be no question about it.

But you had hands and feet. You will be asked, what did you gain with them? You had a tongue, what did you gain with it?

In this way will the inequalities of earthly states be leveled out at God's judgment.[31]

Early Quaker Application of the Parable of the Talents

Isaac Penington (1668):

He that is faithful to the light of the Spirit (and to the discerning that is thereby) in the little, he shall receive more, he shall have his light and discerning thereby increased, as his need requireth. But he that stands disputing, and would have all his way made clear to him, before he sets one step in it; he is far from becoming that child, which the Father teaches, and administereth an entrance into the kingdom . . .[32]

Penington applies the Parable of the Talents to the idea that if a person is open to, paying attention to, and faithfully following guidance from the Spirit, more such gifts/guidance will come to them, along with increased skill in discernment. Those who question spiritual guidance or

---

31. Sanidopoulos, "Parable of the Talents; St Theophan the Recluse."
32. Penington, QBI, "Luke 19:17."

who demand proof of its validity before following it, however, will gradually receive less and less, delaying their ability to enter the Kingdom of God (love). The understanding here (and in the quotation from Barclay below) is that Jesus' teaching "to those who have, more will be given, and from those who have nothing, even what they have will be taken away" refers to spiritual guidance, not to material wealth or possessions.

> Robert Barclay (1678):
>
> ... he that had two talents was accepted as well as he that had five because he used them to his master's profit. And he that had one might have done so: his talent was of the same nature with the rest, it was as capable to have proportionably brought forth its interest as the rest. And so though there be not a like proportion of grace given to all ... yet there is given to all that which is sufficient, and no more is required than according to that which is given: "For unto whomsoever much is given, from him shall much be required" ... [33]

Remember that the Parable of the Talents is not about money. Barclay sees the talents representing God's grace, a currency of love. In his understanding, though each "investor" received a different number of talents (i.e., measures of grace), each had all he needed or could handle. The point was not how much each one had, but what he did with it. Barclay's comments about proportionate grace suggest a comparison with the poor widow in Mark 12:41–44 (a story known from other sources, perhaps quoted by Jesus).

> [Jesus] sat down opposite the treasury and watched the crowd putting money into the treasury. Many rich people put in large sums. A poor widow came and put in two small copper coins, which were worth a penny. Then he called his disciples and said to them, "Truly I tell you, this poor widow has put in more than all those who are contributing to the treasury. For all of them have contributed out of their abundance, but she out of her poverty has put in everything she had, all she had to live on."

The fearful investor hid his talent (i.e., the measure of grace God had given him) and did nothing with it. Had he used it to the fullest to "earn interest" (increase grace), he would have received the same approval the other two investors did, regardless of the differing amounts. To

---

33. Barclay, QBI, "Matt 25:14–30."

paraphrase Mother Teresa, we may not be able to do great things, but we can do small things with great love.

Traditional Interpretation of The Vineyard Workers

Below is a brief commentary from the early Church father, Irenaeus of Lyons, written between 175 and 185 CE. Ireneus links this parable to that of the prodigal son, both of which, he says, teach the same lesson: that God will forgive and welcome home all who wish to return. By the end of his interpretation, he has added a caveat, however: "knowing" God's son (Christ) is a prerequisite for achieving eternal life.

> For He gives existence to all; He, "who maketh His sun to rise upon the evil and the good, and sendeth rain upon the just and unjust."
>
> And not alone by what has been stated, but also by the parable of the two sons, the younger of whom consumed his substance by living luxuriously with harlots, did the Lord teach one and the same Father, who did not even allow a kid to his elder son; but for him who had been lost, [namely] his younger son, he ordered the fatted calf to be killed, and he gave him the best robe.
>
> Also by the parable of the workmen who were sent into the vineyard at different periods of the day, one and the same God is declared as having called some in the beginning, when the world was first created; but others afterwards, and others during the intermediate period, others after a long lapse of time, and others again in the end of time; so that there are many workmen in their generations, but only one householder who calls them together. For there is but one vineyard, since there is also but one righteousness, and one dispensator, for there is one Spirit of God who arranges all things; and in like manner is there one hire, for they all received a penny each man, having [stamped upon it] the royal image and superscription, the knowledge of the Son of God, which is immortality. And therefore, He began by giving the hire to those [who were engaged] last, because in the last times, when 'the Lord was revealed He presented Himself to all [as their reward].'[34]

For Irenaeus, the vineyard represents God's kingdom, the workers represent faithful supporters of God throughout time, and the penny wage

---

34. Irenaeus of Lyons, "Prophets Were Sent from One and the Same Father."

each worker receives—stamped with "the royal image and superscription, the knowledge of the Son of God"—represents knowing Christ/being Christian, which is necessary to receive the ultimate reward of immortality.

To address the unfairness of expecting those from earlier centuries to "know Christ" when they lived well before he did, Ireneus invokes the idea of "dispensations,"[35] referring to different eras when God "dispensed" laws, covenants, grace, etc., through faithful workers like Abraham, Moses, David, Noah, Isaiah, etc. In his interpretation of the workers in the vineyard parable, Irenaeus equates these early workers with the vineyard workers who start early in the day. They do God's work but without knowledge of his Son. The workers last hired Irenaeus equates with Christians in the end times when Christ will return and reveal himself to all humanity. Presumably, this will include those early workers, who at that time will "have knowledge of the Son of God." Christ will reward—equally—all who "know of him" at the end of time. This connection between God's realm, "knowing" his Son/being Christian, and only thereby achieving immortality, became foundational in Christian thought.

Compare Ireneus with the following interpretation of the parable in *Meditations for Every Day in The Year*, the Jesuit devotional written fifteen hundred years later.

From "*Meditations for Every Day in The Year*/Historical Narratives."

The Laborers in the Vineyard.— I.

> I. "The kingdom of heaven is like to a master of a family who went out early in the morning to hire laborers." (Matt. xx. 1.) This "master of a family" is God Himself, who, although He be the Lord of the kingdoms of heaven and earth, nevertheless provides in such a manner for the smallest wants of each individual, that it might seem that He is master only of a small family. His vineyard is the Church, the vines are all the faithful, the workmen are His pastors, and the faithful themselves; for every one must take care of his own soul. What a happiness it is to labor in such a vineyard, under such a master, and in cultivating such precious vines! Let this reflection induce you to labor seriously in performing your task in this vineyard.

---

35. *Strong's Greek Lexicon*, "Dispensation," s.v., G3622. The Greek word (*oikonomia*) translated in the New Testament as "dispensation" meant "the management of a household or of household affairs; specifically, the management, oversight, administration, of others' property; the office of a manager or overseer, stewardship."

II. Consider the solicitude of the master of the family. "He went out early in the morning to hire laborers." From the very commencement of the world, in every age, God calls these workmen. He calls every one to Himself, from the first use of their reason. Although many, nay, even the greatest part of mankind, resist His early call, He still continues to call in every stage of life afterwards, even to their last moment. Some He entices to His service by the hopes of reward, saying, "I will give you what is just." He rebukes others for their slothfulness: "Why stand you here all the day idle?" Examine if you have not been hitherto very idle in the service of God.

III. A part of this great vineyard consists of those whom God has placed under your charge, but particularly your own soul. Examine the present state of this part of the vineyard. See if it be not in the condition described by the author of Proverbs: "Behold it was all filled with nettles, and thorns had covered the face thereof, and the stone wall was broken down." (Prov. xxiv. 31.) Remember that you are sent into a vineyard, and not into a garden of pleasure; to labor, not to enjoy yourself and live at your ease. Encourage yourself to labor hard in this vineyard, for your reward will be very great. "The soul of them that work shall be made fat" (Prov. xiii. 4).

The Laborers in the Vineyard.— II.

I. "When evening was come, the Lord of the vineyard said to His steward: 'Call the laborers and pay them their hire, beginning from the last even to the first.'" (Matt. xx. 8.) This steward is Christ our Lord, to whom the Father "hath given authority to execute judgment." (John v. 27.) The evening of our life is death, for the whole of our life is but one day. "A thousand years," says holy David, addressing his Lord, "in Thy sight are as yesterday, which is past." (Ps. lxxxix. 4.) After death every man receives his hire or wages. In the distribution of rewards, not so much regard is paid to the time employed as to fervor in working. Hence, those who come into the vineyard at the last hour, by conversion, receive as much as the first, because they are generally accustomed to labor with greater fervor and humility, and deem themselves undeserving of any reward, whilst on the contrary the others are often too confident and presumptuous.

II. Those who had been longest in the vineyard, "murmured against the master of the house, saying, these last have worked but one hour, and thou hast made them equal to us that have borne the burden of the day and heats." There can of course be no murmuring in heaven, but the reward "of those who come last" will be so great that, if their state could permit, it would breed envy in those who came first. This kind of envy is unfortunately very common in this world. Examine yourself on the subject; see if your eye be not in some respect evil, because your brother is more favored than you are. Remember the expression of St. Paul, "Charity envieth not" (1 Cor. xiii. 4).

III. The parable closes in these remarkable words "So shall the last be first, and the first last; for many are called, but few chosen." Those that were last employed in the vineyard receive the reward in consequence of their fervor. "God," says St. Gregory, "does not consider so much what is done as the affection with which it is done. Perhaps you may count many years in which you have been employed in the service of God, and not one in which you have served Him with fervor. Let it be said of you, "In a short space he fulfilled a long time" (Wis. iv. 13).[36]

Note the dominance of the Church throughout this interpretation. The Church is God's vineyard, never mind the rest of the world or other faiths and peoples. "The vines are all the faithful, the workmen are His pastors," and particularly, the "steward is Christ our Lord, to whom the Father 'hath given authority to execute judgment.'" The Church-as-God's-vineyard is central now, with Christ himself "managing" it and determining who receives what wages/rewards, based on how fervently the workers worked, not how long. Ordinary people in this interpretation are not only vines in God's vineyard, but workers in it who are urged to consider the state of their own souls. Although God is described as a loving master of the vineyard, he also scolds lazy workers or those overconfident of their own worth.

The devotional writer warns that we are "sent into a vineyard" where hard labor is expected, and "not into a garden of pleasure." The precise nature of the work to be done in God's vineyard is not specified, though there is a suggestion that workers are to weed out the "nettles" and "thorns" (sins) in their own souls and in those "whom God has placed under [their] charge." This attitude encouraged individuals to judge themselves and others by whatever measure church authorities established, i.e., what is unpardonable sin? what is minor sin? how can sins be

---

36. Meditations, "Laborers in the Vineyard."

corrected? how much will it cost (i.e., what is the indulgence I must pay the Church) to escape punishment for a sin, etc.³⁷

At the end of life or the end of time, Christ himself as Steward of the Church-as-God's-vineyard, will "execute judgment" of what reward each worker deserves. Imagine how the gentle rabbi Jesus would react to such an interpretation of his parable.

Early Quaker Application of The Vineyard Laborers

George Fox (1666):

Concerning the women's meetings; encourage all the women of families that are convinced, and mind virtue, and love truth, and walk in it; that they may come up into God's service, that they may be serviceable in their generation, and in the creation, and come into the practice of the pure religion, which you have received from God, from above; that every one may come to know their duty in it, and their service in the power and wisdom of God. For now the practical part is called for. For people must not be always talking and hearing, but they must come into obedience to the great God of heaven and earth. . . . that none may stand idle out of the vineyard and out of the service, and out of their duty . . .³⁸

Katharine Whitton (1681):

But living praises to the Lord, who in every Age is ready to reward the faithful, in what hour soever they labor in his Vineyard; and there is not one Member, though never so little, if in the body, nor Instrument, though never so weak, if prepared of the Lord, but all needful and useful in their places, to the dressing of the Vineyard of the Lord, and for the plucking up of those hurtful weeds that cumber the tender Plants. . . . For thereby, saith he, am I glorified, that ye bring forth much Fruit. Then is the labor of love which the faithful bestows answered, when the Plants prosper, and the Lord is glorified; so in this labour, as co-workers and fellow-helpers, Male and Female, for which we were raised up by the Lord's Power, let us put our hands to the work . . .³⁹

37. An indulgence is "a remission of the temporal punishment due to sin, the guilt of which has been forgiven." See *Catholic Encyclopedia*, s.v. "Indulgence."
38. Fox, QBI, "Matt 20:3, 6."
39. Whitton, "Epistle to Friends Everywhere."

The two quotations above show early Friends applying the lesson in the parable of the vineyard workers to the radical Quaker practice of allowing women to speak during worship.[40] Even more controversial among Friends[41] was the establishment of women's "meetings for worship with attention to business" separate from the men's meeting. Though Fox is credited with establishing them, evidence suggests that Margaret Fell was influential in the decision, concerned that women's voices not be drowned out by men's voices in meetings that included both sexes.[42]

Both Fox and Whitton apply the aspect of the parable of the vineyard in which the owner (God, not the Church) wishes everyone to work in his vineyard and none to be idle. He returns several times to hire whoever is not yet working for him. He hires those not expecting to work, those available only late in the day, those who didn't get hired before, those who were "undesirable" for whatever reason. The early Friends understood this to mean that God welcomes all (including women) to work in his kingdom. No one is passed over, and all receive the same reward.

Traditional Interpretation of The Dishonest Manager

This problematic parable, which follows immediately after the Parable of the Prodigal Son, appears only in the Gospel of Luke. As early as the fourth century, Bishop Asterius of Amasea acknowledged "it is not easy

---

40. Elizabeth Hooton (1600–72), mentioned by George Fox in his journal as "a very tender woman" he met in 1647, is identified by Emily Manners as "The First Quaker Woman Preacher." In her 1914 book by that title, Manners quotes Gerard Croese, author of a 1696 history of Quakers, who described Hooton as "a Woman pretty far advanced in Years . . . the first of her Sex among the Quakers who attempted to imitate Men and Preach." In a footnote in Fox's *Journal*, ed. John L. Nickalls identifies her as "Fox's first convert and preacher of Quakerism." Hooton began preaching as early as 1652, and though frequently beaten and jailed for preaching, she continued to speak and spread the message of Quakers until her death in Jamaica on a mission with Fox and others.

41. Allowing women to conduct their own business meetings was so disturbing that it led to one of the first separations in the Religious Society of Friends. (See Martin, "Tradition Versus Innovation.")

42. In researching the nineteenth-century minutes of a Friends meeting in western Ohio, I saw a clear example of this. The meeting had separate business meetings for men and women from its founding in 1809 until 1895 when the two meetings were combined. In all the early minutes, I heard—clear and strong—the voices of women, especially those who served as Clerk or in other leadership capacities. From 1895 on, women's voices virtually disappeared from the meeting minutes.

APPENDIX: TRADITIONAL INTERPRETATIONS VS. QUAKER APPLICATIONS 197

to convert this into allegory consonant with Scripture."[43] "No parable in the Gospels has been the subject of so much controversy as this," writes New Testament scholar, Henry Alford, in 1868.[44] In the 1905 *Ellicott's Bible Commentary for English Readers*, Rev. E. H. Plumptre offers an interpretation of the parable, then leaves it to the "thoughtful reader" to choose among a catalog of other interpretations.[45] And in 1988, editors of a Jesus Seminar book on the parables commented: "The Dishonest Steward embarrassed Christendom from the beginning."[46]

Below are samples from the above sources which illustrate the confusion around this parable. First, from Bishop Asterius of Amasia (ca. 380 to 390 CE), who, after acknowledging the difficulty or reconciling the parable with other scripture, interpreted it as possibly referring to being charitable, especially as death approaches, to "secure a place" in heaven:

> Asterius "The Unjust Steward":
>
> But what can we say concerning the remission of debts which the unjust steward contrived, that he might through his fellow servants secure relief for himself from the hardships of his downfall? For it is not easy to convert this into allegory consonant with Scripture, but after long reflection something like this occurred to me: All of us who busy ourselves about the rest to which we are destined, by giving what is another's, work to our own advantage; now by what is another's I mean what belongs to the Lord. For nothing is our own, but all things belong to him. When, therefore, any one anticipating his end and his removal to the next world, lightens the burden of his sins by good deeds, either by canceling the obligations of debtors, or by supplying the poor with abundance, by giving what belongs to the Lord, he gains many friends, who will attest his goodness before the Judge, and secure him by their testimony a place of happiness.[47]

Below is the seventeenth-century interpretation from "*Meditations for Every Day in The Year*/Historical Narratives."

---

43. Asterius, "Sermon 2: The Unjust Steward."
44. Alford, "Luke 16," *Greek Testament Critical Exegetical Commentary*.
45. Plumptre, "Luke 16:8."
46. Funk, et al., *Parables of Jesus*, 32.
47. Asterius, "Sermons, The Unjust Steward."

The Wicked Steward.

I. "There was a certain rich man who had a steward, and the same was accused unto him that he had wasted his goods." (Luke xvi. 1.) God is designated under this certain rich man; for "the earth is the Lord's, and the fulness thereof." (Ps. xxiii. 1.) You are the steward to whom God has entrusted many goods, both of soul and body, natural and supernatural. His object was that you might use these goods well; but, by your mismanagement and misadministration, you have deserved to be accused before your employer of having "wasted his goods." What a disgrace it is to misemploy the treasures of God, and to become a bankrupt to heaven!

II. The rich man said to his steward, "Give an account of thy stewardship." When God calls you from this world, you will be obliged to render a strict and severe account of your stewardship. After that moment you cannot imitate the unjust steward any longer, for of the period succeeding this moment it is said, "the night cometh when no man can work." (John ix. 4.) Do good, therefore, whilst you possess the time. Wise and prudent stewards frequently examine their accounts in order to correct any error and be always prepared to settle their accounts. Imitate them by a daily rigorous examination of conscience; for "if we would judge ourselves, we should not be judged." (1 Cor. xi. 31.)

III. This steward acted wisely for himself, though deceitfully in relation to his master, and Christ commends his prudence, though He condemned his fraudulent action. Would to God that we were as prudent in regard to our salvation! Lament that "the children of this world are wiser in their generation than the children of light." Exert yourself for the salvation of your own soul; for "there is a wise man who is wise to his own soul" (Ecclus. xxxvii. 25.).

In the first paragraph, the writer of *Meditations* interprets the "goods" being wasted by the steward as "soul and body, natural and supernatural" gifts, and readers are admonished to not waste their own gifts. In the second paragraph, we learn what happens on Judgment Day to those who waste God-given gifts and do not do enough good while they are alive. In paragraph three, the writer struggles to make sense of the ending of the parable, conflates Christ with the master in the parable, reporting inaccurately that "Christ commends his prudence, though He condemned [the steward's] fraudulent action." (In the parable, Jesus says only that the master "commended" the steward for being shrewd.)

Finally, the *Meditations* writer falls back on the second half of Luke 16:8: "the children of this world are wiser in their generation than the children of light." This summary statement, not considered part of the authentic parable, was probably added by the gospel writer (or a later editor) who struggled to understand the original ending. In fact, biblical scholars believe that the explanations in Luke 16:8b–13 were attempts to soften the master's commendation of the dishonest steward.[48]

Jesus' parables are notably down-to-earth, pithy stories with unexplained metaphors, but in Luke 16:8b, we are whisked away to a lofty comparison that has little to do with the narrative. The odd sentence about "children of this world" and "children of light" refers to the spiritual realm of light, suggesting it is somehow key to the parable's meaning. These references do not appear in the text of the parable, however, but are tacked on at the end.

Anglican theologian J. C. Ryle (in 1859) takes the view that no one who has been dishonest like this steward will be allowed into heaven, even if his master did "commend" him:

> Let us contend earnestly for the glorious doctrines of salvation by grace, and justification by faith. But let us never allow ourselves to suppose that true religion sanctions any trifling with the second table of the law.[49] Let us never forget for a moment, that true faith will always be known by its fruits. We may be very sure that where there is no honesty, there is no grace.[50]

Finally, below is an excerpt from Rev. Plumptre's 1905 all-inclusive but indecisive conclusion which speaks volumes about the confusion surrounding this parable.

> It must be left to the thoughtful reader to judge how far [an] exposition of the parable is coherent and satisfying in itself, and in harmony with the general teaching of our Lord. Those who will may compare it, apart from the real or imagined authority

---

48. Funk, et al., *Parables of Jesus*, 32.

49. The "Second Table of the Law" refers to the last six of the Ten Commandments, which address civic issues such as "adultery, stealing, and murder." "[Roger] Williams also conceived that the first four commandments, or the first table of the law, addressed one's obligations to worship God, while the last six commandments, the second table, addressed one's civil obligations." See Reinach, "Two Tables of the Law."

50. Ryle, "Luke 16."

of this or that name, with the other interpretations which find in it a lesson

(1) to the publicans (like that of Luke 3:13) to exact no more than that which is appointed them; or

(2) to all Christians to be as lenient in dealing with their "debtors" as the steward was with his master's; or

(3) a simple example of quickness and prudence in things temporal, which Christians are to reproduce, mutatis mutandis, in dealing with things eternal; or

(4) which hold, as the main point of the parable, that the steward's master was ignorant of his fraudulent collusion with the debtors; or

(5) find in the call to give an account of his stewardship nothing but the approach of death; or

(6) teach that the master is Mammon, and that the disciples were accused by the Pharisees of wasting his goods when they became followers of Christ; or

(7) that the steward stands for the publicans as a class, and then for all Christians generally; or

(8) for Judas Iscariot; or

(9) for Pontius Pilate; or

(10) for our Lord Himself; or

(11) for St. Paul; or

(12) for an example of the true penitent; or

(13) for the devil.

The wild diversity of interpretations which this list partially represents, should make any commentator more or less distrustful of what seems to him an adequate and complete exposition; and it may well be, even after an exposition as full as the conditions of the case seem to render possible, that there are sidelights in the parable which are yet unnoticed, and further applications which, as being founded on real analogies, might be instructive and legitimate.[51]

---

51. Plumptre, "Luke 16:8."

Early Quaker Applications of The Dishonest Manager

George Fox (1653):

> Hold your freedom, and keep and stand fast in it, that ye may be armed with wisdom, and furnished against your enemies, who are wiser in their generation than the children of light. But the wisdom of the Most High is spreading, and making itself manifest in your hearts, by which ye may comprehend the world's wisdom, the world's worship, and knowledge.

Early Friends made scant reference to this parable, perhaps because like others, they found it puzzling. In the example above, Fox refers to the parable obliquely, skipping the story and going straight to the gospel writer's addition about "the children of this world" being "wiser in their generation than the children of light."

A footnote in the 1599 Geneva Bible, with which early Friends would have been familiar, has a similar take on Luke 16:8.

> This parable doth not approve the steward's naughty dealing, for it was every theft: but parables are set forth, to show a thing covertly, and as it were under a figure to represent the truth, though it agree not thoroughly with the matter itself: so that Christ meaneth by this parable to teach us, that worldly men are more heady in the affairs of this world, than the children of God are careful for everlasting life.[52]

Fox and this footnote suggest that Jesus meant to teach us that "worldly men," i.e., children of this world, are wiser or cleverer about their business dealings than "children of God" are about the state of their souls for eternity. But it is doubtful that the sentence referred to was in Jesus' original parable, which probably ended with the master commending the manager for his wise solution to a problem rather than condemning him for dishonest or immoral behavior.

George Fox (1676):

> For the power and spirit of God gives liberty to all; for women are heirs of life as well as the men, and heirs of grace, and of the light of Christ Jesus, as well as the men, and so stewards of the manifold grace of God. And they must all give an account of their stewardship, and are to be possessors of life, and light, and

---

52. Luke 16:8 (1599 Geneva Bible).

grace, and the gospel of Christ, and to labor in it; and to keep their liberty and freedom in it, as well as the men.[53]

Referring to the rich man calling the steward to account for his management of his employer's resources, Fox notes that all "must give an account of their stewardship," and he applies this to the argument for women's spiritual equality, saying that just as men do, women have an individual accountability for their stewardship of "the manifold grace of God."

During the decades-long process of establishing separate women's meetings for business, Fox and others wrote epistles and pamphlets arguing for the spiritual equality of women. The quotation above comes from a lengthy pamphlet titled *An Encouragement to all the Faithful Women's-Meetings in the WORLD, who assemble together in the Fear of God, for the Service of the Truth. Wherein they may see how the Holy Men encouraged the Holy Women, both in the Time of the Law, and in the Time of the Gospel; though Selfish and Unholy Men may seek to Discourage them. But go on in the Name and Power of Christ and Prosper.* Throughout the many pages of the pamphlet, Fox cites scripture from both the Old Testament ("the Time of the Law") and the New Testament ("the Time of the Gospel") that show individual women as respected and active participants in the spiritual life of their communities. This Quaker application of scripture was considered abhorrent and heretical by the established Church.

Traditional Interpretation of the Unmerciful Servant/Wicked Steward

From "*Meditations for Every Day in The Year/ Historical Narratives.*"

Christ a Patient Creditor.

"And forgive us our debts, as we forgive our debtors." (Matt. 6. 12.)

I. Imagine yourself to be that servant, who in this day's gospel is said to have owed his master " ten thousand talents." (Matt, xviii. 24.) The debt, which a sinner owes to God for one mortal sin, is in a certain manner infinite. He is unable to pay this debt, and to make satisfaction for his sins, although he, and everything which belongs to him, were sold, and himself reduced to perpetual slavery. What then would become of you, were your Lord to call you to an account this very day? You are charged with a great debt, and are, unable to pay it.

53. Fox, "Encouragement to all the Faithful Women's Meetings."

II. God's goodness prompts Him to be willing to forgive even more than man can owe. He is "rich in mercy" (Ephes. ii. 4), "patient, and plenteous in mercy." (Ps. cxliv. 8.) "Come and accuse Me, saith the Lord; if your sins be as scarlet, they shall be made as white as snow." (Joel, ii. 13, and Is. i. 18.) He will visit you today in the Eucharist, which He wishes to make a sanctuary or place of refuge for all His debtors, who cannot pay their debts. Hence David says, "The Lord is become a refuge for the poor." (Ps. ix. 10.) O how ought you to wish for the coming of your great and good creditor!

III. From this parable we learn what preparations are necessary for His coming—"I forgave thee all the debt, because thou besoughtest Me." Therefore, He is to be entreated by earnest prayer. You must approach Him with the most profound humility; for "the servant falling down, besought Him." You are to make a firm resolution of amendment. "Have patience with Me, and I will repay thee all." You must forgive your brother, if you have any uncharitable feeling against him—"Should not thou, then, have had compassion also on thy fellow servant, even as I had compassion on thee? Forgive, and you shall be forgiven." (Luke vi. 37).[54]

While the writer of this meditation ends with Jesus' clear statement of the need to forgive our debtors because God forgives us, the need to do so is predicated on the idea of "mortal sin," for which we can never "repay" God. The question, "What then would become of you, were your Lord to call you to an account this very day?" seems calculated to evoke fear of being punished by God as the king in Matthew's version punishes the unmerciful servant.

Early Quaker Application of the Unmerciful Servant

James Naylor (1655):

To all the children of darkness, that stumble at the light wherewith Christ hath enlightened everyone that cometh into the world. . . . Who would have believed within these few years that you had been of them of which Christ spoke, by which his messengers should be shamefully entreated, beat in the synagogues, haled before rulers, falsely accused and imprisoned? Who would have thought you had been the men who should

---

54. *Meditations*, "Wicked Steward."

have been found beating your fellow servants, suing, and imprisoning for tithes and hire?

William Penn (1679):

But now let us Protestants examine, if we have not departed from this Sobriety, this Christian Temperance? how comes it, that we who have been forgiven much, have our selves fallen upon our fellow Servants, who yet owe us nothing? have not we refused them this reasonable choice? have we not threatened, beaten, and imprisoned them? Pray Consider, have you not made Creeds, set Bounds to Faith, form'd and regulated a Worship and strictly enjoined all men's obedience by the help of the Civil Power upon pain of great Sufferings, which have not been spared to Dissenters, though in Common, Renouncers and Protestors with you against the Pope & Church of Rome; for this the Land mourns, Heaven is displeas'd, and all is out of due course.[55]

In the two quotations above, both James Naylor and William Penn allude to the Parable of the Unmerciful Servant in reference to Protestants and their treatment of fellow Christians.[56]

In 1651, Protestants led by Oliver Cromwell (i.e., Puritans) won the English Civil War and overturned the monarchy. King Charles was beheaded, England declared a Commonwealth, and in 1653, Cromwell was named Lord Protector of England. The episcopal system long in place in the Church of England (Anglican) was dismantled with the goal of establishing a uniform Protestant Church tolerant of differences. In this time of turmoil and change, however, Puritan Protestants were no more tolerant than the Catholic Church and Anglican Protestants had been. Writing in 1655, Naylor alludes to the Parable of the Unmerciful Servant: "Who would have believed within these few years . . . [that you would] have been found beating your fellow servants, suing, and imprisoning for tithes and hire."

By 1660, the monarchy had been restored along with the Church of England. Religious chaos characterized the following three decades (known as "The Restoration") as Puritans were unseated and Anglican control reinstated. Religious dissenters, i.e., non-Anglican Protestants,

---

55. Penn, *The Second Part of the Address to Protestants*.

56. The Catholic Church used the word "Protestant" to refer to anyone who opposed Catholicism, but the Church of England (i.e., Anglican Church) distinguished between "orthodox" Protestants, like the Lutherans and Calvinists, and those they considered unorthodox, like the Quakers and the Baptists.

were persecuted by the Anglican church, some more than others; for instance, the English Parliament passed a series of laws to silence Quakers, beginning with the Quaker Act of 1662 which made it illegal for Quakers to worship together; in 1670, the Conventicle Act prohibited religious meetings of any kind except those of the official Church of England.

In 1679, William Penn set down his serious concerns about the state-of-affairs among English Protestants.[57] The first Protestants, Penn says in his address, went to scripture seeking truth; they asked for patience, brotherly love, and moderation in the inquiry into their objections to the Catholic Church. Penn asks, "how comes it, that we who have been forgiven much, have our selves fallen upon our fellow Servants [i.e., fellow Protestants], who yet owe us nothing? have not we refused them this reasonable choice? have we not threatened, beaten and imprisoned them?" Like the unmerciful servant, Protestants were inflicting on other Protestants pain and punishment they themselves had experienced.[58]

---

57. He signed the Address, "by a Protestant, William Penn."

58. After a dark period of religious persecution, in 1688 Parliament passed the Act of Toleration which allowed Protestants who dissented from the Church of England to have their own places of worship provided they took oaths of allegiance. Toleration did not extend, however, to Catholics, Jews, atheists, or those who denied the Trinity.

Bibliography

Alford, Henry. "Luke 16." *Greek Testament Critical Exegetical Commentary*. Bible Hub. https://biblehub.com/commentaries/alford/luke/16.htm.
Asterius of Amasea, "Sermon 2: The Unjust Steward." Early Christian Writings.com. http://www.earlychristianwritings.com/fathers/asterius_02_sermon2.html.
Atkinson, John. "The Celtic Way: From Patrick to Cuthbert." Christian History Institute.org. https://christianhistoryinstitute.org/magazine/article/celtic-way-from-patrick-to-cuthbert.
"'Love and Do What You Will.' #110: Augustine's Love Sermon." The Christian History Institute. https://christianhistoryinstitute.org/study/module/augustine/.
Bacon, Nathaniel, et al. *"Meditations for every day in the year: collected from different spiritual writers and suited for the practice called 'Quarter of an hour's solitude."* New York: Benzinger Brothers, 1884.
Barclay, Robert. *An Apology for the True Christian Divinity*, 1678. Online edition. Quaker Heritage, 2002. http://www.qh.org/texts/barclay/apology/.
———. *Christian Faith and Practice in the Experience of the Society of Friends*. London: London Yearly Meeting of the Religious Society of Friends, 1972.
———. Quaker Bible Index. "Main Scripture Index: New Testament: Gospel and Acts, Mark 4:31 and Matt 13:31." Earlham School of Religion. https://qbi.earlham.edu/5syn/mat13.htm#S48D.
———. Quaker Bible Index. "Main Scripture Index: New Testament: Gospel and Acts, Matt 13:33." Earlham School of Religion. https://qbi.earlham.edu/5syn/mat13.htm#mat13:33q.
———. Quaker Bible Index. "Main Scripture Index: New Testament: Gospel and Acts, Matt 25:14–30." Earlham School of Religion. https://qbi.earlham.edu/5syn/mat24-25.htm.
Baeker, Stephen. "Parable of the Prodigal Son–Bible Braddock." BibleStudyTools.com. https://www.biblestudytools.com/bible-stories/the-prodigal-son-parable-bible-story.html.
Barrier, Katherine. "Clifton Heights' Good Plates Eatery to Hand Out Free Thanksgiving and Christmas Meals: Anyone Can Get a Free Meal from Good Plates on Nov. 22, No Questions Asked." *CityBeat Magazine*, Nov 10, 2023. https://www.citybeat.com/food-drink/clifton-heights-good-plates-eatery-to-hand-out-free-thanksgiving-and-christmas-meals-16284451.

BIBLIOGRAPHY

Barron, Bishop Robert. Excerpts from "The Deeper Meaning of the Parable of the Talents." *The Catholic World Report*, Sep 22, 2014. https://www.catholicworldreport.com/2014/09/22/the-deeper-meaning-of-the-parable-of-the-talents/.

Bloomberg, Craig L. *Interpreting the Parables*. Downers Grove, IL: InterVarsity, 1990.

Bolz-Weber, Nadia. "Benediction, Funeral Liturgy for Rachel Grace Held Evans, June 1, 2019." https://rachelheldevans.com/funeral.

———. *Pastrix: The Cranky, Beautiful Faith of a Sinner and Saint*. Nashville: Jericho, 2013.

Boorstein, Michelle. "Bolz-Weber's Liberal, Foulmouthed Articulation of Christianity Speaks to Fed-Up Believers." *The Washington Post*, Nov 3, 2013. https://www.washingtonpost.com/local/bolz-webers-liberal-foulmouthed-articulation-of-christianity-speaks-to-fed-up-believers/2013/11/03/7139dc24-3cd3-11e3-a94f-b58017bfee6c_story.html.

Brinton, Howard. *Friends for 350 Years*. Wallingford, PA: Pendle Hill, 2002.

———. *Prophetic Ministry*. Wallingford, PA: Pendle Hill, 1950. http://www.pendlehill.org/pendle_hill_pamphlets.htm.

"Canting." *The Century Dictionary*. Wordnik.com. https://www.wordnik.com/words/canting.

Cassidy, Cody. "Who Figured Out How to Make Leavened Bread?" *Slate*, May 4, 2020. https://slate.com/human-interest/2020/05/leavened-bread-yeast-invention-history.html (accessed December 2023).

Christian History Institute. "'Love and Do What You Will.' #110: Augustine's Love Sermon." https://christianhistoryinstitute.org/study/module/augustine/.

Crawford, Jack. "The Cathars: Persecuting Heretical Christians in the 13th Century." The Collector. https://www.thecollector.com/cathars-persecution-of-christians-13th-century/.

Dalrymple, Galen C. "Everything Counts All the Time." DayBreaks Devotions. https://daybreaksdevotions.word.com/2018/01/11/daybreaks-for-1-11-18-everything-counts-all-the-time/.

"Debate Over Canceling Student Debt." Opinion, Letters to Editor. *New York Times*, May 28, 2022. https://www.nytimes.com/2022/05/28/opinion/letters/college-debt-cancellation.html.

"Dispensation." Dictionary.com. https://www.dictionary.com/browse/dispensation.

Dodd, C. H. *The Parables of the Kingdom*. New York: Charles Scribner & Sons, 1961.

Douglas-Klotz, Neil. *The Hidden Gospel: Decoding the Spiritual Message of the Aramaic Jesus*. Wheaton, IL: Quest, 2001.

Elnes, Eric. *Asphalt Jesus: Finding a New Christian Faith Along the Highways of America*. San Francisco: Jossey-Bass, 2007.

"*Ekklēsia*." Bill Mounce Greek Dictionary. https://www.billmounce.com/greek-dictionary/ekklesia.

Erasmus, Desiderius. *An Exhortation to the Diligent Study of Scripture*. Unio Cum Christo. https://uniocc.com/archive/an-exhortation-to-the-diligent-study-of-scripture.

Evans, Rachel Held. "Let the World Change You: A Commencement Address Do-Over," May 21, 2016. https://rachelheldevans.com/blog/commencement-do-over-world-change-you.

Faggin, Federico. "Awakening." In *Spiritual Awakenings: Scientists and Academics Describe Their Experiences*, edited by Marjorie Woollacott and David Lorimer, 79. Battle Ground, WA: Academy for the Advancement of Postmaterialist Sciences, 2022.

Fox, George. *The Journal of George Fox*. Edited by John L. Nickalls. London: Religious Society of Friends, 1975.
———. "An Encouragement to all the Faithful Women's-Meetings in the World." *A Collection of many Select Epistles to Friends, of that Ancient, Eminent and Faithful Minister of Jesus Christ George Fox*. Ann Arbor: Text Creation Partnership, 2011.
———. "Epistle 17." *Selections from the Epistles of George Fox*. Edited by Samuel Tuke. London: Society of Friends, 1879.
———. "Epistle 24." *Selected Epistles of George Fox*. Renascence Editions. https://www.luminarium.org/renascence-editions/foxep.htm.
——— QBI. "Epistle 265." *George Fox's Epistles*. Earlham School of Religion. https://qbi.earlham.edu/gfe/e265-273.htm.
———. QBI. "Main Scripture Index. New Testament: Gospel and Acts Matt 13:44-46." Earlham School of Religion. https://qbi.earlham.edu/5syn/mat13.htm#S48D.
———. QBI. "Main Scripture Index. New Testament: Gospel and Acts, Matt 20:3, 6." Earlham School of Religion. https://qbi.earlham.edu/5syn/mat19-20.htm#S118.
———. *The Pearle Found in England*. London: Thomas Simmons, 1658.
———. *A Word From the Lord, to All the World, and All Professors in the World; Spoken in Parables*. London: Printed for Giles Calvert, at the Black Spread-Eagle, at the West end of Pauls, 1654.
Fox, George, et al. "Declaration from the Harmless and Innocent People of God called Quakers." Digital Quaker Collection. Earlham School of Religion. http://dqc.esr.earlham.edu:8080/xmlmm/docButton?XMLMMWhat=builtPage&XMLMMWhere=E11229469.P000000032&XMLMMBeanName=toc1&XMLMMNextPage=/builtPageFromBrowse.jsp.
Funk, Robert. *Honest to Jesus: Jesus for a New Millenium*. San Francisco: Harper, 1996.
Funk, Robert W., Bernard Brandon Scott. Edited by James R. Butts. *The Parables of Jesus: Red Letter Edition: The Jesus Seminar*. Sonoma, CA: Polebridge, 1988.
Funk, Robert W., and Roy W. Hoover. *The Five Gospels: What Did Jesus Really Say? The Search for the Authentic Words of Jesus*. San Francisco: HarperCollins, 1997.
"G93 – *adikia* – Strong's Greek Lexicon (rsv)." Blue Letter Bible. https://www.blueletterbible.org/lexicon/g93/rsv/mgnt/0-1/.
"G264 – *hamartanō* – Strong's Greek Lexicon (rsv)." Blue Letter Bible. https://www.blueletterbible.org/lexicon/g264/rsv/mgnt/0-1/.
"G1342 – *dikaios* – Strong's Greek Lexicon (kjv)." Blue Letter Bible. https://www.blueletterbible.org/lexicon/g1342/kjv/tr/0-1/.
"G3622 – *oikonomia* – *Strong's Greek Lexicon* (kjv)." Blue Letter Bible. https://www.blueletterbible.org/lexicon/g3622/kjv/tr/0-1/.
"G3875 – *paraklētos* – Strong's Greek Lexicon (kjv)." Blue Letter Bible. https://www.blueletterbible.org/lexicon/g3875/kjv/tr/0-1/.
Garcia, Feliks. "6 Years Later, The Double Rainbow Guy Still Wonders What It All Means." *DailyDot*, Jan 8, 2016. https://www.dailydot.com/unclick/double-rainbow-guy-interview/.
Garner, Tonya. "Progressive Christians Spread Message in Clovis." *The Clovis News Journal*, May 19, 2006.
Garver, Jaclyn Youhana. "During Partial Restaurant Closures, This Couple Started Their Own Eatery." *Cincinnati Magazine*, May 28, 2020. https://www.cincinnatimagazine.com/article/during-partial-restaurant-closures-this-couple-started-their-own-eatery/.

Goodacre, Mark. "Q Source." Bible Odyssey. https://www.bibleodyssey.org/ask-a-scholar/q-source/.

Gordon, Ernest. *Through the Valley of the Kwai*. New York: Harper & Row, 1962.

Grace Thru Faith. "About Our Beliefs." https://gracethrufaith.com/about/about-our-beliefs/.

"H4912 – *māšāl* – Strong's Hebrew Lexicon (kjv)." Blue Letter Bible. https://www.blueletterbible.org/lexicon/h4912/kjv/wlc/0-1/.

Hinds, Arthur. "The Compiler's Purpose." *The Complete Sayings of Jesus*. The Internet Sacred Text Archive. https://sacred-texts.com/bib/csj/csj002.htm.

Hultgren, Arland J. *The Parables of Jesus: A Commentary*. Grand Rapids: Eerdmans, 2000.

Irenaeus of Lyons. "The Prophets Were Sent from One and the Same Father from Whom the Son Was Sent." Early Christian Writings.com. http://www.earlychristianwritings.com/text/irenaeus-book4.html.

Jefferson, Thomas. "Letter to John Adams, 12 October 1813." Founders Online. https://founders.archives.gov/documents/Jefferson/03-06-02-0431.

Jeremias, Joachim. *Jesus and the Message of the New Testament*. Minneapolis, MN: Fortress, 2002. Kindle.

Jewish Virtual Library. "Ancient Jewish History: Pharisees, Sadducees, and Essenes." https://www.jewishvirtuallibrary.org/pharisees-sadducees-and-essenes.

Julian of Norwich. "The Highest Form of Prayer." *Devotional Classics: Selected Readings for Individuals and Groups*. Edited by Richard J. Foster and James Bryan Smith. Renovaré.org. https://renovare.org/books/devotional-classics.

Kelley, Jack. "The Lost Sheep, The Lost Coin, And The Lost Son." Grace Thru Faith, June 29, 2022. https://gracethrufaith.com/topical-studies/parables/the-lost-sheep-the-lost-coin-and-the-lost-son/.

———. "Thinking You Are Saved But Aren't?" Grace Thru Faith, July 3, 2015. https://gracethrufaith.com/ask-a-bible-teacher/thinking-you-are-saved-but-arent/.

"Kenosis." *New World Encyclopedia*. https://www.newworldencyclopedia.org/entry/Kenosis.

Kimmel, Jimmy. Twitter.com. July 3, 2010. https://twitter.com/jimmykimmel/status/17665533038.

Klopsch, Louis. "Explanatory Note." *The Holy Bible: Red Letter Edition*. New York: Christian Herald, 1901.

Knecht, Friedrich Justus. "XLV. The Parable of the Prodigal Son." *A Practical Commentary on Holy Scripture*. Freiburg: Herder, 1910.

"Koan." Buddhism Guide.com. https://buddhism-guide.com/koan/.

Kraybill, Donald B. *The Upside-Down Kingdom*. Revised Edition. Harrisonburg, VA: Herald, 2011.

Krueger, Michael J. "Early Christianity Was Mocked for Welcoming Women." The Gospel Coalition, Aug 27, 2020. https://www.thegospelcoalition.org/article/early-christianity-welcoming-women/.

"Laborers in the Vineyard (Matt 20:1–16)." Theology of Work Project. https://www.theologyofwork.org/new-testament/matthew/living-in-the-new-kingdom-matthew-18-25/the-laborers-in-the-vineyard-matthew-201-16/.

Louw, J.P. and Eugene Nida. *Greek-English Lexicon of the New Testament Based on Semantic Domains*. Minneapolis, MN: Fortress, 1988.

Luttrell, Marcus and Patrick Robinson. *Lone Survivor: The Eyewitness Account of Operation Redwing and the Lost Heroes of SEAL Team 10*. Boston: Little, Brown & Company, 2007.

Martens, John W. "His Master Commended the Dishonest Manager." *America: The Jesuit Review*, Sep 19, 2010. https://www.americamagazine.org/content/good-word/his-master-commended-dishonest-manager.

Martin, Clare J. L. "Tradition Versus Innovation: The Hat, Wilkinson-Braddock and Keithian Controversies." *Quaker Studies* 8.1 (2003).

"Mercy, Corporal and Spiritual Works of." *The Catholic Encyclopedia*. https://www.newadvent.org/cathen/10198d.htm.

"Mold vs. Yeast." Moldbusters.com. https://www.bustmold.com/resources/about-mold/mold-vs-yeast/.

Moore, Russell. "He Was a Top Church Official Who Criticized Trump. He Says Christianity Is in Crisis." NPR, Aug 8, 2023. https://www.npr.org/2023/08/08/1192663920/southern-baptist-convention-donald-trump-christianity.

Nayler, James. *A Discovery of Faith, Wherein is laid down The Ground of True Faith . . . The difference betwixt The Living Word and the Letter*. London: Printed for Giles Calvert, at the Black Spread Eagle at the west end of Paul's, 1653.

———. QBI. "Main Scripture Index. New Testament Gospel and Acts, Luke 15:16-20." Earlham School of Religon. https://qbi.earlham.edu/5syn/luk13-17.htm#S105Dqtext.

Nuttall, Gregory F. "Introduction to George Fox and His Journal." *The Journal of George Fox*. Edited by John L. Nickalls. London: Religious Society of Friends, 1975.

"Origins of the Red-Letter Bible." Crossway, March 23, 2006. https://www.crossway.org/articles/red-letter-origin/.

Pagels, Elaine. "What is the Gospel of Thomas and Why is it Important?" *U.S. Catholic Magazine*, May 2, 2019. https://uscatholic.org/articles/201905/matthew-mark-luke-and-thomas/.

"Parable of the Dishonest Steward." United States Conference of Catholic Bishops. https://bible.usccb.org/bible/luke/16.

"Parable of the Unmerciful Servant." Bible Study Resources, Oct 30, 2020. https://biblestudyresources.org/parable-of-the-unmerciful-servant.

Penington, Isaac. "Of The Pure, 'Constant, Eternal, Unchangeable Nature of God's Truth." *The Works of Isaac Penington, A Minister of the Gospel in the Society of Friends*. Fourth Edition. Vol. III. Philadelphia: Religious Society of Friends, 1863.

———. "An Examination of The Grounds or Causes Which Are Said To Induce The Court Of Boston In New England To Make That Order Or Law Of Banishment, Upon Pain Of Death, Against The Quakers." Quaker Heritage. http://www.qh.org/texts/penington/boston.html#385.18.

———. QBI. "Main Scripture Index. New Testament: Gospel and Acts, Luke 19:17." Earlham School of Religion. https://qbi.earlham.edu/5syn/mat21-22.htm#S123.

———. QBI. "Main Scripture Index. New Testament: Gospel and Acts, Matt 13:44–46." Earlham School of Religion. https://qbi.earlham.edu/5syn/mat13.htm#S48N.

———. QBI. "Main Scripture Index. New Testament: Gospel and Acts, Mark 4:31 and Matt 13:31." Earlham School of Religion. https://qbi.earlham.edu/5syn/mat13.htm#S48D.

———. QBI. "Main Scripture Index. New Testament: Gospel and Acts, Matt 13:33." Earlham School of Religion. https://qbi.earlham.edu/5syn/mat13.htm#mat13:33q.

———. "Some Deep Considerations Concerning the State of Israel . . ." *The Works of Isaac Penington.* 4 vols. Quaker Heritage, 1995. http://www.qh.org/texts/penington/editor.html.

Penn, William. *Fruits of Solitude. Vol. I, Part 3: Religion.* The Harvard Classics. New York: P.F. Collier & Son, 1909–14.

———. *Twenty-First Century Penn.* Translated by Paul Buckley. Richmond, IN: Earlham College Press, 2003.

———. QBI. "Main Scripture Index. New Testament and Acts, Luke 10:30-35." Earlham School of Religion. https://qbi.earlham.edu/5syn/luk10-12.htm#S83.

———. QBI. "Main Scripture Index. New Testament and Acts, Luke 14:18-20." Earlham School of Religion. https://qbi.earlham.edu/5syn/luk13-17.htm#S105D.

———. "The Second Part of the Address to Protestants Upon the Present Conjuncture." Early English Books Online Text Creation Partnership. https://quod.lib.umich.edu/e/eebo/A54098.0001.001/1:4?rgn=div1;view=fulltext.

Phelps-Roper, Megan. *Unfollow*, Episode 2. "Something is Wrong." Podcast. BBC Sounds, Radio4, Dec 9, 2019. https://www.bbc.co.uk/sounds/play/p07wp38f.

———. "How I Escaped the Notorious Westboro Baptist Church." Introduction to *Unfollow.* Podcast. BBC Sounds, Radio4, Dec 9, 2019. https://www.bbc.co.uk/programmes/articles/17ZFny3GkPmQv4BxqRZPC3f/how-i-escaped-the-notorious-westboro-baptist-church.

———. "Megan Phelps-Roper on Remorse over Westboro Baptist Church." BBC, Dec 9, 2019. https://www.bbc.com/news/world-us-canada-50518466.

"Phoenix Affirmations Summary Version 3.8." *Progressive Christianity.org.* https://progressivechristianity.org/12-phoenix-affirmations/.

"*Phronimos.*" Strong's Definitions and Thayer's Greek Lexicon. Study Tools: Reverse Interlinear Text." Blue Letter Bible. https://www.blueletterbible.org/lexicon/g5430/rsv/mgnt/0-1/.

Plumptre, Rev. E. H. "Luke 16:8." Bible Hub. https://biblehub.com/commentaries/ellicott/luke/1.htm.

Reinach, Alan J. "The Two Tables of the Law." *Liberty Magazine*, May/June, 2005. https://www.libertymagazine.org/article/the-two-tables-of-the-law.

Rohr, Richard. "Mystical Holism." Daily Meditations, April 9, 2021. https://cac.org/daily-Meditations/mystical-holism-2021-04-09/.

Rollins, Peter. *The Orthodox Heretic: And Other Impossible Tales.* Brewster, MA: Paraclete, 2009.

Ryle, John Charles. "Luke 16." *Ryle's Expository thoughts on the Gospels, with the text complete, vol 2.* StudyLight. https://www.studylight.org/commentaries/eng/ryl/luke-16.html.

Sanidopoulos, John. "The Parable of the Talents; St Theophan the Recluse." *Orthodox Christianity Then and Now*, Feb 7, 2021. https://www.johnsanidopoulos.com/2021/02/the-parable-of-talents-st-theophan.html.

"Saying 64: The Parable Of The Dinner Party." *Gospel of Thomas.* Translated by Mark M. Mattison. https://www.academia.edu/15107954/The_Gospel_of_Thomas_A_Public_Domain_Translation.

Spillane, Edward P. "Nathanial Bacon." *Catholic Encyclopedia.* https://www.catholic.com/encyclopedia/nathaniel-bacon.

Spurgeon, Charles Haddon. "'George Fox': An Address Delivered by Charles Haddon Spurgeon to the Society of Friends in the Devonshire House Meeting House,

Bishopsgate Street, London, on Tuesday Evening, November 6th, 1866." *Internet Archive*. https://archive.org/details/georgefoxanaddroospurgoog/page/n5/mode/2upen.

Surangama Sutra. ABuddhistLibrary.com. https://www.abuddhistlibrary.com/Buddhism/C%20-%20Zen/Sutras/The%20Shurangama%20Sutra/Shurangama%20Sutra.htm.

Tennyson, Alfred Lord. "The Higher Pantheism." Poetry.com. https://www.poetry.com/poem/1082/the-higher-pantheism.

Tertullian. *The Apology of Tertullian for The Christians*. Translated by Bindley T. Herbert. Oxford: Parker and Co., 1890.

The New Encyclopaedia Britannica. 15th ed. 32 vols. Chicago: Encyclopaedia Britannica, 2010. Final print version. Continued online, as *Encyclopaedia Britannica*, at https://www.britannica.com/.

Thomas, Gospel of. Translated by Thomas O. Lambdin. The Nag Hammadi Library. http://www.gnosis.org/naghamm/gthlamb.html.

Treybig, David. "The Prodigal Son: Parable With Overlooked Meaning." July/August 2016. *Discern Magazine*. https://lifehopeandtruth.com/change/repentance/the-prodigal-son/.

Vasquez, Paul. "Yosemitebear Mountain Double Rainbow 1-8-10." YouTube video, 03:29. https://www.youtube.com/watch?v=OQSNhk5ICTI&t=35s.

Westar Institute. "About Us." https://www.westarinstitute.org/about/us.

Westar Institute. "Bob Funk." https://www.westarinstitute.org/about/bob-funk.

"What Do Quakers Believe?" Quaker.org. https://quaker.org/faith-and-practice/ .

"What is the Meaning of the Parables of the Hidden Treasure and Pearl of Great Price?" GotQuestions.org. https://www.gotquestions.org/parable-treasure-pearl.html.

"What Is the Meaning of the Parable about the Unmerciful Servant?" Jesus Film Project. December 31, 2018. https://www.jesusfilm.org/blog/parable-unmerciful-servant/.

Whelchel, Hugh. "Five Lessons for Our Lives from the Parable of the Talents." The Institute for Faith, Work & Economics, March 14, 2013. https://tifwe.org/five-lessons-for-our-lives-from-the-parable-of-the-talents/.

Whitton, Katherine. "An Epistle to Friends Everywhere." In *Hidden in Plain Sight: Quaker Women's Writing, 1650-1700*, edited by Mary Garman, Judith Applegate, Margaret Benefiel, and Dorta Meredith. Wallingford, PA: Pendle Hill, 1996.

Wiles, Martin. "The Pharisee and the Tax Collector." *Martin Wiles' Lessons for Children and Youth*. Theology Mix.com, June 18, 2017. https://theologymix.com/sunday-school/the-pharisee-and-the-tax-collector-martin-wiles-lessons-for-children-and-youth/.

Williams, Justin. "Houses of the Holy." *Cincinnati Magazine*, April 5, 2016. https://www.cincinnatimagazine.com/citywiseblog/houses-of-the-holy/.

Woolman, John. *The Journal of John Woolman*. Vol. I, Part 2. The Harvard Classics. New York: P.F. Collier & Son, 1909-14.

Ziv, Shahar. "Which Would You Pick: $1,000,000 Or A Magical Penny?" *Forbes*, July 30, 2019. https://www.forbes.com/sites/shaharziv/2019/07/30/can-you-correctly-answer-the-magical-penny-question/?sh=165690061a64.

Subject Index

abundant, 20, 25, 36, 39, 62, 64, 75, 79, 93, 103, 118, 131, 137, 155
accessible, 13, 18, 26, 29, 49, 110, 168
Alford, Henry, 197
allegory/allegorical, xiv, 13, 34–35, 103, 197
ambiguity, 30, 160
An Apology for the True Christian Divinity, 7, 144, 179
Anglican (see "Church of England"), 151, 167, 171, 199, 204–5, 204n56
Apology of Tertullian, 94
"applied" theology vs. "theoretical" theology, 46–47
apostasy, 45, 73, 171, 171n8, 172
Aramaic, 24, 29n7, 162, 163
Asterius of Amasia, Bishop, 197
Augustine, 173, 186,
authentic parables/teachings/words of Jesus, xi, xiii–xiv, 8, 11, 13, 18, 30, 30–31n11, 33–38, 40–60, 66–67, 85, 97, 116, 129–31, 135–36, 138, 150, 154, 156–57, 159–61, 171, 199

Bacon, Robert, 167
Baptist church, ix–x, 69, 122, 132–33
    preacher/minister, 122, 152
    Southern Baptist, 69, 150
    Westboro Baptist Church, 132–33

Barclay, Robert, 7, 99, 117–18, 144, 162, 163, 165–66, 179–80, 184, 190
Barclay's Sixth Proposition, 179
Barclay's Third Proposition, 7, 99
Barron, Bishop, 118
"be perfect," 63, 130
Bible, Geneva, 3, 147, 201
    Jefferson, 8–9
    King James Version, 3–4, 10, 147, 148, 154
    Red-Letter Edition, 9–10
    translations, 3, 60, 74, 147
blood of Christ, 132, 146–48
Bolz-Weber, Nadia, 138–40
Bovina, Texas, 66–68
Brinton, Howard, 7, 144–45
Buddha/Buddhism/Zen, 2n2, 26, 88, 99, 99n4, 164

Cadbury, Henry J., 46
"canting," 43
Catholic, xv, 41, 67–68, 131, 143, 144, 151, 167–68, 174n12, 180, 205, 205n58
changeable,/unchangeable 4–5, 171–73
child/children (see "little ones"), ix, x, 15, 20, 25n2, 28, 29n, 40, 41, 62, 63, 65, 73, 74, 79, 80–81, 83, 87, 87n4, 89, 91, 98, 106, 120n5, 128, 129, 133, 134, 137, 138, 158 (chart), 177, 183, 189, 198–99, 201, 203

"Christ has come to teach his people himself," 6, 45, 47, 49, 154
Christian doctrine, xiii, xiv, 4–5, 6, 9, 11, 30, 131, 143, 171, 173, 180–81, 182, 183–84, 199
  dogma, 9, 14, 30, 171, 187
  tradition, xiv, 4, 9, 11, 13, 14, 16, 18–20, 28n7, 30, 39–42, 47, 54, 66, 73–74, 76, 99, 116, 132, 146, 168, 173, 181–82, 187
Christianity, three kinds, 144–45
Christianity, xi, xiv–xv, 9, 13, 14, 15n3, 16, 20, 21, 30, 31, 39, 40, 41, 45, 66, 67, 73–74, 76, 87, 87n4, 99, 105–7, 123–24, 132, 139, 143–45, 149–51, 155, 171, 173, 180, 184, 188
Church of England (see "Anglican"), 143, 204–5, 204n56, 205n58
CityBeat Magazine, 104–5
Clovis, New Mexico, ix, 67–68, 121–23
"Codex 16," 9
Coffin, William Sloan, 71, 149
commandments, 16–18, 36, 118, 151, 181, 199n49
"common purse," 95
communion, 5–6, 7, 140, 147, 147n12, 148
community, 28, 34, 40, 41, 88, 89, 93–96, 121n7, 122, 130, 135, 140, 156, 167
compassion, x, xi, xiv, 13, 19, 20, 36, 37, 38, 41, 47, 60, 63–64, 66, 68, 72, 84, 101, 105, 110–11, 118–19, 123–24, 127, 149, 151, 159 (chart), 160, 163, 173, 177, 203
Complete Sayings of Jesus, The, 8, 10
conditional/unconditional, 20, 36, 38, 75, 76, 79–80, 93, 100–101, 103, 130–33, 136, 155, 158 (chart), 173
consistency, xi, xiii, 4, 8, 13, 19, 20, 26, 30–31, 42, 118, 131, 135, 136, 153, 154, 157, 173
control/controlled, 20, 29, 30, 100, 149, 151, 174, 204
Crosswalk America, 66–68, 121–23

crucifixion/Jesus' death and resurrection, 6, 8, 19, 20n11, 24, 28, 32, 60, 93, 99, 132, 147, 149–50, 151, 153, 154, 164, 184,
currency, 38, 63–64, 93, 103, 118, 136, 159 (chart), 190

direct/directly re teaching of Jesus (also see "spiritual experience"), xi, 7, 13, 20, 25, 27, 28, 64, 87, 169
dispensation, 178–79, 192, 192n35
Dodd, C. H., 11, 30
double-rainbow guy (see Vasquez, Paul), 56–57
Douglas-Klotz, Neil, 162, 163

early Christians, xi, xiv, 6, 19, 34, 39, 41, 87, 93, 130, 147n12, 151, 156, 160
earning interest 115–21, 165, 190
Easter, 40, 150
economics, 30n9, 91, 118
Elnes, Eric, 121–22
"end times"/"end of time," (see "judgment") 39, 192, 195, 198
enemy/enemies, 15, 61, 61n1, 63–64, 65–66, 68, 70, 133, 159 (chart)
enlighten/enlightened/enlightenment, 14n2, 26, 171, 182, 203
Erasmus, 3
eternal, 20, 21, 29, 36, 38, 40–42, 54, 60–62, 67, 79, 93, 103, 131, 137, 150, 155, 165, 169–70, 171, 177, 191, 200
Evans, Rachel Held, 140n7
"experimentally" (see "spiritual experience") 143–44
exponential growth, 109–111, 119, 120–21, 123–24, 127

factual details vs. higher Truth, 25–26
Faggin, Federico, 58–59
fair/fairness/unfairness, 75–77, 91–93, 172
"fearful investor(s)," 116–17, 121–23, 188, 190–91
Fell, Margaret, 196

SUBJECT INDEX

finger pointing at moon (see "fountain"), 99, 99n4
first/last/first/least/greatest, 86, 102, 148n13
Five Gospels, The, xiii–xiv, 12, 34, 40, 97n1, 103, 129–30, 135, 170n5
forgive/forgiveness, x, 15–16, 18, 27, 35, 47, 74–76, 83, 84, 87, 92, 130–32, 135–37, 140, 148, 158 (chart), 173, 174n12, 191, 195n37, 202–3, 204–5
fountain, 99, 171
Fox, George, 3–7, 21, 39, 42–46, 47–49, 53, 54, 89, 143–44, 145–48, 152–53, 154, 167, 170, 181–82, 184–85, 195–96, 196n40, 201–2
Franklin, Benjamin, 115, 120
Friends (see "Quakers")
Friends Theological College, 112, 113
Funk, Robert W., 9 (quoted), 11–12, 30n11, 46n14

"gathered meeting," 88
generous/generosity, 63–64, 68, 90, 91, 93, 94, 130, 159 (chart)
"God is Love," 20, 131, 154, 163
God, Jesus' understanding of, x, xi, xiii–xiv, xv, 7, 13, 14–22, 25, 26–29, 31, 36–38, 40–41, 45, 47, 49, 54, 59, 62–64, 66–67, 73, 75, 79, 84, 86, 87, 93, 100–101, 102–4, 105, 107, 109–111, 116–21, 123, 127, 129–32, 133, 136–37, 138, 145, 147, 151, 153, 154, 155, 158–59 (chart), 171–73, 175–76, 178, 181, 190
"good news," 14, 18–21, 24, 29–30, 33, 38, 41, 62–64, 66, 93
Good Plates Eatery, 104–5
Gordon, Ernest, 123–27
Gospel of John, 10, 20n11, 24, 36, 98–99, 98n2, 154
Gospel of Luke, 32, 34, 39, 60, 72–73, 86, 97, 97n1, 97, 102, 102n8, 196–97
Gospel of Mark, 32, 33, 34–36, 35n6, 39, 40, 41, 73, 82, 97, 98, 102n8, 117, 190

Gospel of Matthew, 32, 33, 34, 39, 40, 41, 54, 73, 97, 97n1, 98, 102, 102n8, 130
Gospel of Thomas, 26, 39, 87, 97, 98–100, 102
gospel(s) xi, 3, 8–9, 17, 18–19, 20, 26, 32, 46n14, 98, 98n2, 132, 140, 172, 197, 202
 canonical, 17, 24
 editing/editors of, 8, 10, 20, 27, 31, 97, 130, 149, 156, 199
 "sayings gospel," 98
 synoptic, 23–24, 28, 32–33, 40, 41, 85–86, 87, 98, 136, 147, 154
 writers of, xi, xiii, 9, 12n27, 18, 19, 24, 25, 27, 31, 32, 33, 34, 36, 37, 39, 41, 42, 87, 97, 116, 129, 130, 156, 158, 160, 199, 201
grace, xii, 55, 56, 77, 86, 117, 165–66, 176, 177, 179, 187–88, 190, 192, 199, 201–2
Grace through Faith website, 77–78
Great Biblical Commentary of Cornelius á Lapide, The, 187–88
"guilty of Christianity," 105–7
Gulab (Pashtun elder), 65

"hard sayings," 27
"hardening theory," 34, 35
Hebrew scripture, 14–18, 19, 23, 26, 29
"here and now," xii, 13, 19, 36, 40, 62, 113, 147
heresy/heretic/heretical, 98, 182, 202
hidden, xiii, 38, 44, 46, 47, 49, 54, 59, 98, 117, 123, 150, 153, 163, 168–70
hierarchy, x, 87, 102, 158 (chart), 182
Hinds, Arthur, 10–11, 10n22
Hooton, Elizabeth, 196n40
Hultgren, Arland J., 13 (quoted), 24, 75–76, 86, 135
humanity, x, xiii, 4, 19, 36, 40, 57, 105, 153, 160, 192
human reaction/response, 101, 129, 131
humor, Jesus' use of, 12, 135, 138
hypocrisy, ix, 86, 122, 130

infinite/infinity, 13, 20, 36, 38, 62, 79, 93, 103, 110, **119**, **137**, 202
Inner Teacher/Inner Christ, 6, 42, 44, 45, 47, 145, 146, 154
interpretation, xi, xiv, 5, 9, 13, 14, 18, 24, 25, 28–29n,7 30, 34–37, 39–42, 46–47, 54, 67, 73–74, 85, 91, 98–99, 116, 132, 138, 145, 153, 157, 160, 165, 167, 170–71, 173, 176, 178, 180–81, 182, 183, 185–88, 191–95, 196–200, 202–3
invite/invitation, 68, 100–104, 122, 177
Irenaeus, 191–92
Isaiah, 33, 33n2, 34n4, 192

jealousy/envy, 14, 75, 79, 91, 126, 132, 137, 157, 179
Jefferson, Thomas, 8–9, 10, 11, 44n7
Jesus' parables/teachings/words (see "authentic")
Jesus Seminar, 10–12, 30, 34–36, 36n7, 97, 103, 129, 134–35, 136, 197
Jesus the teacher, xi, xiii, xv, 4–6, 8–11, 13, 14, 16, 18–21, 24–30, 33, 36, 36n7, 40–43, 44–45, 47, 48–49, 53, 54, 61–62, 63–64, 66, 68, 72, 73, 75, 84, 85–87, 99, 101–2, 104, 106, 116–18, 121, 123, 124, 129, 130–33, 136–38, 149–51, 153–55, 157, 159, 160, 168, 169, 171, 174, 176, 178, 182, 190, 201
Job, Book of, 42
judgment/Judgment Day, x, 14, 31, 40–41, 64, 76–77, 84, 129, 132, 137, 158 (chart), 183, 188–89, 193–95, 198
Julian of Norwich, 21
Julicher, Adolf, 13

Kelly, Jack, 77n6
kenosis (see "self-emptying"), 164
Kenya, 112–14
key to Jesus' message, xi, 13, 21, 27, 36, 38, 54, 62, 79, 87, 103, 110, 118, 131, 145
Keys to Meaning in Jesus' Parables (chart), 158–59
Kimmel, Jimmy, 57

King Lear, 25n2, 74n2
Kingdom of God, xiii, xiv, xv, 5, 7, 13, 14, 18–20, 23–27, 29, 31, 33, 34–38, 40–42, 49, 54, 55, 59, 62–64, 70, 73, 75–76, 79, 84, 87, 91, 93, 94, 101–5, 108–111, 112, 116–20, 123–24, 129–38, 140, 153, 155, 157, 158 (chart), 162–63, 169, 171, 173, 175–76, 178, 182–84, 190
Kingdom of Heaven, 54
Klopsch, Louis, 9–11
koan, 26, 164

Lapide, Cornelius á, 187–88
judgment, x, 14, 31, 40–41, 64, 76–78, 84, 129, 132, 137, 158 (chart), 183, 188–89, 193–95,
leaven/leavening, 109–110, 113, 120, 123–24, 137, 162, 163
Letter/letter of the law/spirit of the law, 43, 45–46, 86, 99n6, 145–46, 153, 176, 176n15, 178–79
Light (of Christ), the, xi, xii, 4, 6, 43, 53, 59, 77, 89, 98–99, 171, 179–80, 181–82, 189, 201, 203
"little ones," (see "children") 73, 168
Lone Survivor, 65n2
love/compassion, x, xi, xiv–xv, 7, 13, 16–27, 31, 36–38, 40–41, 43, 47, 49, 53–55, 58–59, 60–64, 66–68, 72, 75–76, 78–84, 86–87, 93, 94, 96, 97, 100–101, 102n8, 103–5, 110–11, 116–23, 124, 126–27, 129–33, 136–38, 140, 149–50, 153–55, 157, 158–59 (chart), 160–61, 163, 168, 169–70, 173, 175–80, 182, 183, 186, 190–91, 195, 203, 205
Luke, 9, 10, 12n27, 19, 24, 25, 32, 32n1, 33, 33n2, 34, 36, 39, 40, 46n14, 60–62, 63, 72, 73, 86, 97, 97n1, 98, 101–3, 116–17, 135–36, 196, 199, 200, 201
Lutheran, 139, 204n56
Luttrell, Marcus (US Navy Seal), 64–65, 65n2

Madison Place Community, 95–96
"magic penny," 120–21, 121n5
Making of Luke-Acts, The, 46n14
Mark, 10, 12n27, 17n7, 19, 24, 28n6, 32n1, 33, 34, 35n, 36, 39, 40, 41, 73, 82, 97, 98, 117, 190
Matthew, 10, 12n27, 19, 24, 32n1, 33, 34, 34n4, 36, 39, 40, 41, 54, 63, 72–73, 97, 97n1, 98, 101, 102, 102n8, 103, 116–17, 129–30, 203
"measure of," 38, 77, 93, 103, 109, 110, 117, 162, 170, 172, 179, 185, 190
Meditations for every day in the year, 41–42, 167–70, 173–74, 176–78, 180–81, 183–84, 185–87, 192–95, 197–99, 202–3
mercy/merciful, x, 6, 20, 40, 61n1, 61–64, 66, 77, 85, 87, 105–6, 118, 124, 126, 128–33, 136, 173–76, 177, 179, 186, 202–5
message of Jesus, x, xi, 6, 13, 16, 19–20, 26–27, 30, 31, 38, 42, 54, 67, 100, 104, 105, 118, 120, 121, 123, 131, 133, 149, 150, 153, 155, 157, 160, 173
Methodist, x, 80, 138
Metropolitan Community Church (MCC), 121, 121n7
"Mind the Light," 53
money, 26, 74, 88, 91–93, 94, 100, 115–16, 120, 127, 131, 135, 136, 186–87, 188, 190
moneylender, 136
Moore, Russell, 150–51
Moses, 16–17n6, 17–18, 29, 147, 177, 179, 192
Mürer, Esther Greenleaf, 8
mustard plant, 108–9, 109n1, 183n24
mustard seed, 35, 105, 108–110, 120, 123, 124, 127, 137, 162, 163, 183–85

Naylor, James, 153, 178, 203–4
neighbor, 7, 16, 16n5, 17, 36, 61–64, 66, 70, 71, 113, 124, 133, 159 (chart), 161, 175–76, 181–82, 186, 187

new covenant, 99n6, 146–48, 153, 179

offerings, 14n, 15–16, 18, 94
"older brother attitude/righteousness," 74, 75–80, 86, 92–93
"opening/openings," xi, xiv, xv, 4, 5, 6, 13, 21–22, 44, 45, 104, 143–44, 146–48, 156, 184
organized religion, 151, 174

Pagels, Elaine, 98–99
parables of Jesus, definition, 11, 30
    characteristics of authentic Jesus parables, 11–12, 30, 135
    consistency in, 13, 30–31, 135
    Dishonest Manager, 134–38, 196–202
    Good Samaritan, 60–66, 68, 70, 86, 103, 116, 121, 173–76
    Great Dinner/Feast/Wedding Banquet, 97–107
    Hidden Treasure and Pearls, 46, 54, 59, 168–71
    Lost Coin/Lost Sheep, 71–73, 180–82
    Mustard Seed/Leaven, 35–36, 105, 108–110, 113, 120, 123, 124, 127, 137, 162–63, 183–85
    Pharisee and Tax Collector, 76, 85–87, 137,
    Prodigal Son, 71–80, 86, 92, 93, 153, 154, 176–79, 191, 196
    Talents, 109, 115–21, 123, 124, 137, 165–66, 169, 185–91
    Unmerciful Servant, 128–33, 202–5
    Vineyard Workers, 24, 38, 90–94, 102n8, 191–96
Parables of Jesus, Red Letter Edition, The, 11
paradigm shift, xi
Pashtun villagers, 64–65
Paul, 3, 10, 19, 20, 41, 99, 148, 151, 153, 169–70, 173, 194, 200
"pay attention," 37, 117, 189
"pearl of great price," 46–49, 54–55, 58, 59, 164–65, 168–71, 172
"Pearle Found in England, The," 47–49

Penington, Isaac, 46–47, 76–77, 78–79, 85, 164–65, 170–73, 178–79, 184, 189–90
Penn, William, 5, 6, 175, 204, 205, 205n57
persecution, 35, 41, 168, 205n58
Pharisees, 16, 28–29, 68, 76, 85–87, 103, 136, 200
Phelps-Roper, Megan, 132–33
Phoenix Affirmations, 66–67, 160–61
Pine Creek Meeting, 80n10, 80–84
Plumptre, Rev. E. H., 197, 199–200
power/powerful/empowerment, xi, xiv, 6, 14, 15, 19–20, 26, 27, 29, 38, 44, 54, 56, 58–59, 62, 73, 103, 109–110, 118, 120–21, 123, 127, 138, 150, 152, 159 (chart), 162, 175, 182, 183, 187–88, 195, 201–2, 204
pre-Christianity, 155, 173
"professor(s)," 43, 45, 146–47, 184
progressive, 66–67, 79, 111, 122
Protestant, xv, 41, 121n7, 139, 143, 144, 168, 204–5, 205n57, 205n58
punish/punishment, x, 14, 15, 28, 31, 40, 93, 100, 116, 129, 131, 132, 156, 158 (chart), 187–88, 195, 195n37, 203, 205
Puritan/Puritans, 4, 43, 48, 151, 204

Q source/*Quelle*, 97–98
Quaker application of parables, xv, 42–49, 170, 175–76, 178–80, 181–82, 184–85, 189–91, 195–96, 201–2, 203–5
  Hidden Treasure & Pearl, 170–73
  Dishonest Manager, 201–2
  Good Samaritan, 175–76
  Lost Coin and Lost Sheep, 181–82
  Mustard Seed, 184–85
  Prodigal Son, 178–80
  Talents, 189–91
  Unmerciful Servant, 203–5
  Vineyard Workers, 195–96
Quaker Bible Index/QBI, 7–8, 46
Quakers/Friends, xv, 4, 45, 48–49, 80, 83n12, 84, 87–89, 104, 105, 112–14, 144–45, 169, 170, 196n40, 41, 42, 204n56, 205
  early Friends, xv, 3–7, 38, 42–47, 99n6, 105, 145, 148n13, 151, 153–54, 167, 171, 179, 182, 196, 201
  early Quakers, xi, 7–8, 42, 46–47, 99, 154, 170, 175, 178, 181, 184, 189, 195, 201, 204
  peace testimony, 5, 7, 68, 88, 89
  "SPICES," 89
  women as spiritual equals, 110, 138, 180, 181–82, 195–96, 196n40–42, 201–2
  women's meetings, 195–96, 202

radical, 29–30, 47, 62, 93, 94, 96, 138, 151
  equity, 91, 93–96
"rainbow man" (see "Vasquez, Paul")
red letters/red-letter, x–xi, xiv, 8–10
Reynolds, Malvina, 120n5
righteousness, 28, 29, 76, 78–79, 84, 86, 136
Rohr, Richard, 19
Rollins, Peter, parable by, 105–6
Ryle, J.C., 199

sacraments, 5–6, 7, 144, 176, 180
sacrifice, xiv, 14n1, 15–16, 18, 19, 20, 42, 49, 92, 126, 146
Sadducees, 28, 86
salvadora persica 109, 109n1
Samaritan, 38, 60–70, 86, 103, 116, 121, 138, 173–76
"saved/salvation," 19, 29, 41, 48, 54, 76–78, 86, 103, 144, 150, 162, 163, 172, 176, 184, 198, 199
Schumacher, E.F., 30n9
scribe(s), 16, 17, 28–29, 86
"second coming," 154
"Second Table of the Law," 199n49
secret, 23, 25, 35–36, 98, 117, 162, 163, 180
seed(s), 34, 35, 35n6, 37, 48, 105, 108–9, 110–13, 119, 120, 120n4, 123, 124, 127, 137, 157, 162–63, 172, 183, 183n24, 184–85

SUBJECT INDEX

"self-emptying," 163–65
Sermon on the Mount, 63, 150–51
Shakespeare, 3, 25n2, 43–44, 74n2
silent worship/silence, 44n, 87, 88–89, 111n–112n, 144
Son of Man, 28–29, 28–29n7, 39
Spirit of Truth, 4, 153, 154
spiritual experience/encounter/ epiphany, xi, xv, 5, 7, 21–22, 26, 42, 44, 47, 54, 57, 59, 126, 143–48, 151, 152, 164, 165
Spurgeon, Charles Haddon, 39, 152, 152n4
"surprise and/or shock," 12, 129, 135

talents, 109, 115–27, 128, 130, 137, 165, 169, 185–91, 202
teaching style(s), 145
Tertullian, 94
testimony, testimonies, 7, 88, 89, 160
Theophan the Recluse, St., 188–89
Through the Valley of the Kwai, 123–27
"Time of the Law/Time of the Gospel," 202
Torah, the, 15n3, 16, 28, 60, 61–62, 61n1, 176, 176n15
treason/traitor, 28, 150

United Society of Friends Women, 113n5

universal, 10, 20, 25n2, 38, 47, 62, 97, 131, 176, 180, 185

value, in the Kingdom of God, xi, 7, 20, 37, 38, 47, 54, 62, 73, 93, 96, 103, 110, 131, 136, 138, 157–59 (chart)
Vasquez, Paul, 56–57
vineyard, 24, 38, 90–96, 191–96
violent/violence, ix, xi, 5, 7, 19, 31, 106, 111, 113, 116, 150, 156, 159 (chart)
vocal ministry, 44n6

way of Jesus, xi, xv, 5
wealth, 20, 26, 35, 38, 40, 71, 74, 101, 110, 118, 136, 137, 138, 159 (chart), 165, 190
Westboro Baptist Church, 132–33
Whitton, Katharine, 195–96
Woolman, John, 47, 58, 97, 175–76
women, 3, 87, 87n4, 110, 112, 114, 138, 180, 182

yeast (see "leaven/leavening"), 109–110, 162

Zander, Dieter, 151
Ziv, Shahar, 120–21

Scripture Index

Old Testament / Hebrew Bible

Exodus

20:2–3	17
23:4–5	61n1

Leviticus

19:18	16

Numbers

11:29	178

Deuteronomy

5:6–7	17
6:4–5	17
10:4	17
10:12	17
10:13	18
30:11–14	29

Psalms

9:10	203
21:7	183
23:1	198
89:4	193
118:155	176
118:179	181
119:155	176
140:4	186
144:8	203

Proverbs

13:4	193
19:24	186
24:31	193
26:13	186

Ecclesiastes

1:18	x
4:5	186
7:30	176

Song (Canticles)

2:3	183

Isaiah

1:18	203
6:9–10	34n4
28:19	177
53:6	181
61:1–2a	33

Jeremiah

3:14	177
31:31–34	148

Ezekiel

12:2	33

Joel

2:13	203

Micah

6:6–8	16

New Testament

Matthew

3:11	5
5:7	174
5:17	176n
5:44	27, 36
5:43–45, 48	63
5:43–46, 48	130
6:12	202
7:7–8	27, 78
8:24	202
11:25	168
11:28	174
13:10, 13	23
13:12	117
13:13	32, 34
13:13–15	34
13:31	35, 183
13:31–32	108
13:33	109
13:31–33	162
13:44	168
13:44–46	47, 54
13:45	169
18:10–12	73
18:12–13	71
18:23–24	128, 202
19:28	41
19:30	86
20:1	192
20:1–15	90
20:6	102n
20:8	193
20:16	86, 87
22:1–14	102
22:37	17
25:14	185
25:14–28	116
25:16	185, 187
25:18	186, 187
25:24	186
25:28	116
25:31–34, 41	40

Mark

1:8	5
1:14–15	14
1:40–45	82
2:27–28	28
4:3–9	35
4:9	32
4:10	23
4:11–12	35
4:12	23
4:13–20	12, 35
4:25	117, 117n
4:26	35
4:26–27	120, 162
4:26–29	157
4:30–31a	35
4:30–32	108
8:18	32
9:42	73
10:24b–25	41
10:29–30	41
10:26	41
10:30	42
10:31	86, 87
12:1–8	156–57
12:28	16
12:30	17
12:41–44	190
14:22–24	147

Luke

1:1–4	32
3:13	200
6:27, 35	36
6:35–36	62
6:37	203
7:41–43	136
7:47	136
8:9	23
8:10	23
8:11–15	12
8:18	117, 117n
10:27	17
10:30	174
10:30–35	60
11:33	169
13:18–19	35, 108
13:30	86, 87, 102n
14:11	85
14:15–24	101
14:16–24	97
14:33	169
15:4	180
15:8–9	71
15:11	174
15:11–24	72
15:20	177
15:25–32	72
16:1	198
16:1–8a	134
16:8	199
16:8b–13	199
17:2	73
17:20–21	29
18:2–5	157
18:10–14a	85
18:24	41
18:29–30	41
19:13	169, 185
19:13, 15–24	116
19:26	117n
19:27	116
19:47	174
20:9–15a	156–57
22:26–27	102
35–36	62

John

5:27	193
9:4	198
14:26	154
16:13–15	154

Acts

2:44–47	93, 94
10:38	174

1 Corinthians

2:9	185
4:7	185
11:31	198
13:4	194

2 Corinthians

3:2–3, 6	99
3:5–7	153
12:10	183

Ephesians

2:4	203

Philippians

2:3–8	163
3:8	170

Colossians

2:3	183

1 Timothy

6:9	41

Hebrews

12:24	148

James

5:2	169

1 Peter

2:5	49

Apocryphal / Deuterocanonical Books

Wisdom

4:13	194
5:4	183
7:9	169

Sirach (Ecclesiasticus)

37:25	198

Canticles (Song)

2:3	183

Nag Hammadi Codices

Thomas

4:2	87
64:1–12	97, 98, 100
65:1–7	156–57

Early Christianity

Celsus

Fragments from Origen, Book 3:44	87

Ireneus of Lyons

Against Heresies, Book 4, Chapter 36, 7	191–92

Tertullian

Apology, Chapter 39	94

www.ingramcontent.com/pod-product-compliance
Lightning Source LLC
Chambersburg PA
CBHW062018220426
43662CB00010B/1377